Tourism Spaces

Geographic space is a fundamental and essential construct of the physical reality within which we live, move, and construct our world. Through space we create 'others' (anything that is any distance from 'us') and we experience time (by moving from one place point to another). Because it is so fundamental to our experience, we often take geographic space for granted.

Tourism Spaces: Environments, Locations, and Movements shows some of the ways that geographers and other social scientists bring spatial considerations to the forefront of our research and understanding of tourism. This is seen through the spatial arrangements and distributions of tourism phenomena, such as attractions, destinations, and in the spatial behaviour of tourists themselves. Today, these spatial arrangements and patterns are increasingly being captured, analysed, and understood through various forms of formal and informal digital data.

The chapters in this book were originally published as a special issue of *Tourism Geographies*.

Alan A. Lew is Professor Emeritus of Geography and Planning at Northern Arizona University. He is the founding Editor-in-Chief of *Tourism Geographies* (Routledge/Taylor & Francis), and has primarily researched and written about tourism development and landscapes of East and Southeast Asia.

Tourism Spaces
Environments, Locations, and Movements

Edited by
Alan A. Lew

LONDON AND NEW YORK

First published 2022
by Routledge
2 Park Square, Milton Park, Abingdon, Oxon, OX14 4RN

and by Routledge
605 Third Avenue, New York, NY 10158

Routledge is an imprint of the Taylor & Francis Group, an informa business

© 2022 Taylor & Francis

All rights reserved. No part of this book may be reprinted or reproduced or utilised in any form or by any electronic, mechanical, or other means, now known or hereafter invented, including photocopying and recording, or in any information storage or retrieval system, without permission in writing from the publishers.

Trademark notice: Product or corporate names may be trademarks or registered trademarks, and are used only for identification and explanation without intent to infringe.

British Library Cataloguing-in-Publication Data
A catalogue record for this book is available from the British Library

ISBN13: 978-0-367-71528-1 (hbk)
ISBN13: 978-0-367-71529-8 (pbk)
ISBN13: 978-1-003-15245-3 (ebk)

Typeset in Myriad Pro
by codeMantra

Publisher's Note
The publisher accepts responsibility for any inconsistencies that may have arisen during the conversion of this book from journal articles to book chapters, namely the inclusion of journal terminology.

Disclaimer
Every effort has been made to contact copyright holders for their permission to reprint material in this book. The publishers would be grateful to hear from any copyright holder who is not here acknowledged and will undertake to rectify any errors or omissions in future editions of this book.

Contents

Citation Information vii
Notes on Contributors ix

Introduction 1
Alan A. Lew

1 Spatial arrangements of tourist villages: implications for the integration of residents and tourists 2
Dawid Soszyński, Barbara Sowińska-Świerkosz, Patricia A. Stokowski and Andrzej Tucki

2 Selecting the best route in a theme park through multi-objective programming 23
Beatriz Rodríguez-Díaz and Juan Ignacio Pulido-Fernández

3 Pattern of Chinese tourist flows in Japan: a Social Network Analysis perspective 42
Bindan Zeng

4 Understanding visitors' spatial behavior: a review of spatial applications in parks 65
Geoffrey K. Riungu, Brian A. Peterson, John A. Beeco and Greg Brown

5 Leveraging physical and digital liminoidal spaces: the case of the #EATCambridge festival 90
Michael Duignan, Sally Everett, Lewis Walsh and Nicola Cade

6 Proximate tourists and major sport events in everyday leisure spaces 112
Katherine King, Richard Shipway, Insun Sunny Lee and Graham Brown

7 Big data and tourism geographies – an emerging paradigm for future study? 131
Jie Zhang

8 The impact of distance on tourism: a tourism geography law 137
Bob McKercher

9 Sensing tourists: geoinformatics and the future of tourism geography research   142
   Noam Shoval

10 The more-than-visual experiences of tourism   145
   Tim Edensor

11 The end of tourism? A Gibson-Graham inspired reflection on
   the tourism economy   148
   Patrick Brouder

   Index   151

Citation Information

The chapters in this book were originally published in the *Tourism Geographies*, volume 20, issue 5 (2018). When citing this material, please use the original page numbering for each article, as follows:

Introduction
Tourism spaces
Alan A. Lew
Tourism Geographies, volume 20, issue 5 (2018) pp. 769

Chapter 1
Spatial arrangements of tourist villages: implications for the integration of residents and tourists
Dawid Soszyński, Barbara Sowińska-Świerkosz, Patricia A. Stokowski and Andrzej Tucki
Tourism Geographies, volume 20, issue 5 (2018) pp. 770–790

Chapter 2
Selecting the best route in a theme park through multi-objective programming
Beatriz Rodríguez-Díaz and Juan Ignacio Pulido-Fernández
Tourism Geographies, volume 20, issue 5 (2018) pp. 791–809

Chapter 3
Pattern of Chinese tourist flows in Japan: a Social Network Analysis perspective
Bindan Zeng
Tourism Geographies, volume 20, issue 5 (2018) pp. 810–832

Chapter 4
Understanding visitors' spatial behavior: a review of spatial applications in parks
Geoffrey K. Riungu, Brian A. Peterson, John A. Beeco and Greg Brown
Tourism Geographies, volume 20, issue 5 (2018) pp. 833–857

Chapter 5
Leveraging physical and digital liminoidal spaces: the case of the #EATCambridge festival
Michael Duignan, Sally Everett, Lewis Walsh and Nicola Cade
Tourism Geographies, volume 20, issue 5 (2018) pp. 858–879

Chapter 6
Proximate tourists and major sport events in everyday leisure spaces
Katherine King, Richard Shipway, Insun Sunny Lee and Graham Brown
Tourism Geographies, volume 20, issue 5 (2018) pp. 880–898

Chapter 7
Big data and tourism geographies – an emerging paradigm for future study?
Jie Zhang
Tourism Geographies, volume 20, issue 5 (2018) pp. 899–904

Chapter 8
The impact of distance on tourism: a tourism geography law
Bob McKercher
Tourism Geographies, volume 20, issue 5 (2018) pp. 905–909

Chapter 9
Sensing tourists: geoinformatics and the future of tourism geography research
Noam Shoval
Tourism Geographies, volume 20, issue 5 (2018) pp. 910–912

Chapter 10
The more-than-visual experiences of tourism
Tim Edensor
Tourism Geographies, volume 20, issue 5 (2018) pp. 913–915

Chapter 11
The end of tourism? A Gibson-Graham inspired reflection on the tourism economy
Patrick Brouder
Tourism Geographies, volume 20, issue 5 (2018) pp. 916–918

For any permission-related enquiries please visit:
http://www.tandfonline.com/page/help/permissions

Contributors

John A. Beeco National Park Service, Natural Sounds & Night Skies Division, Fort Collins, USA.

Patrick Brouder Vancouver Island University Ringgold Standard Institution, Nanaimo, Canada. University of Johannesburg Ringgold Standard Institution, Auckland Park, South Africa.

Graham Brown School of Management, University of South Australia, City West Campus, Adelaide, Australia.

Greg Brown California Polytechnic State University, College of Agriculture Food and Environmental Sciences, Natural Resource Management & Environmental Sciences, Center for Science, San Luis Obispo, USA.

Nicola Cade Lord Ashcroft International Business School, Anglia Ruskin University, Cambridge, UK.

Michael Duignan Lord Ashcroft International Business School, Anglia Ruskin University, Cambridge, UK.

Tim Edensor Department of Geography and Environmental Management, Manchester Metropolitan University, UK.

Sally Everett Lord Ashcroft International Business School, Anglia Ruskin University, Cambridge, UK.

Katherine King Faculty of Management, Bournemouth University, Talbot Campus, Poole.

Insun Sunny Lee School of Management, University of South Australia, City West Campus, Adelaide, Australia.

Alan A. Lew Editor-in-Chief, Tourism Geographies. Department of Geography, Planning, and Recreation Northern Arizona University, Flagstaff, USA.

Bob McKercher School of Hotel and Tourism Management, The Hong Kong Polytechnic University, Kowloon, Hong Kong.

Brian A. Peterson Department of Social and Health Sciences, Parks, Recreation and Tourism Management, Clemson. University College of Behavioral, Clemson, USA.

Juan Ignacio Pulido-Fernández Laboratory of Analysis and Innovation in Tourism, Department of Economics, University of Jaen, Spain.

Geoffrey K. Riungu Department of Social and Health Sciences, Parks, Recreation and Tourism Management, Clemson. University College of Behavioral, Clemson, USA.

Beatriz Rodríguez-Díaz Department of Applied Economics (Mathematics), University of Malaga, Spain.

Richard Shipway Faculty of Management, Bournemouth University, Talbot Campus, Poole.

Noam Shoval Department of Geography, The Hebrew University of Jerusalem, Israel.

Patricia A. Stokowski Rubenstein School of Environment and Natural Resources, Aiken Center, University of Vermont, Burlington, USA.

Dawid Soszyński Institute of Landscape Architecture, The John Paul II Catholic University of Lublin, Poland.

Barbara Sowińska-Świerkosz Department of Hydrobiology and Ecosystems Protection, University of Life Sciences in Lublin, Poland.

Andrzej Tucki Department of Regional Geography and Tourism, Maria Curie-Skłodowska University in Lublin, Poland.

Lewis Walsh Lord Ashcroft International Business School, Anglia Ruskin University, Cambridge, UK.

Bindan Zeng Regional Geography, Graduate School of Life and Environmental Sciences, University of Tsukuba, Japan.

Jie Zhang Nanjing University, School of Geography and Ocean Sciences, PR China.

INTRODUCTION

Alan A. Lew

This special issue is a compilation of articles that have been independently submitted to *Tourism Geographies*, but which fall under the general theme of 'tourism space'. Geographic space is a fundamental and essential construct of the physical reality within which we live, move and construct our world. Through space we create others (anything that is any distance from 'us') and we experience time (by moving from one place point to another). Because it is so fundamental to our experience, we often take geographic space for granted. The selection of papers in this special issue show some of the ways that geographers and other social scientists bring spatial considerations to the forefront of our research and understanding of tourism. This is seen through the spatial arrangements and distributions of tourism phenomena, especially the spatial behavior of tourists themselves, which is increasingly being captured through various forms of digital data.

http://orcid.org/0000-0001-8177-5972

Spatial arrangements of tourist villages: implications for the integration of residents and tourists

Dawid Soszyński ⓘ, Barbara Sowińska-Świerkosz ⓘ, Patricia A. Stokowski and Andrzej Tucki

ABSTRACT

In assessing the sustainability of tourism development and tourism impacts on rural communities, researchers have analyzed a variety of personal, social, and economic factors. Rarely, however, have they devoted attention to the spatial characteristics of rural tourism places. Yet spatial factors may be important for quality of life and positive relationships among local residents and tourists, as suggested by the theoretical perspectives of the 'New Urbanism.' This concept proposes that the arrangement of the built environment influences residents' level and quality of social interactions and their overall sense of community – an idea also relevant for communities wishing to initiate tourism development projects. Thus, the research described here asks: How do different spatial arrangements in tourist villages affect the quality of public spaces and the level of integration between locals and tourists? To address these questions, we used cartographic spatial analysis and semi-structured interviews with community residents to study 17 tourist villages in the Łęczna-Włodawa Lake District of eastern Poland. Results show that the spatial integration of residents and second home users is generally beneficial for both locals and tourists. The greatest benefit is received by residents of the smallest villages, where levels of spatial integration are the highest under moderate levels of tourism development. Spatial isolation of tourist and residential zones, as well as excessive dominance of tourism development, however, negatively impact community social relationships and reduce quality-of-life benefits. This research suggests that spatial arrangements should be considered to a greater extent in planning and managing rural tourism development.

摘要

在评估旅游发展的可持续性和旅游业对乡村社区的影响时，研究人员分析了个人、社会与经济各个方面的因素，但是他们对乡村旅游地方的空间特征现有鲜有关注。正如新城市主义理论观点所示，空间因素对当地居民与旅游者的生活质量和积极关系可能很重要。新城市主义这个概念主张人造环境的空间安排影响居民社会互动的水平与质量以及他们总体的社区感。这个思想对于那些希望启动旅游发展项目的社区也很有参考价值。所以，我们的研究问题是旅游村落的不同空间安排是如何影响公共空间质量和主客互动水平的?为解决该问题，我们采用了地图空间分析和对社区居民半结构访谈的方法研究了波兰东部拉孜娜-沃达瓦(Łęczyńsko-Włodawskie)湖区17个旅游村落。结果显示，居民与第二住宅用户的空间融合总体上对双方都有益。在中等旅游发展水平下，空间互动水平最高、规模最小的村落，居民获益最大。但是，旅游者与住宅区的空间隔离，以及旅游开发过分的主导地位会负面影响社区的社会关系，减低双方的生活质量。本研究建议，在乡村旅游发展规划与管理中应当最大程度上考虑主客双方的空间布局因素。

Introduction

Current approaches to tourism development emphasize sustainability, i.e. management and protection of the long-term viability and quality of both natural and human resources (Hardy, Beeton, & Pearson, 2002) associated with tourism development projects. Within sustainability agendas, the concept of community-based tourism (CBT) specifically directs attention to local residents' involvement in tourism ventures that aim to enhance a community, conserve its resources, and develop the industry itself (Ghasemia & Hamzah, 2014; Johnson, 2010; Murphy, 1985). One central goal of CBT is to enable opportunities for personalized contacts between hosts and guests (Kastenholz & Sparrer, 2009; Suansri, 2003; Tucker, 2003) within tourism development and implementation processes.

Although sustainable development offers a basis on which many community tourism projects are founded, there is nevertheless an extensive literature documenting the negative impacts of tourism – not only on natural and cultural resources but also on the local community itself, as well as on relations between residents and tourists (Jokinen & Sippola, 2007; Ko & Stewart, 2002; Stokowski, 1996; Tosun, 2002; Weaver & Lawton, 2001; Tsartas, 2003). One approach to mitigating negative impacts is to consciously shape the spatial structure of tourist destinations to meet the needs of both residents and visitors, while also enhancing social interactions between these groups. With this in mind, the concept of the 'New Urbanism,' drawn from urban planning, can inform discussions about the spatial structure of tourism destinations (Katz, Scully, & Bressi, 1994).

One of the key ideas of New Urbanism is the assertion that the quality and arrangement of the built environment may influence residents' level and intensity of use of public spaces, the quality of their social interactions, and their overall sense of community. Because public places are considered to be central to community design, these are theorized to play significant roles in shaping social relationships and interactions among residents (Szeszuła, 2010; Talen, 1999). Despite numerous critics, the New Urbanism remains a resilient, practical and well-founded alternative to conventional land development practices (Ellis, 2002) – and it offers lessons for communities wishing to initiate tourism development programs.

New Urbanism also raises many questions about spatial planning in amenity areas. Should tourists and residents be integrated, or isolated? Should planners create compact or scattered villages? If compact villages are desired, then what type of spatial structure is preferable, and how strong should the spatial link be between tourists and residents? To some extent, the answers to these questions depend on local conditions. But, efforts to identify positive and negative consequences associated with varying spatial patterns may allow community planners to choose appropriate designs for different types of tourist villages – and can help researchers better understand tourism planning processes.

Thus, the purpose of the research reported here is to address the question of how different kinds of tourist community spatial arrangements may affect the quality and functions of public spaces and the level of integration between local residents and tourists. The research was conducted in 17 rural villages situated in the Łęczyńsko-Włodawskie Lake District in eastern Poland (Lublin Province) – raising further important issues about tourism spatial planning in Polish villages and the consequences of these development processes.

Literature review

Spatial issues and community social functions

In analyzing the impacts of tourism development on village social life and relationships between residents, many researchers emphasize the significance of tourism intensity. Doxey (1975) suggested that resident attitudes shift from euphoria, to apathy, annoyance and finally antagonism as tourism growth and number of visitors increase. Thus, communities have a 'social carrying capacity' above which irritation occurs, a pattern confirmed by Wall (1996) in eight villages in Bali, Indonesia. Other researchers also describe increasing stress on residents, and negative changes in a destination's physical, economic, and sociocultural characteristics, as a consequence of excessive tourism development (Jokinen & Sippola, 2007; Puczkó & Rátz, 2000; Vargas-Sánchez, Porras-Bueno, & Plaza-Mejía, 2011). Counter to this, studies conducted in small villages with low tourism intensity indicate that inhabitants described almost entirely positive tourism impacts for their village Kastenholz, João Carneiro, Peixeira Marques, & Lima, 2012, including attitudes of 'euphoria' suggested in Doxey's theory. Yet, the intensity of tourism development is not the only (or the main) factor determining the impacts of tourism on residents, as shown by numerous studies describing residents' positive attitudes to tourism, even in destinations with high degrees of tourism development (e.g. Horn & Simons, 2002; Lawson, Williams, Young, & Cossens, 1998.

The intensity of tourism is also strongly linked to its type. There is growing evidence of the negative consequences of mass tourism and the promotion of alternative, sustainable types of tourism that have significantly lower social and environmental costs (Bramwell, 2004). Milne and Ateljevic (2001) use the term 'new tourism' to refer to flexibility and variety in development projects that are appropriately scaled to community size (e.g. rural areas rejecting big hotels and holiday resorts in favor of small guest houses, tourist farms or second homes).

Beyond the scale and type of tourism, spatial relationships between tourist areas within a community and other areas inhabited by local residents are also important. In Polish tourist villages, Kowalczyk and Derek (2010) have distinguished four types of spatial arrangements: 'planned tourist villages,' 'chaotic colonization on agricultural parcels,' 'planned tourist estate isolated from the village,' and 'mixed villages' of tourist/residential construction. A related scheme is identified by Xi, Wang, Kong, and Zhang (2015) in

Yesanpo area in China; these authors describe three types of spatial development: 'intensive reconstruction type,' 'enclave extension type,' and 'in-situ utilization type.' In both settings, these categories are based largely on the degree of integration of tourist and residential areas of a village.

The spatial integration of tourist and residential areas seems to be crucial for planning in villages intending to serve as tourism or recreation sites. Unfortunately, there is little published research that analyzes the impacts of various types of spatial arrangements on quality of life and social functioning of a village. Freitag (1994), however, emphasizes the negative social consequences and the adverse economic effects of tourist enclave development. Development of housing with integrated tourism and residential functions may offer a solution, but in conjunction with high-intensity tourism development, it can cause problems similar to those associated with counter-urbanization (Nepal, 2007) and can intensify any negative impacts of tourism on rural population.

The tourism literature does confirm, however, that negative effects of tourism development can adversely affect communities (e.g. Jokinen & Sippola, 2007; Tosun, 2002; Vargas-Sánchez et al., 2011; Tsartas, 2003). Some authors suggest that the proximity of tourist zones and local residential areas may increase resident-tourist tensions (Erotokritakis & Andriotis, 2007; Overvåg & Berg, 2011), and they argue for providing buffer zones between residential and tourist areas to create more dispersed community spatial patterns (Overvåg & Berg, 2011). Tourist enclaves or dispersed tourist housing may reduce some of these problems because it restricts contacts between tourists and local residents.

Many researchers have described, however, positive community impacts associated with the presence of tourists, providing a rationale for promoting the creation of tourist zones that are integrated within residential areas. Positive impacts include opportunities for modernization, improving and developing new local attractions and public services, preserving local culture and reviving old customs, protecting cultural heritage, and enhancing the sense of place and place identity (Jokinen & Sippola, 2007; Tosun, 2002; Tucki & Soszyński, 2012; Weaver & Lawton, 2001). In addition, Kastenholz et al. (2012) discussed the example of residents of a small Portuguese historical village who felt that the presence of tourists made the village more famous, enhanced the community's self-image, and made the community livelier and more enjoyable. A suitable spatial structure, however, is needed to allow visitors to contribute to the host community (Farstad, 2011). Such contact is implied within the CBT framework, and is a hallmark of rural tourism, which can be defined as 'small scale, personalized contacts, the presence of nature and of traditional community structures, reflected in a specific way of life, that tourists are curious about and eventually wish to participate in' (Kastenholz & Lima, 2013, p. 194).

The creation of an integrated tourist/resident spatial structure is possible with a long-term, participatory planning process which is included in theories of CBT (Murphy, 1985; Suansri, 2003). Within these, spatial issues are very important in order that tourist services can also be accessed by residents (Vargas-Sánchez et al., 2011). Additionally, planning can help to create accessible, coherent spatial arrangements in a destination, with paths, edges, districts, nodes, and landmarks that strategically enhance or inhibit the ability of people to move around and use common places (Fennell, 1996; Lynch, 1960). Such planned, realized and used 'good spaces' can be the foundation for establishing multiplex social relationships (Richards & Hall, 2000). Furthermore, according to the recommendations of Kim and Choi (2012) based on the renewal of Gu-Ryong village in South Korea, a good plan must first take care of all key spaces: public places (created as outdoor activity and meeting places for residents, as well as integration sites for residents and tourists), and areas creating diverse experiences for visitors.

Public spaces and rural tourism development

'Public space' can be defined as places that are open and freely accessible to all people and which are used as settings for social interaction (Habermas, 1991; Lorenz, 2010). Scholars agree that the basic indicators influencing the quality or attractiveness of public space include the vitality and diversity of those spaces (Gehl, 1987; Montgomery, 1998; Whyte, 1980). Vitality refers to the number of people present within a space, and their activities. Diversity refers to combinations of activities, especially as these are associated with a variety of users (Montgomery, 1998). Gehl (1987) proposed that activities that are crucial for creation of a good space can be divided into three main types: necessary/functional activities, optional/recreational activities, and social activities. Whyte (1980, p. 19) emphasized the interactions between different types of activities, and argued that, 'what attracts people most (…), is other people.' High activity levels and diversity results not only from the use of a space, but is also determined by the physical features of the space and by its development processes.

Chmielewski (2004, p. 205) noted that the quality of public space depends primarily on general availability, safety in use and the information obtained by 'the architectural and urban symbolism, general aesthetics, the ideological expression, cognitive and instrumental layer (signs, inscriptions, advertising, posters).' According to Whyte (1980), the primary, essential component of urban public spaces is comfortable seating choices; thus, a good space means for him a 'sittable space.' Montgomery (1998) argues that good spaces arise from promoting pedestrian flows and movement, services and attractions for people, extended hours of operation, an active street life, people watching opportunities, and economic values. Other researchers argue that the best way to achieve site vitality and diversity is to organize cultural and commercial events (Holland, Clark, Katz, & Peace, 2007). Permanent public and commercial services which are crucial for communications and social exchange are also very important (Aubert-Gameta & Covab, 1999). Heffernan, Heffernan, and Pan (2014) showed that the quality of an 'active frontage' view can significantly affect people's perceptions of a public space in terms of its safety, comfort, sociability and liveliness.

Community public spaces that serve local residents may also be spaces that serve tourists. The social and cultural (and sometimes economic) value of these integrated spaces is enhanced as a result of increases in the number and diversity of users and the variety of their activities. Because such places also present themselves as living public spaces, they also contribute to the authenticity of a destination. As MacCannell (1973, p. 594) wrote, a tourist's desire is 'to share in the real life of the places visited, or at least to see that life as it is really lived.'

Of course, processes of community change and tourism development are dynamic, and change over time. In recent decades in Europe, land tenure, rural communities, and village life all have undergone transformation. After the 1989 political changes in Poland and other places in Central and Eastern Europe, for example, public places seemed to become less important to rural villages, as individualism increased, and interest groups gained in importance (Oncescu & Robertson, 2010). The past several years, however, have seen a gradual revival of communal and neighborly relations, and new development of rural meeting places (Soszyński, Jaruga, & Sowińska-Świerkosz, 2015; Sotiropoulou, 2007).

Relative to recent trends in tourism in European rural areas, Pitkanen, Adamiak, and Halseth (2014) suggest that differences in outdoor activities between local residents and second-home owners are declining due to changes in the agricultural sector along with the intentional efforts of villages to develop their communities for tourism and second home construction. Leisure in rural areas is no longer only the domain of the tourists, just as involvement in village life is no longer just the domain of locals (Jennings & Krannich, 2013). Rural life and development may be influenced by individuals and formal or informal groups who wish to shape the social, economic and environmental character of the village where they live, visit or feel an attachment (Sotiropoulou, 2007). Tourist villages (especially those that are rural) may be most susceptible to this because they are often small and have migratory populations. Within this context, elements of traditional culture, history and community are transformed, and a new type of village, formed by people with different origins and aspirations, begins to emerge. New social relationships are also reflected in the spatial arrangements of these villages.

Below, we address the primary research questions of this paper: how are tourist villages, and public places within them, spatially organized, and what is their importance for the functioning of community tourism and for the quality of local social relationships. The paper concludes with a discussion about tourism spatial planning in Polish villages, and the consequences of these development processes.

Context and methods

Study area

The research was conducted in 17 villages situated in the Łęczyńsko-Włodawskie Lake District in eastern Poland (Lublin Province). This region was chosen as the case study area because it is the only – and therefore very popular – lake district in central-eastern Poland. Although this region is also a peripheral agricultural and mining area with a depressed economy, there is a very clear distinction between residents (mainly farmers and other laborers, generally with low income) and tourists (mainly residents of large cities from this part of Poland, generally with high income) (Flaga & Łoboda, 2011; Krukowska & Świeca, 2012). The entire study area is notable because it is part of the UNESCO Biosphere Reserve 'West Polesie.' Within this district, we selected all the villages with a tourist function that were located close to lakes. The 17 study villages are mainly very small (less than 200 inhabitants) and small (200–500 inhabitants) localities (Figure 1). Within these villages, the relationships between residents and tourists are visible and obvious because residential neighborhoods and tourist areas are spatially situated quite near to one another.

The social structure of the region is dominated by elderly residents (on average, about 19% of the total population). The entire region is characterized by high unemployment, low levels of economic prosperity and high migration of young people to the cities, especially in the smallest villages (Flaga & Łoboda, 2011). Most residents depend on agriculture, though the number of operating farms has dropped significantly in recent years. In the southern part of the area, a relatively large number of people are employed in the

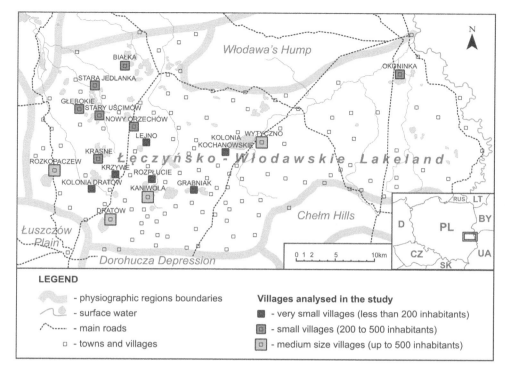

Figure 1. Location of the analyzed villages in the Łęczyńsko–Włodawskie Lakeland (51.2012°N, 22.4849°E to 51.3147°N, 23.3359°E) (own work: using Arc Gis and Corel Draw).

mining industry. In the vicinity of the most attractive lakes in this region, a considerable proportion of the residential population is employed in the tourism sector. This work is mainly in tourist resorts or in services provided for second home owners, while a small percentage of residents have their own tourist businesses. According to Krukowska and Świeca (2012), most tourists stay at resorts on the most attractive lakes, while only about 17% of all visitors rent private rooms or stay on agrotourism farms. These authors also emphasize the seasonal nature of employment related to tourism. The resorts function primarily in the summer season, while tourists staying in second homes and agritourism farms may visit in other seasons and tend to stay a little longer (mainly over weekends).

Tourism in the Łęczyńsko-Włodawskie Lake District has developed in two phases: exploration and colonization. In the first stage of regional development, tourist investments began along the shores of the most attractive lakes, and construction of social holiday resorts (owned by public companies and institutions) occurred from 1956-1989. In the second stage (from the 1980s until today), an intensive process of second home development began across the region, including in areas adjacent to the less attractive lakes (Krukowska, 2009). Over time, the Łęczyńsko-Włodawskie Lake District has become a supraregional destination area with a significant domination of summer time, water-based recreational activities (Krukowska & Świeca, 2012).

Lakes located in the vicinity of study villages are of two basic types. First, some lakes are intensively developed and used for tourist purposes, with vast beaches providing good conditions for swimming and water sports (9 lakes). Second, other lakes are less accessible and are poorly developed, with only small areas for bathing. The main activities associated with these lakes are fishing and walking (8 lakes). All the lake basins are either circular or oval in shape.

Methods

The research method combined two main types of analysis: social and spatial. Social analyses were based on semi-structured interviews with local community members. Interviews were conducted in person by the first author at the interviewee's home or in public places. Between 2012 and 2015, a total of 93 people were interviewed across the 17 villages (Table 1). In each village, four to eight persons of different ages, sexes, and professions were interviewed; these included key individuals (the grocery saleswoman or the village head) or active individuals representing different age and social groups. In case of refusal to be interviewed, another person from the same village and social group was sought. The average duration of an interview was 45 minutes.

The interviews were intended to obtain information from a range of local people about the location and importance of village public places, their use of these places for recreational and social activities, and local perspectives about tourism. Interviews included open-ended questions and were divided into four parts: (1) the main physical features of the community; (2) types and locations of outdoor activities (especially social); (3) identification, characteristics and importance of public places (with particular reference to the presence of tourists); and (4) any problems and suggestions associated with the development and social functioning of the village (both in terms of resident quality of life, and also with regard to tourists). Interviews were structured in such a way as to provide information about the behavior and opinions of the entire population (not just the individual behavior and opinions of the people being interviewed). During these interviews, the researcher sketched on a map of the village the information provided by the interviewee: the location of public spaces, descriptions of their users (local residents as well as tourists), types of activities and intensity of use. At the end of each conversation, interviewees were asked to review the drawing and its information, and to clarify anything that was unclear. In this way, the map served as both a summary of the interview and, simultaneously, as a form of member checking.

Public spaces in each village were then classified by researchers on a 4-point scale, with 4 = very important, a multi-functional space ('functions' refer to the main types of activity, such as playing, walking, swimming, socializing, religious meetings, fleeting conversation, grilling, etc.) that is frequently used and with a high variety of users (a vibrant place); 3 = important, a space with at least two functions, often used or a multi-functional space,

Table 1. Selected demographic statistics of interviewees.

Socio-economic variables	Classes
Sex	Males – 47%; females – 53%
Age	Under 18 years – 15%; 19-35 years – 24%; 36-65 years – 43%; 66 years and over – 18%
Educational status	Primary education – 23%; secondary education – 65%; tertiary education – 12%
Local community function/ position	Village head – 14%; grocery saleswoman/man – 16%; employees of other important rural institutions (library, office, church) – 15%; local activists – 10%; other people indicated as familiar with the village and residents – 45%

used moderately frequently; 2 = moderately important, a space with at least two functions, moderately frequently used, or a space with only one function, often used; 1 = of little importance, a space with only one function, rarely and moderately frequently used, or space of two functions rarely or very rarely used. The intensity of use was determined with respect to the number of inhabitants and from the perspectives of key local leaders in each village.

Spatial analyses were divided on two parts. The first concerned the spatial arrangement of the village, especially the relation of residential buildings, recreational buildings and lake. Analyses was based on topographic maps at the scale 1:10 000 from the years 1976, 1984, and 2001, and orthophotomaps of pixel size 0.25 m from 2009 and 2012 and executed using the ArcGIS software. Maps included elements such as residential buildings (permanent housing or homesteads), recreational buildings (summer housing or second homes), tourist resorts (the former state-owned tourist centers), service facilities, roads and lakes. Lakes were marked according to the availability and attractiveness of the coastline using a four-item scale: available and most attractive shorelines (large attractive beaches); available and less attractive (small beaches and other places with a possibility of bathing); moderately available (possible access to the shoreline but no bathing, but including fishing platforms or grassy shores); poor access (mainly bulrush and peat bogs).

The second part of the spatial analysis concerned public places and was completely based on the data collected in the interviews. It consisted of aggregating the interview information from each village and creating a comprehensive overview map of the public places for that community, with the location and importance of each place also noted on this overall map.

Spatial data were also supplemented by field observations made on-site by researchers during both the first and second parts of the spatial analyses. With regard to the first part, field inspections were carried out only in places where it was necessary, mainly for determining the availability and attractiveness of the lake shoreline, and buildings function, where it was not clearly stated on the map or readable in aerial photography. With regard to the second part, field observations related to each of the identified public spaces, in order to define the approximate boundaries, connections and state of development (such as bus stops, playgrounds, sports facilities, benches, gazebos, bonfires, bridges and platforms, trodden paths and fences). Field observations were carried out by the first two authors, after the completion of all interviews and cartographic analysis, as a one-time visit to each village and each public place.

Thus, drawing from both the social analyses (interviews) and spatial analyses (cartographic analysis and field observations) conducted for each village, we characterized the spatial-functional structure of the village (the area of various forms of development, communication links, distances, dense or scattered housing, mixed or separated recreational and residential housing) and public place characteristics (system and arrangement of public places, locations and development level of each place, diversity and intensity of social activities and place importance to the community). All results were aggregated and 'village socio-spatial charts' were constructed. Each chart contained a general map, and a brief description (developed by researchers) of spatial and social characteristics and issues (see Figure 2). Then, the relationships and dependencies between social and spatial characteristics within each village and between villages were evaluated to assess patterns in the data and trends across the 17 study sites and the rural region as a whole.

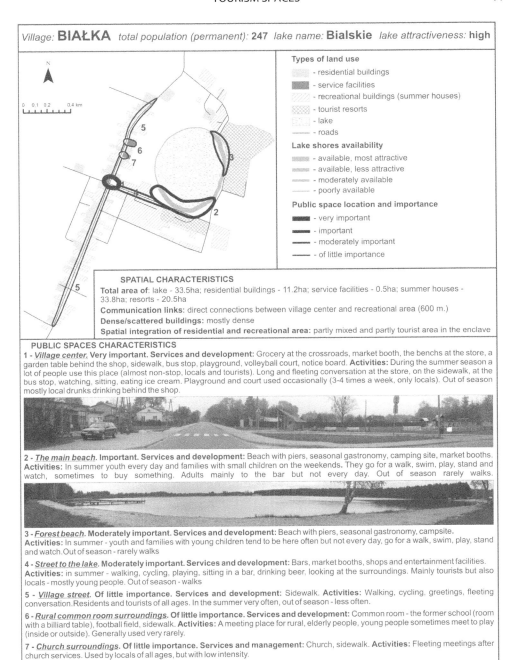

Figure 2. Socio-spatial village chart of Białka (own work: using Arc Gis and Corel Draw).

Results

The spatial arrangements of villages

Study villages are primarily small. Observations made by researchers show that, in some cases, a 'patchy' development pattern is evident, with homes, buildings and open spaces arranged along a single street. A 'dense' development pattern, with buildings concentrated along main streets, is visible in only four villages. Four other villages have 'scattered' settlement patterns, with homes and buildings dispersed across the landscape.

All study villages are adjacent to lakes, but lakes are located directly adjacent to the built-up area in only four cases. In other cases, village centers are from 0.4 to 1.0 km away from accessible parts of the lakeshore. The spatial arrangement of each village has also been modified by development of tourist buildings. In villages with patchy or scattered building patterns, second homes are often located together in a single line. More often, however, they are clustered in micro subdivisions, usually built on former agricultural plots at the back of homestead parcels or on a large housing estate at the edge of a village. These areas were often located between the village and the lake, though some were completely isolated from the village and situated nearer to the lake. Both of these types of spatial arrangement are visible, e.g. in the village of Białka (Figure 2).

Near the most attractive lakes, second homes proliferate, and in some villages there are 100%–600% more second homes than local homesteads. These have been built as estates on homestead parcels in the village, surrounding agricultural parcels, and in former meadows by the lake; second homes sometimes almost completely encircle the lake basin. Near moderately attractive lakes, second homes usually account for about 20% of the homesteads, complementing rural housing (by densification) or forming a second line of development in the farthest parts of agricultural parcels. According to interviewees, second home estates were created and still largely arise in an unplanned manner, and sometimes are based on ill-conceived plans aimed mainly at attracting taxpayers. The result is the rise of vast, mono-functional 'urban' areas of chaotic spatial arrangement, devoid of well-planned communication systems or common areas, and degrading natural and landscape values.

The most developed tourist villages are supplemented by resorts, which interviewees identified as former state-owned recreation centers located adjacent to the most attractive sections of lakeshore. In contrast to second home estates, resorts were created using village spatial development plans that were well-conceived in terms of functionality and composition, but gave little attention to environmental (or village quality of life) issues. Structurally, resorts are usually independent tourist enclaves, separate from villages, with an independent technical and communication infrastructure. Roads linking resorts and villages usually emerge later, without comprehensive planning; as on-site observations showed, these may lack pedestrian and bike connections.

The intensive tourism development of the region is the main reason that villages, despite their small residential populations, are characterized by sprawling development patterns and sometimes elaborate spatial arrangements. Spatial and interview data suggest that these patterns have created chaotic and poorly functional systems. This may be due to a weak spatial planning system, where regional planning is very limited (spatial planning takes place mainly at the municipality/commune level) and public participation is almost absent. Planning therefore, takes into account the interests of individual investors, marginalizing the interests of the whole community. Selected spatial features of particular villages are presented in Table 2.

Table 2. Selected characteristics of the study villages.

Village name (lake name)	Tourist attractiveness of the lake*	Total population (people)**	Homsteads area – including residential and farmhouse (ha)***	Second houses (summer cottage) area (ha)***	Resorts area (ha)***	The distance between the build-up area of the village and recreation areas on the lake (meters)***	The dominance of mixed homesteads and recreational buildings***	Recreational buildings partially mixed with homesteads and partly in the enclave***	The dominance of recreational buildings in the enclave***	The importance of respective everyday public spaces****	The importance of respective lakeside public spaces****
Białka (Białka)	High	247	11.2	33.8	20.5	600		+		4,1,1,1	3,2,2
Dratów (Dratów)	Middle	604	23.2	4.7	–	400	+			1,3,3,3,3	1,1
Głębokie (Głębokie)	Middle	248	24.8	1.0	–	50	+			3,2,1	1
Grabniak (Rotcze)	High	159	8.0	34.1	7.1	100	+			1	2
Kaniwola (Piaseczno)	High	561	32.7	31.3	25.4	1000				3,3,3,2,2,1	2
Kolonia Dratów (Krzczeń)	Middle	143	12.1	4.1	–	900	+			3,2,1	–
Kolonia Kochanowskie (Wytyckie)	Middle	~50	6.9	18.0	–	450				3,1,1,1	3
Krasne (Krasne)	High	~250	11.1	46.7	15.3	50		+		3,2,1,1	2,1,1,1
Krzywe (Łukcze)	High	~150	13.2	79.9	8.1	250		+		3,3,2,2,1	3,3,2
Lejno (Zagłębocze)	High	158	12.8	70.6	6.9	850		+		3,3,2	3,1
Nowy Orzechów (Tomaszne)	Middle	308	25.2	42.5	–	550		+		2,2,2,1,1	1
Okuninka (Białe)	High	393	11.6	62.6	66.4	450		+		3,2,2,2,1	2,2
Rozkopaczew (Mytycze)	Middle	1100	91.6	23.4	–	300		+		3,2,2,2,1	1
Rozpłucie-Grabów (Piaseczno)	High	130	4.5	59.9	3.9	500		+		3,3,2,1,1,1	3
Stara Jedlanka (Gumienko)	High	382	17.1	6.9	6.1	350			+	3,2,2,1,1	3
Stary Uścimów (Maśluchowskie)	Middle	411	20.0	2.9	–	200	+			3,3,2,1,1	2,1
Wytyczno (Wytyckie)	Middle	~500	26.7	4.8	–	800			+	4,3,3,2,1,1	3

*Evaluated on the basis of presence and scale of tourist development and the diversification of tourism forms (especially the presence of beaches for swimming).
**Evaluated on the basis of statistical data of municipal offices.
***Evaluated on the basis of GIS analysis.
****Determined on the basis of semi-structured interviews (4 = very important; 3 = important; 2 = moderately important; 1 = of little importance).

Public places and social interactions

Interviews revealed two basic types of public places in study villages: 'everyday places' focused around rural services, and 'recreation places' located near the lake. Everyday places are usually more permanent, and the greater diversity of users and activities, as indicated by the interviewers, confirm their importance. Recreational places at lakes fulfill a variety of functions: some are sites for activities, but they are also seasonal sites, often used by only limited numbers and groups of people. Yet, recreational public places also function within the system of rural public space, and may play a key role in the integration of residents and tourists. The type, number and importance of public places in particular villages are presented in Table 2.

Everyday public places are often organized around service facilities, generating the necessary activities crucial for the existence of optional and social activities. Lack of these services (e.g. in the Grabniak village) equates with a lack of suitable integrating spaces in a village. Everyday public places are those that are visited frequently and by various social groups – e.g. grocery stores. Interviewees explained that stores can be sites for fleeting conversation, longer meetings, eating and drinking (often alcohol), observing the environment and walking (with the shop as destination). Community notice boards are located there, and it is at central shops that the postman sometimes distributes mail and deliveries for residents (e.g. Kaniwola village). Local shops are a meeting place for many residents (especially for adult men and youth), and serve as centers for wide-ranging social interactions.

These vibrant public places also serve to facilitate encounters and interactions between tourists and residents, especially during summers when tourists and children with their parents are frequent visitors to markets and grocery stores. The quality and development of every day public places is thus an important factor determining the presence of tourists. In 10 of the 17 villages, the central everyday public place serves the needs of both local residents and tourists. The spatial arrangements of all of these villages include at least partially mixed tourist and residential housing. In other villages, where residential and tourists zones are clearly separated, the presence of tourists in a village is rare. In these settings, the tourist zone tends to feature seasonal shops and bars that are public spaces primarily intended for use by tourists. In such spatially divided villages, relations between tourists and locals are very limited.

In all study villages, interviewees felt that tourism was a significant driver in making vibrant community public places, both in economic and social terms. The social analysis showed that when there are stores in a village, and others close to a lake or summer cottage estates, tourists and residents use the stores closest to where they live (as seen in Wytyczno, Kaniwola, Krzywe, Rozpłucie, and Okuninka). Often services in the tourist area are open only during summertime. In contrast, where services are located centrally, near to the intersection of residential and tourist (seasonal) housing, they become a use and interaction center for both local residents and visitors. These also become, according to interviewees, examples of good public places, integrative and well-functioning (e.g. Krasne, Białka; see Figure 2).

Thus, the data suggest that public places function best when service facilities are concentrated in a relatively small area, and when they are complemented by a playground, sports facility or even bus stop (a frequent meeting place for young people). In villages that lack this type of development, residents described taking the initiative themselves to create a sports field on a private meadow (e.g. Kolonia Dratów, Krasne) or a playground in a private garden (e.g. Kolonia Dratów). Nevertheless, single investments arising in separate, random locations – while supporting local functions and adding value to a locale – do not necessarily result in common village places. When primary services are centrally located and the space around them developed properly, local centers emerge as often-vibrant public places (e.g. Rozkopaczew).

Interviewees also identified other important public spaces in villages, including service facilities such as the school, church, chapel, fire station-community room, and library. Though frequency of use may be low, these sites accommodate casual meetings as well as organized events, feasts, team games, and religious services. Moreover, these sites are typically used by a variety of adult groups and young people from the local area. With the exception of the church, however, they are rarely a place of meetings with tourists.

In addition to every-day places related to services, roads were seen to play an important role in the social functioning of villages. In traditional villages, roads were often the sole or primary common space. Though in some villages roads serve mainly as transportation corridors, in villages with little traffic, roads remain important meeting places. In 10 (of 17) villages studied, interviewees reported that rural roads are important or moderately important public spaces. Local residents often use the street as a place of casual meetings, long conversations, ball games, skating, biking or even hanging out on traditional benches and just watching people passing (e.g. Wytyczno, Białka). An interviewee who was a resident of Kochanowskie said that, 'the locals on the road often talk but tourists just walk because they do not know each other.' But a shop assistant from Lejno explained that many older people like to stand and watch the tourists walk in these areas. In this way, tourists from second homes located within the village helped to maintain the vibrant social spaces on local roads.

The social role of beaches and resorts

Beaches are important public spaces, and data show that during the summer season they almost always enrich and invigorate the social life of a village. Residents in about half of the study villages identified at least one lakeside beach as important (typically at the most attractive lakes); there was only one village in which residents did not reference the lake as a public space (a village with poor access to the lake). Beaches provided space for public activities including bathing, meetings and casual conversations, picnics, bonfires and barbecues, visits to bars and fast-food outlets, playing on adjacent playgrounds, ball games, festivals, walking, Nordic-walking, biking, year-round fishing, and winter ice skating. Some residents also visited beaches for purposes of people watching and the possibility of meeting non-local visitors. Beaches are used mainly by young people and families with young children, and occasionally elderly people. Other lakeside areas are primarily used by adults and elderly men (for fishing, mushroom picking, walking).

Generally, the most attractive and best-developed beaches are located within tourist resorts. Resorts, in fact, first initiated lakeside tourism development, as they were located in the most valuable and attractive areas. Resort-based beaches tend to be highly appreciated by local residents, who would like to have regular access to them for purposes of recreation. New owners of former state-owned recreation centers, however, often built fences and introduced paid attractions and services that excluded local residents. Even now, beaches are sometimes appropriated by resorts, and residents may not feel comfortable even at sites that are public property and where access is unlimited. At the same time, beaches fully managed by local governments and accessible for residents are often of much lower quality.

Therefore, much depends on the availability of beaches and the spatial and political connections between the village, the resort owners, and the lake. In Krzywe and Krasne, for example, the beaches are located within the resorts (access to the beach through the fenced area of the resort) and interviewees reported that residents often do not feel welcome. Meanwhile, in Lejno, where access to the beach and the public promenade is unlimited despite the presence of a large resort, interviewees described a very attractive place often used by adult residents, local youth, and tourists.

Even when high quality lakeside space exists, though, varying circumstances determine whether a resort will contribute to improving the quality of rural life, and whether residents and tourists become integrated within those spaces. For example, beaches at the most attractive lakes tended to be both vast and crowded – though in these places, despite many attractions, residents and tourists do not always interact. These beaches are mainly tourist attractions and places of recreation, not meeting and integration spaces, except in the off season, when local residents are more likely to use these sites as places for walks and recreation.

Attractive beaches are also common meeting places and important social spaces for residents when these are located closer to villages. Less important for residents are lakes where recreational areas are scattered or where less attractive beaches are closer to a village. An important social role is played by the beaches in very small villages, which lack services and other meeting points; in these cases, tourist areas are sometimes the only lively, vibrant places. A good example is the village of Kochanowskie where villagers described the beach as a 'community summer cultural center.' An interviewee who is a resident of Grabniak claimed that, 'if there were no tourists, there would be no public place in the village.' Interviews also reveal that residents valued even less attractive beaches at lakes where there are few tourists (e.g. Lakes Tomaszne, Głębokie, Wytyczno).

As for the resorts themselves, it is important to mention the frequent opinions of local resident interviewees regarding the nuisance nature of some resorts. Interviewees who reside in Krzywe village, e.g., complained about noise, public disputes and fighting, litter, parking problems, heavy traffic, and the fenced shore of the lake. On the other hand, second home owners in all villages had only positive opinions about 'resort people': 'There are no problems with them, they are polite because they are families," said a resident of Lejno. Another interviewee who was a resident of Uścimów explained, "Some of them we know since they were a child, they are part of our community.'

Negative effects of growth

Spatial integration can benefit both residents and tourists, but the social data show that there are limits related to intensity of growth. Exceeding the limits will produce negative impacts in villages and result in tourist enclaves that ignore local history, culture and society. In this study, residents reported that limits were exceeded in the village Okuninka, where the lake area is 106 hectares, rural housing occupies 12 hectares and tourism and recreation housing up to 129 hectares. Opinions on tourist overcrowding during the summer season also appeared in other villages. The inhabitants of Białka, where recreational buildings occupy more and more space around the lake, appealed to tourists, saying, 'Vacationists, I say, do not cut the branches on which you sit' – in other words, please protect the positive qualities of the local place that is valued by residents as well as visitors. Other negative opinions appear mainly among people living in the vicinity of the resorts or on main roads leading to lakes. A resident of Kaniwola provides a succinct summary about the presence of tourists in the village: 'At the end of July, I have had enough of them, but when in September they leave, it makes me sad.'

Discussion

How do different spatial arrangements in tourist villages affect the quality of public spaces and the level of integration between locals and tourists? The analysis presented here shows that the spatial integration of permanent and summer housing is beneficial for both locals and tourists, even if the number of second homes exceeds the number of permanent houses. In small villages and those with lower to medium tourism intensity, the optimal solution seems to involve the spatial integration of residential and tourist zones, or even mixed housing. The data showed that development of second homes supports local services and invigorates public spaces. Villages are the focal point for tourists living in summer housing estates, while also providing organized, year-round, common spaces for activities and social interactions for residents. This vitality is missing in mono-functional recreational housing estates, dominated by private property.

This study also suggests that proper deployment of services in the context of rural and tourist housing is essential for the quality of village public places. Furthermore, it is beneficial for community interaction to locate services either in the center of a village using mixed-type development (combining homesteads and recreational buildings), or in contact areas between homesteads and tourist housing estates (which often do not have their own public spaces).

Resorts, on the other hand, are designed mainly for tourist use, and data showed that spatial relations between resorts and villages did not significantly affect the quality of their local services and recreational offerings. Yet, resorts play an important role for residents – although there are sometimes problems and limitations in public access and use of resort amenities. For villages with low populations and limited services, however, the presence of tourism infrastructure (especially at lakesides) is an opportunity to raise local standards of living by creating new public places that otherwise may not have developed. In this case, the key is cooperation between resort owners and local governments, which limit the negative impact of the resorts on the village while still allowing residents easy access to major recreational areas and culturally beneficial contact with the visitors. The spatial integration of tourist and residential buildings should be as strong as possible, providing that an appropriate proportion of the local population and tourists is maintained. Extensive and intensive spatial development for tourism, or the appropriation of local public places and recreational spaces for primarily tourist activity, often causes conflicts and lowers the quality of life for villagers.

The study described here confirms the conclusions of prior research about the spatial impacts of tourism development (Doxey, 1975; Jokinen & Sippola, 2007; Puczkó & Rátz,

2000; Vargas-Sánchez et al., 2011; Wall, 1996), especially with respect to the negative impacts of over-investment and mass tourism. In agreement with Kastenholz et al. (2012), we found that residents of smaller villages where tourism is an important factor in enhancing the attractiveness of rural life tend to hold positive attitudes to tourism. But even in small villages, resident attitudes toward second-home residents are much more favorable than their attitudes toward resort users. This confirms the conclusions of Milne and Ateljevic (2001) concerning the introduction in the villages of projects that are appropriately scaled to community size.

We also documented negative opinions about the creation of tourist enclaves as related to the intensity of tourism and spatial arrangement of local buildings. In most of the villages studied, spatial arrangements integrating the residential and tourist zones were beneficial to the social functioning of public spaces. Buffer zones that limit the resident-tourist tensions proposed by Overvåga and Bergb (2011) are in our opinion, justified only in the case of high tourism intensity and more so in relation to resorts than to second housing estates. According to our research, in the case of the tourist enclave, greater emphasis should be placed on good connections and availability of the main recreational areas for residents, which will minimize the nuisance effects and provide equal local and visitor rights and an opportunity for their integration.

There are several limitations of the study presented here. Though a broad selection of villages was chosen for study, and nearly 100 interviews were conducted across the study sites, the actual number of interviews per village was relatively small. Furthermore, interviewees were persons who were well-known within villages, those with longevity, and those holding positions of importance (key leaders or business persons). These individuals may express particular kinds of orientations to growth compared to other local residents, and so future research should seek to expand and diversify the set of interviewees consulted. In addition, future studies should also interview second-home owners and tourists to assess their perspectives on village spatial arrangements and relationships with local residents.

Conclusions

The research described here has importance for tourism spatial planning in rural villages and amenity regions of Poland and elsewhere, particularly in places that are attempting to develop within weakly institutionalized spatial planning systems. Bearing in mind the hitherto chaotic development that was typical in this region of Poland, and with respect to the 'best' village spatial arrangements suggested by our research, we offer several practical planning suggestions. In small villages or areas with a low summer housing intensity, tourism development should complement street-adjacent buildings, and spatially mixed permanent and summer housing should be introduced. With higher tourism intensity, development of homogeneous holiday estates adjacent to a village may be desired – but services and public places should located in areas accessible to both local residents and tourists in an effort to avoid nuisances while creating opportunities for social interaction among groups. In the case of holiday resorts, tourist enclaves are acceptable, but these require maintaining good connections with the village, and openness and availability of recreation areas and lakes for all. The implementation of these guidelines in spatial planning would create conditions for synergic social and economic development and revival of village public places.

Thus, congruent with theoretical approaches to both sustainable tourism development and New Urbanism spatial planning, we encourage sensitive tourism development toward creating more compact, built-up areas while reducing the annexation of new land for dispersed development. Higher density areas will typically have mixed functions and well-connected residential and recreational areas. This also increases the availability of services whose importance to public places is emphasized by, among others, Aubert-Gameta and Covab (1999) and Heffernan et al. (2014). Maintenance services with a small population, however, are difficult in many villages. As our research shows, though, the spatial integration of tourist and residential housing allows maintenance of services and ensures the viability of common public spaces.

These ideas are consistent with CBT, and with the vision of rural tourism as a contributor to local sustainability (Jennings & Krannich, 2013; Pitkanen et al., 2014; Sotiropoulou, 2007). CBT also fosters a notion of the social values of tourism based on personalized contacts among villagers and tourists, and participation in the daily activities of a community (Farstad, 2011; Kastenholz & Lima, 2013). Although spatial planning is central to effective tourism development, it cannot be the sole basis for decision-making. Wise planning based on a forward-looking vision of an entire region is ultimately a necessity (Anselmi & Genna, 2007; Kim & Choi, 2012; Ko & Stewart, 2002). This vision, along with the level of its implementation, determines whether tourism will fully contribute to and enhance the sustainable development of rural areas and their desirable amenity values.

Acknowledgements

We are grateful to the residents who gave their time and constructive comments to our interviews and Cyprian Jaruga for assisting with the GIS analysis.

Disclosure statement

No potential conflict of interest was reported by the authors.

ORCID

Dawid Soszyński http://orcid.org/0000-0002-3071-7008
Barbara Sowińska-Świerkosz http://orcid.org/0000-0002-0276-7809

References

Anselmi, F. A., & Genna, V. D. (2007). Sustainable tourism development: Guide for local planners. In *Local governance and sustainable development* (pp. 1–17). Cergy: Paris.

Aubert-Gameta, V., & Covab, B. (1999). Servicescapes: From modern non-places to postmodern common places. *Journal of Business Research, 44*(1), 37–45. doi:10.1016/S0148-2963(97)00176-8

Bramwell, B. (2004). Mass tourism, diversification and sustainability in southern Europe's coastal regions. In B. Bramwell (Ed.), *Coastal mass tourism. Diversification and sustainable development in southern Europe. Aspects of tourism* (pp. 1–31). Clevedon: Channel View.

Chmielewski, J. M. (2004). *Teoria urbanistyki w projektowaniu i planowaniu miast* [Theory of urbanism in town design and planning]. Warszawa: Oficyna Wydawnicza PWN.

Doxey, G. V. (1975). A causation theory of visitor-resident irritants: Methodology and research inferences. In *Proceedings of Travel and Tourism Research Associations Sixth Annual Conference* (pp. 195–198). San Diego, CA: Travel Research Association.

Ellis, C. (2002). The new urbanism: Critiques and rebuttals. *Journal of Urban Design, 7*(3), 261–291. doi:10.1080/1357480022000039330

Erotokritakis, K., & Andriotis, K. (2007). Residents' perceptions towards tourism in a rural Cretan community. In *International Conference of Trends, Impacts and Policies on Tourism Development, Heraklion, Greece, 15-18 June 2007*. Retrieved from http://eprints.mdx.ac.uk/13231/3/Residents,perceptions,towards,tourism,in,a,rural,Cretan,communit.pdf

Farstad, M. (2011). Rural residents' opinions about second home owners' pursuit of own interests in the host community. *Norsk Geografisk Tidsskrift – Norwegian Journal of Geography, 65*(3), 165–174. doi:10.1080/00291951.2011.598551

Fennell, D. (1996). A tourist space-time budget in the Shetland Islands. *Annals of Tourism Research, 23*(4), 811–829. doi:10.1016/0160-7383(96)00008-4

Flaga, M., & Łoboda, K. (2011). Sytuacja demograficzna Polesia Lubelskiego jako skutek i przyczyna marginalizacji regionu [Demographic situation of Polesie Lubelskie as a result and cause of marginalization of the region]. *Barometr regionalny, 3*(25), 67–78.

Freitag, T. G. (1994). Enclave tourism development: For whom the benefits roll ? *Annals of Tourism Research, 21*(3), 538–554. doi:10.1016/0160-7383(94)90119-8

Gehl, J. (1987). *Life between buildings: Using public space*. New York, NY: Van Nostrand Reinhold.

Ghasemia, M., & Hamzah, A. (2014). An investigation of the appropriateness of tourism development paradigms in rural areas from main tourism stakeholders' point of view. *Procedia – Social and Behavioral Sciences, 144*, 15–24. doi:10.1016/j.sbspro.2014.07.269

Habermas, J. (1991). *The structural transformation of the public sphere: An inquiry into a category of bourgeois society*. Cambridge: The MIT Press.

Hardy, A., Beeton, J. S., & Pearson, L. (2002). Sustainable tourism: An overview of the concept and its position in relation to conceptualisations. *Journal of Sustainable Tourism, 10*(6), 475–496. doi:10.1080/09669580208667183

Heffernan, E., Heffernan, T., & Pan, W. (2014). The relationship between the quality of active frontages and public perceptions of public spaces. *Urban Design International, 19*(1), 92–102. doi:http://dx.doi.org/10.1057/udi.2013.16

Holland, C., Clark, A., Katz, J., & Peace, S. (2007). *Social interactions in urban public places*. London: The Policy Press.

Horn, C., & Simmons, D. (2002). Community adaptation to tourism: Comparisons between Rotorua and Kaikura, New Zealand. *Tourism Management, 23*(2), 133–143. doi:10.1016/S0261-5177(01)00049-8

Jennings, B. M., & Krannich, R. S. (2013). Bonded to whom? social interactions in a high-amenity rural setting. *Community Development, 44*(1), 3–22. doi:10.1080/15575330.2011.583355

Johnson, P. A. (2010). Realizing rural community-based tourism development: Prospects for social economy enterprises. *Journal of Rural and Community Development, 5*(1), 150–162. Retrieved from http://journals.brandonu.ca/jrcd/article/view/349

Jokinen, M., & Sippola, S. (2007). Social sustainability at tourist destinations – local opinions on their development and future in northern Finland. *University of Lapland – Arctic centre reports, 50*, 89–99. Retrieved from http://urn.fi/URN:NBN:fi:uLa-20116161147

Kastenholz, E., & Sparrer, M. (2009). Rural dimensions of the commercial home. In P. Lynch, A. MacIntosh, & H. Tucker (Eds.), *Commercial homes in tourism: An international perspective* (pp. 138–149). London: Routledge

Kastenholz, E., João Carneiro, M., Peixeira Marques, C., & Lima, J. (2012). Understanding and managing the rural tourism experience – The case of a historical village in Portugal. *Tourism Management Perspectives, 4*, 207–214. doi:10.1016/j.tmp.2012.08.009

Kastenholz, E., & Lima, J. (2013). Co-creating quality rural tourism experiences – the case of a Schist Village in Portugal. *International Journal of Management Cases, 15*(4), 193–204. Retrieved from http://www.ijmc.org/IJMC/Vol_15.4.html

Katz, P., Scully, V. J., & Bressi, T. W. (1994). *The new urbanism: Toward an architecture of community*. New York, NY: McGraw-Hill.

Kim, Y-G., & Choi, J-M. (2012). Preliminary landscape improvement plan for Guryong village. *Journal of the Korean Institute of Landscape Architecture, 40*(6), 23–34. doi:10.9715/KILA.2012.40.6.023

Ko, D-W., & Stewart, W. P. (2002). A structural equation model of residents' attitudes for tourism development. *Tourism Management, 23*(5), 521–530. doi:10.1016/S0261-5177(02)00006-7

Kowalczyk, A., & Derek, M. (2010). *Zagospodarowanie turystyczne* [Tourist development]. Warszawa: PWN.

Krukowska, R. (2009). Pojezierze Łęczyńsko-Włodawskie – funkcja turystyczna regionu [Łęczyńsko-Włodawskie Lake District – tourist function of the region]. *Folia Touristica, 21*, 165–184.

Krukowska, R., & Świeca, A. (2012). Tourism and recreation in the Łęczyńsko-Włodawskie Lake District (middle-east Poland) survey results. *Polish Journal of Natural Science, 27*(4), 393–405. Retrieved from http://www.uwm.edu.pl/polish-journal/sites/default/files/issues/articles/krukowska_and_swieca_2012.pdf

Lawson, R. W., Williams, J., Young, T., & Cossens, J. (1998). A comparison of residents' attitudes towards tourism in 10 New Zealand destinations. *Tourism Management, 19*(3), 247–256. doi:10.1016/S0261-5177(98)00018-1

Lorens, P. (2010). Definiowanie współczesnej przestrzeni publicznej [Defining contemporary public space]. In P. Lorens & J. Martyniuk-Pęczek (Eds.), *Problemy kształtowania przestrzeni publicznych* (pp. 6–22). Gdańsk: Wydawnictwo Urbanista.

Lynch, K. (1960). *The image of the city*. Cambridge: MIT Press.

MacCannell, D. (1973). Staged authenticity: Arrangements of social space in tourist settings. *The American Journal of Sociology, 79*(3), 589–603. doi:10.1086/225585

Milne, S., & Ateljevic, I. (2001). Tourism, economic development and the global-local nexus: Theory embracing complexity. *Tourism Geographies, 3*(4), 369–393. doi:10.1080/146166800110070478

Montgomery, J. (1998). Making a city: Urbanity, vitality and urban design. *Journal of Urban Design, 3*(1), 93–116. doi:10.1080/13574809808724418

Murphy, P. E. (1985). *Tourism: A community approach*. New York, NY: Methuen.

Nepal, S. K. (2007). Tourism and rural settlements in Nepal's Annapurna region. *Annals of Tourism Research, 34*(4), 855–875. doi:10.1016/j.annals.2007.03.012

Oncescu, J., & Robertson, B. (2010). Recreation in remote communities: A case study of a Nova Scotia village. *Journal of Rural and Community Development, 5*(1/2), 221–237. Retrieved from http://journals.brandonu.ca/jrcd/article/view/350

Overvåg, K., & Berg, N. G. (2011). Second homes, rurality and contested space in Eastern Norway. *Tourism Geographies, 13*(3), 417–442. doi:10.1080/14616688.2011.570778

Pitkanen, K., Adamiak, C., & Halseth, G. (2014). Leisure Activities and rural community change: Valuation and use of rural space among permanent residents and second home owners. *Sociologia Ruralis, 54*(2), 143–166. doi:10.1111/soru.12023

Puczkó, L., & Rátz, T. (2000). Tourist and resident perceptions of the physical impacts of tourism at lake Balaton, Hungary: Issues for sustainable tourism management. *Journal of Sustainable Tourism, 8*(6), 458–478. doi:10.1080/09669580008667380

Richards, G., & Hall, D. (2000). *Tourism and sustainable community development.* London: Routledge.

Soszyński, D., Jaruga, C., & Sowińska-Świerkosz, B. (2015). A river in a rural public space in the early 1940s: A case study of the Bug river valley (East Poland). In V. Ivanišević, T. Veljanovski, D. Cowley, G. Kiarszys, & I. Bugarski (Eds.), *Recovering lost landscapes* (pp. 35–44). Belgrade: Institute of Archaeology and Aerial Archaeology Research Group.

Sotiropoulou, E. Ch. (2007). Tourism, village, space and the re-appropriation of rural: Towards a new social organization of the countryside. *Tourismos: An International Multidisciplinary Journal of Tourism, 2*(2), 113–128. Retrieved from https://mpra.ub.uni-muenchen.de/id/eprint/6371

Stokowski, P. A. (1996). *Riches and regrets.* Niwot: University Press of Colorado.

Suansri, P. (2003). *Community based tourism handbook.* Bangkok: Responsible Ecological Social Tours.

Szeszuła, W. (2010). Kryteria oceny rozwiązań przestrzennych zespołów zabudowy jednorodzinnej [The criteria for the assessment of spatial solutions in the family housing]. *Architecturae et artibus, 1,* 76–84. Retrieved from http://www.wa.pb.edu.pl/uploads/downloads/11-Kryteria-oceny-rozwiazan-przestrzennych-zespolow-zabudowy-jednorodzinnej.pdf

Talen, E. (1999). Sense of community and neighborhood form: An assessment of the social doctrine of New Urbanism. *Urban studies, 36*(8), 1361–1379. doi:10.1080/0042098993033

Tosun, C. (2002). Host perceptions of impacts: A comparative tourism study. *Annals of Tourism Research, 29*(1), 231–253. doi:10.1016/S0160-7383(01)00039-1

Tucker, H. (2003). The host–guest relationship and its implications in rural tourism. In D. L. Roberts & M. Mitchell (Eds.), *New directions in rural tourism* (pp. 80–89). Ashgate: Aldershot.

Tucki, A., & Soszyński, D. (2012). Postawy społeczności lokalnej miasta Kazimierz Dolny wobec rozwoju turystyki [Resident's attitudes toward turism development in Kazimierz Dolny]. *Problemy Ekologii Krajobrazu, 34,* 245–252. Retrieved from agro.icm.edu.pl/agro/element/bwmeta1.element.../c/vol34_32_Tucki___i_in.PDF

Wall, G. (1996). Perspectives on tourism in selected Balinese villages. *Annals of Tourism Research, 23*(1), 123–137. doi:10.1016/0160-7383(95)00056-9

Weaver, D., & Lawton, L. (2001). Resident perceptions in the urban–rural fringe. *Annals of Tourism Research, 28*(2), 439–458. doi:10.1016/S0160-7383(00)00052-9

Whyte, W. H. (1980). *The social life of small urban spaces.* Washington, DC: The Conservation Foundation.

Vargas-Sánchez, A., Porras-Bueno, N., & Plaza-Mejía, M. A. (2011). Explaining residents' attitudes to tourism: Is a universal model possible ? *Annals of Tourism Research, 38*(2), 460–480. doi:10.1016/j.annals.2010.10.004

Xi, J. C., Wang, X. G., Kong, Q. Q., & Zhang, N. (2015). Spatial morphology evolution of rural settlements induced by tourism: A comparative study of three villages in Yesanpo tourism area, China. *Journal of Geographical Sciences, 25*(4), 497–511. doi:10.1007/s11442-015-1182-y

Tsartas, P. (2003). Tourism Development in Greek Insular and Coastal Areas: Sociocultural Changes and Crucial Policy Issues. *Journal of Sustainable Tourism, 11*(2-3), 116–132. doi:10.1080/09669580308667199

Selecting the best route in a theme park through multi-objective programming

Beatriz Rodríguez-Díaz and Juan Ignacio Pulido-Fernández

ABSTRACT
The theme park industry has grown intensely in recent times and offer every day a greater number of attractions and activities to visit. The problem is that, when a tourist visits a theme park, he has a short space of time and he wants to maximize the usefulness of the visit, such as enjoying as many attractions as possible. Visitors face a serious selection problem – they must identify the best alternatives so as to optimally utilize their time and visit to the attractions that most interest them, besides keeping a check on the money spent during the visit. It would be very useful if they had a tool to help them take an optimum decision from among the different alternatives, considering their goals, restrictions and preferences. Therefore, we are going to develop a tool that, through a multi-objective model, helps theme park visitors who want to obtain an ideal route, helping them choose among the various alternatives: what activities to pursue, in what order, at what time, etc. The system can be used from home through a web page or application, or when present in the park, which also allows the tourist to incorporate the suggestions that arise in the park on the fly. This tool could improve the satisfaction of tourists visiting the park as it offers the maximum utility with regard to the activities undertaken within the timeframe available to them, thus also rendering added value to the theme park. One of the challenges facing theme parks management is the management of visitor flow, characterized by the dual objective of ensuring the highest quality experience for the tourists and reducing the risks arising from congestion of the different areas and/or most visited attractions, and we consider that this tool can help them to do it.

摘要:
近年来,主题公园产业蓬勃发展,每天都有更多的景点和活动可供参观。问题是,当一个游客参观一个主题公园时,他有很短的时间,他想最大化这次访问的效用,比如尽可能多地欣赏旅游景点。游客们面临着严重的选择问题——他们必须找到最佳的选择,以便最佳地利用他们的时间,去参观他们最感兴趣的景点,同时还要确保参观期间的花费不超支。考虑到他们的目标、限制和偏好,如果他们有一个工具帮助他们从不同的选择中获得最佳决策,那将是非常有用的。因此,我们通过多目标模型要开发一个工具,帮助主题公园游客获得理想的路线,帮助他们从不同的游览方案中选择一个理想的获得路线: 在什么时刻以什么顺序游览什么活动,等。该系统通过一个web页面或应用程序在家里就可以使用,或者当出现在公园时,还可以允许旅游者采用即时生成的游览建议。这个工具可以提高游客参观公园的满意度，因为它给游客提供了在时间框架内开展活动的最大效用，从而为主题公园提升了价值。主题公园管理面临的挑战之一是游客流的管理，该项管理具有双重目标，既确保为旅游者提供最佳的游览体验，又减少因不同区域和/或最常访问的景点游客拥堵产生的风险，我们认为这个工具对此可以有所帮助。

1. Introduction

The study of tourist behavior is one of the major topics of tourism research. However, as Shoval and Isaacson (2010) admit, until the end of the last century, little attention had been given to the spatial and temporal behavior of tourists. This aspect, nevertheless, is key to improving the management of attractions, optimizing the administration of basic services, expanding the flow of visitors or renewing marketing strategies, among other things (Grinberger, Shoval, & McKercher, 2014; Thornton, Williams, & Shaw, 1997).

As documented Xiang, Wang, O'Leary, and Fesenmaier (2014), the influence of the Internet and the massive use of mobile devices by tourists are facilitating their access to a vast volume of tourist information. Tourists today can easily find out the smallest details about different tourist destinations, activities that can be pursued at these destinations, up-to-date prices, visiting times and so on.

At present, the problem for the tourists is not the lack of information, but rather, when faced with the amount of information available, the difficulty lies in knowing (and, above all, evaluating) all the possible trip alternatives, which translates into a lot of time spent. On the other hand, even when able to know all the possible alternatives, there is no guarantee of choosing the best option, since their goals are in conflict.

Although this problem can be generalized to tourism as a whole, we focus on theme parks, because nowadays the number of activities that can be carried out in these areas has increased largely. So the visitors are faced with a problem of choosing from a wide variety of activities to do in a limited timeframe and they may need help to organize their visit in an optimal way. We want to propose a tool that develops a route as appropriate as possible for each tourist and this tool can be especially significant in the management of such parks (Birenboim, Antón-Clavé, Russo, & Shoval, 2013; Xu et al., 2015). Simultaneously, park managers are faced with a problem that stems from the possible congestion due to visitors deciding to pursue the same type of activity at the same time, a situation that lengthens the waiting time to enjoy the attractions (Birenboim et al., 2013; Meijles, de Bakker, Groote, & Barske, 2014). If we offer each tourist a different route according to their needs, it is possible that the problem in congestion and waiting times will improve, since not all visitors will follow the same standard route.

Theme parks, which spread endemically across the United States in the late 1960x and 1970s, include attractions such as rides, shows, food services and retail shops. In the 1980s and the 1990s, the majority of the parks emerged, including Disney World, Universal Studios, and Disneyland (Tsai & Chung, 2012). In 2015, the main destinations for theme parks were the United States and China, with a revenue of US$8 billion and US$4.6 billion, respectively, and China expected to overtake the United States by 2020 (Brzeski, 2017).

As Birenboim et al. point out (2013, p. 607), scientific literature has clearly identified 'temporal qualities (such as duration of activity, waiting time, time of arrival, and time of the day) as significant factors that strongly influence visitor decision-making.' It is, therefore, a key aspect that should be considered in any analysis of the selection process conducted by a visitor in a theme park.

On the other hand, tailored services increase visitor satisfaction. As Jung, Chung, and Leue (2015, p. 75) state: 'questionnaires administered to 241 theme park visitors revealed that content, personalized service, and system quality affect users' satisfaction and intention to recommend augmented reality applications.'

On the other hand, as Kemperman, Borgers, Oppewal, and Timmermans (2003) reported, in the case of amusement parks, it must be borne in mind that the visitor activity options and activity preferences may vary at different times of the day. Furthermore, the researchers postulate that the popularity of certain attractions means that visitors are willing to wait for more time to enjoy them, since the expected quality of the experience is higher. They also show that in the visitor's decision-making process, there are activities that are not alternatives, but rather mutually dependent (for example, one can enjoy an attraction at the beginning of the visit to the park in order to repeat it at a later time in the day, while other less attractive attractions or places can be visited to fill the time between the more attractive ones). Therefore, it would be very useful to manage an optimal route for the visitors that maximizes their preferences and minimizes their costs.

In short, we are confronted with a problem of selection (to decide what activities to perform from among all the existing choices) and sequencing (to indicate the order of performing these activities during the visit to the theme parks) of activities. In order to choose an alternative, there will be a conflict between the multiple objectives of the decision-maker, among others, in equal conditions, the tourists would like to minimize costs of the activities, and maximize the utility that the activities deliver. As Xu et al. point out (2015, p. 208), the solution to this problem could be 'personalizing the visiting routes and enhancing the enjoyment of the tour for individual visitors.'

It is interesting, therefore, to help the visitor organize a tailor-made visit, an aspect that is not novel, since, during the first decade of this century, several help-systems have been proposed in the general tourism ambit that aim at helping tourists (Camacho, Borrajo, & Molina, 2001; Castillo et al., 2008; Colineau & Wan, 2001; Godart, 2003; ahmood, Ricci, Venturini, & Höpken, 2008; Paris, 2002; Ricci, 2002; Schmidt-Belz, Laamanen, Poslad, & Zipf, 2003; Sun, Fan, Bakillah, & Zipf, 2015; Ten Hagen, Modsching, & Krarner, 2005; Yu, Spaccapietra, Cullot, & Aufaure, 2003; Zipf, 2002). However, the proposals made so far have certain limitations, not taking into consideration all the elements that are needed to give each visitor the most appropriate option. This drawback gives us the opportunity to propose a new system that covers these shortcomings.

In particular, there have not been many studies in the domain of theme parks. The relevant literature is very recent and includes the works by Tsai and Chung (2012), Tsai and Lai (2015), and Xu et al. (2015).

The objective is to develop a tool that helps theme park visitors who want to obtain an ideal route overcome the difficulty that they may face when planning their visit, and help them choose among the various alternatives, such as what activities to do, what order to do them in, at what time, etc. It is particularly useful for tourists who have not defined their visit and want help in organizing it. The system can be used from home through a web page or application, or when present in the park, which also allows, on the fly, the tourists to incorporate the different suggestions, considering they can change their mind once they are at the park. This tool could help improve the satisfaction of the tourists as it maximizes the utility they derive from the activities pursued within the limited time on hand, minimizing costs and adjusting to their preferences. This would, in turn, add value to the theme park.

The system we propose allows a problem that combines the problems of selection and sequencing of activities to be solved as one, since the selection of the activities will depend on where they are located in relation to the others. The first problem is to select activities that are well valued, in accordance with the preferences of the decision-maker, and the second, once they have chosen the activities to be performed, is to draw a route to visit these activities, so that the solutions are determined by considering the criteria of the decision-maker.

Comparing with similar problems analyzed in the literature, our problem has added difficulties as we must select and order the different points to be visited and consider four criteria in addition to the time windows for each of the activities.

The tourist has many destinations to visit and several activities to pursue. One of the factors that can help him decide where to go is the added value he obtains from a particular destination. A personalized help system for organizing his trip can be a reason behind making that decision. Managers of theme parks could be interested in these types of tools. In addition, such tools can aid in tail management and in assessing the impact of the carrying capacity, waiting time, and so on. Likewise, it could be very useful in other areas of the sector.

In the following section, we will see the methodological development of the model in order to obtain a customized route in a theme park; we will then proceed to present the solution to the model; in section 4, a practical application will be illustrated with the example of a visitor to a theme park; lastly, we present the conclusions.

2. Methodological approach

An in-depth analysis of the literature reveals that the problem we face is very similar to what is known as Travelling Salesman Problem with Profits (TSPP), considered a variant of the well-known Travelling Salesman Problem (TSP). According to Schrijver (2005), the TSP is to find the shortest path for a travelling salesman to visit 'n' given cities. The number of possible routes will grow exponentially as the number of cities grows, which makes resolving it very complex for a large number of cities to visit.

As examples of other variations of the TSP, we can highlight the so-called Prize Collecting (Ausiello, Bonifaci, & Laura, 2008; Balas, 1989), Travelling Salesman Problem (PCTSP), the so-called Orienteering Problem (OP) (Chao, Golden, & Wasil, 1996), Selective Travelling Salesman Problem (STSP), or Maximum Collection Problem

(Laporte & Martello, 1990) applied by several authors (Chao et al., 1996; Leifer & Rosenwein, 1994).

In the specific case that concerns us, the TSPP, the intention is to meet two objectives: minimize the distance traveled and maximize the profit at each point visited, where visiting all existing points is not necessary (Feillet, Dejax, & Gendreau, 2005). Among the methods that have been used to resolve this issue, local search combined with a multi-objective evolutionary algorithm (Jozefowiez, Glover, & Laguna, 2008), and the exact ε-constraint method (Bérubé, Gendreau, & Potvin, 2007) stand out.

We will be incorporating temporary restrictions through time windows, which have been used by authors such as Focacci, Milano, and Lodi (1999), Bar-Yehuda, Even, and Shahar (2005), Kantor and Rosenwein (1992), and Muñuzuri, Grosso, Cortés, and Guadix (2013).

Thus, we are going to consider more than two goals, as well as time windows, taking into account the schedule of the activities, entailing an even more complex approach that we will lay out below. Elements not addressed by other systems, such as the conflict between the objectives of the visitor, the time available to perform various activities, the duration of each activity or attraction, the time to get from one attraction to another, and how much the visitor wants to spend, will be taken into account.

In short, the proposed tool ensures the design of an itinerary customized to each visitor, by selecting a series of activities to pursue through the day, set out chronologically, considering all possible restrictions. For this purpose, an activity is understood as a combination of various activities that can be carried out in the park (observation, participation, and free time, including restaurants and refreshments).

The tool developed will provide the theme park visitors a detailed itinerary with all the activities to be carried out at each moment of their visit, taking into account their needs and preferences, making it the best possible route.

In order to provide an optimal route, we will use a model that makes up the base of the system and takes into account the objectives and constraints of the problem. We will interrelate this with previously developed databases, some with information about activities and others holding information about distances and travel times. Lastly, the system must have an interface through which the information required from the user will be collected, returning the optimal solution.

2.1. Formulation of the model

We apply a model that can be applied to any visitor who wishes to spend a day at a theme park, where a series of activities '1 to M' can be carried out. The set of activities, $j = 1, 2, \ldots, M$, which will be part of the decision process, will be sorted into different types, since each group of activities will behave in a different way, and therefore can be grouped into different sets to determine their characteristics.

For example, in the case presented, the theme park has the following activities: observing animals (birds, mammals and reptiles), observing plants, leisure (adventure activities, meetings with animal keepers, exhibitions and safari), restaurants, and free time. For a better understanding of the nomenclature, we are going to use this example to express the variables, but it can be applied to any other park that offers other activities.

We are going to consider these activities: observing animals belonging to the subset V_1, observing plants in the subset V_2, leisure in the subset V_3, restaurants in V_4, and free time in V_5. That is to say, we divide the activities into five subsets V_s ($s = 1-5$), the union of which forms the total set of activities V, as we shall see in expression (1). The observation of animals and leisure groups, in turn, contain different subtypes of visits represented, respectively, as V_{11}, V_{12} & V_{13} (birds, mammals and reptiles) on one hand and V_{31}, V_{32}, V_{33} & V_{34} (adventure activities, encounters with keepers, exhibits and safari) on the other; in other words: V_{1k} ($k = 1, 2, 3$) and V_{3k} ($k = 1, 2, 3, 4$).

The set made up by all the activities will be referred to as V, which represents the union of all the subsets of activities of each type, V_s:

$$V = \bigcup_{s=1}^{5} V_s \tag{1}$$

Other sets that we need to define for our model are as follows: V_y, which refers to the activities established by the decision-maker to be carried out during the tour; V_i, the set of activities preferred by the decision-maker that he/she would like to pursue if possible; and V_n, the set of activities that the visitor does not wish to pursue at any point.

The set of alternatives will be formed by the different routes that the visitors can take in the period of time that they establish for the visit, once the appropriate restrictions are incorporated. Each route is an ordered set of activities that visitors will carry out throughout the day.

This ordered set of activities is expressed by the decision variables in our model, which are binary variables x_{ij}:

$$x_{ij} = \begin{cases} 1 & \text{if they go from activity } i \text{ to activity } j \\ 0 & \text{otherwise} \end{cases} \quad i, j = 1, \ldots, M, i \neq j \tag{2}$$

We need to define some auxiliary variables; y_j is the number of times that the activity j is performed, which is to say, the times that the tourist switch activity j from any other activity i,

$$y_j = \sum_{i=1}^{M} x_{ij} \quad i, j = 1, \ldots, M, \quad i \neq j \tag{3}$$

Then, goals are established along with the set of constraints that the model must meet. The objectives under consideration were:

- Minimize travel time to switch from one activity to another: This time would depend on the distance between activities, since the tourists would walk. Therefore, this objective will be equivalent to minimizing the distance traveled throughout the day:

$$\text{Min} \sum_{i=1}^{M} \sum_{j=1}^{M} d_{ij} x_{ij} \quad i \neq j \tag{4}$$

where d_{ij} denotes the distance covered when moving from activity i to activity j.

- Minimize the cost of the activities: Some of the activities to be carried out may have an extra cost on top of the park's ticket price:

$$\text{Min} \sum_{j=1}^{M} c_j y_j \qquad (5)$$

where c_j is the cost of activity j.

- The third objective collects visitor preferences, trying to maximize their satisfaction with the activities they carry out. A value must be obtained that defines the interest/utility of each activity for the visitor, which must correspond to the visitor's preferences:

$$\text{Max} \sum_{j=1}^{M} u_j y_j \qquad (6)$$

Where u_j is the utility value obtained from activity j. This value depends on the visitor's preferences. The visitor's preference level is considered for each type of activity as well as for the quality of the activity.

- Another objective to consider is the diversity of activities to be pursued by the visitor at the park. This will be measured by the percentage of time that each type of activity takes compared to the total time spent on all the activities pursued. We try to minimize the deviation between the diversity offered in the final route and the visitor's wishes – in other words, the distance between the time used by the visitor on each type of visit in the route (real time for type of visit, tv_{sk}) and the desired time for each type of visit (desired time for type of visit, td_{sk}). This objective seeks to adjust the time devoted to each type of visit depending on the preferences indicated by the visitor. The formula is as follows:

$$\text{Max} \sum_{s=1}^{S} \sum_{k=1}^{K} |tv_{sk} - td_{sk}| \qquad (7)$$

where tv_{sk} is an auxiliary variable that indicates the total time spent on type s and subtype k visits, and td_{sk} is an auxiliary variable that indicates the total time the visitor wants to devote to the type s and subtype k visit. We define these auxiliary variables as follows:

$$tv_{sk} = \sum_{j \in V_{sk}} d_j y_j, \quad s = 1, \ldots, S\, k = 1, \ldots, K \qquad (8)$$

where d_j is the duration of activity j. The duration of the activities will be determined by several factors: the average duration of the activity, the preferences of the decision-maker (Botti, Peypoch, & Solonandrasana, 2008), and a percentage over the duration for downtime (or rest between activities).

$$td_{sk} = p_{sk} T, \quad s = 1, \ldots, S, \ k = 1, \ldots, K \qquad (9)$$

where p_{sk} is the percentage of time that the visitor wants to devote to the type of visit s sub k, over the total time of the visit; T is the total time of the visit:

$$T = \sum_{j=1}^{M} d_j y_j \qquad (10)$$

With regard to the restrictions, some are considered as belonging to the model, as there must be consistency in the instructions that the program offers; That is, if the visitor arrives at an activity, he/she should continue from thereon. Other restrictions are constraints specific to each decision-maker. This ensures that each decision-maker can choose certain features of the tour. This information is obtained by directly prompting the visitor at the beginning of the process:

- Each activity will be carried out a specific number of times, depending on the type of activity or visitor preferences:

$$\sum_{h=1}^{M} x_{hj} \leq \text{Max}_j, \; j = 1, \ldots M \quad \sum_{k=1}^{M} x_{jk} \leq \text{Max}_{jk}, \; j = 1, \ldots, M \quad (11)$$

- We need to know how long the visitors want to remain in the park, 'Max Time':

$$T_{\text{desp}} + T \leq \text{Max Time} \quad (12)$$

Where T_{desp} represents the time taken to move around the park, and T is the time used for pursuing activities throughout the day.

- In the case of the restaurant activities, two circumstances may occur if tourists eat in the park: the visitors want to eat at a restaurant at the park or they bring their own food. If they state that they want to eat at a restaurant, the following restriction is applied:

$$\sum_{j \in V_4} y_j = 1 \quad (13)$$

In the event that the tourists bring their own food, fictitious restaurants are included at the same location as each activity, so that they can eat near the place where they are at that moment.

$$y_j \leq y_i \forall (j, i) \in V_f \quad (14)$$

where V_f, is a set of pairs of activities made up by each visit and its corresponding fictitious restaurant.

- The visitor will be able to determine which activities they want to prioritize, implying that they must be pursued.

$$\sum_{h=1}^{M} x_{hj} = 1, j = \text{present activity} \quad (15)$$

acting similarly, if they indicate the type of activity that they want.

- They will also be able to indicate the visits or types of visits they do not want to carry out.

$$y_j = 0 \quad j = \text{activity not to be carried out} \quad (16)$$

- Each activity or show has a certain duration, which must be taken into consideration. The time at which an activity ends shall be equal to the time at which the activity begins, plus the duration of the visit. This will always be so when this activity is carried out; when it is not carried out, this number will be zero:

$$HF_i = HI_j + ta_j y_j \forall, j = 1, \ldots, M; j \neq i_0 \quad (17)$$

where HI_j is an auxiliary variable that indicates the time at which the visitor begins activity j ($j = 1, 2, \ldots, M$), and HF_j the time at which the activity ends.

- The time of arrival at the park is defined as the time of completion of the start point activity:

$$HF_{i0} = \text{time of arrival} \tag{18}$$

- The time at which an activity j ($j = 1, \ldots, M$) starts must be greater than, or equal to, the finish time of the activity preceding i, ($i = 1, \ldots, M$), in addition to the time taken to switch from one activity to another:

$$HI_j \geq HF_i + tr_j + td_{ij} - 10^6(1 - x_{ij}), \quad i,j = 1, \ldots, M; i \neq j \tag{19}$$

where td_{ij} denotes the time needed to move from activity i to activity j; meanwhile, tr_j is the leisure time associated with an activity.

- The time that the tourist begins activity j must be greater than, or equal to, the activity's opening time. This will be so, assuming the visitor performs activity j. Therefore, we incorporate the variable y_j so that when activity j is not carried out, this restriction does not affect the model:

$$HI_j \geq e_j y_j \tag{20}$$

where e_j is the time at which activity j can be started at the earliest, i.e. the opening time for that activity.

- The time at which the tourist begins activity j must be lower than, or equal to, the activity's latest starting time.

$$HI_j \leq l_j y_j \tag{21}$$

where l_j is the latest time at which activity j can start, which is the difference between the closing time for activity j and the duration of the activity, i.e. $l_j = cierre_j - ta_j$, where $cierre_j$ is the time at which activity j closes.

- Lastly, the visitor will also be able to indicate the pace of visit that they want, if they prefer to enjoy a relaxed route, with a rest period between one activity and another, or if, on the contrary, they want to carry out the greatest possible number of activities.

$$tr_j = d_j m \tag{22}$$

where tr_j is the time for relaxation (or downtime between activities) associated with an activity and 'm' is the percentage of time applied.

2.2. Databases

The information about the activity characteristics that are to be analyzed is collated in a database, so that the system can contrast it with visitors' preferences and provide the best path based on their preferences.

The main data that must be collected from each of the activities are, on one hand, location, type, duration, maximum number of times an activity can be enjoyed, utility, price, and visit schedule. On the other hand, distances between all the activities must be obtained using a Geographic Information System (GIS), generating a distance array that gathers the distances between each point and all others.

2.3. Interface

Information pertaining to the decision-makers will be gathered through a computer program that will serve as a platform for the tool that is proposed. The decision-makers will be presented with several questions through simple forms. Maximum time at the park will be gathered. The decision-makers will be offered the possibility to select, from a list of options, the activities they want to prioritize and the ones they do not want to pursue; the same procedure is followed for activity subtypes.

Subsequently, a valuation for each activity, according to visitors' preferences, must be obtained. Since they are not familiar with the activities, they cannot assign a value to each one. Therefore, they will be offered the possibility to indicate their preferences toward the generic features of the activities. The features been grouped together in different types, which the tourists will rate. In cases where there are subcategories, the visitors have the option to rate only the general classifications or the various subcategories.

The solutions that the visitors will receive will be a detailed itinerary that will show them the activities to be carried out, the travel times from one activity to another, the duration and the final rating for each of the activities, as well as a final summary.

One limitation is that it does not consider the actual environment and situation in the park, which would help manage queues and other aspects of management. This could be remedied by combining this technique with some others in the literature. It would also be interesting to have a prior analysis of the tourist behavior in the park, which would help improve the accuracy and model response time; for example, Birenboim et al. (2013) carried out a study of patterns of theme park visitors in PortAventura.

2.4. Resolution

Multi-objective problems are decision problems that are characterized by the presence of multiple objective functions in conflict. In this type of problem, faced with the general difficulty of finding a single solution, the objective becomes to find a set of efficient solutions, where a better solution, by improving certain attributes, is not possible without, at the same time, worsening others. This suite of solutions is called the Pareto frontier, and the concept of an optimal solution disappears, giving rise to the concept of efficient solution.

In order to arrive at a suitable solution, first, visitors' preferences regarding the fourth objective are adjusted by programming; once this is achieved, the efficiency of the rest of objectives is considered.

To do this, with regard to the fourth objective, we will understand it as a goal, with a valid margin of deviation that we will set at 10% of the time the visitor wishes to invest in each type of activity. We consider the objective to obtain a maximum deviation of 10% from the time wished by the visitor in the difference between the time spent and the desired time for each type of visit, thus obtaining the following statement:

$$|tv_{sk} - td_{sk}| \leq 0.1 td_{sk}, \quad k = 1, \ldots, 6 \tag{23}$$

The absolute value takes the form of two inequalities:

$$tv_{sk} \leq 1.1 td_{sk}, \quad k = 1, \ldots, 6 \tag{24}$$
$$tv_{sk} \leq 0.9 td_{sk}, \quad k = 1, \ldots, 6 \tag{25}$$

We seek to minimize the deviation in both directions. To do this, we define several deviation variables: for the first constraint (which represents a higher figure), the variables are n_{usk} and p_{usk}; for the second constraint (which is the lower figure), the variables are n_{dsk} and p_{dsk}:

$$\text{Min} \sum_{k=1}^{K} p_{usk} + n_{dsk} \tag{26}$$

Subject to:

$$tv_{sk} + n_{usk} - p_{usk} = 1.1 td_{sk}, \quad k = 1, \ldots, 6 \tag{27}$$
$$tv_{sk} + n_{usk} - p_{usk} = 0.9 td_{sk}, \quad k = 1, \ldots, 6 \tag{28}$$

as well as the rest of the model's restrictions.

Once this is achieved, we will determine efficient solutions, taking into consideration the rest of the objectives.

We have used linear programming solvers since the problem has a reduced dimension and these programs offer a satisfactory solution in a short time.

However, in some cases, such as when we work with a greater number of alternatives, traditional operational research techniques are not sufficient for the complexity that the resulting problem of selecting and sequencing multi-purpose activities would entail. In this case, we advise the use of meta-heuristics methods. Heuristic methods are methods of approximation that offer a quick and simple path to a good solution, even if it is not necessarily optimal (Zanakis & Evans, 1981). Meta-heuristic methods are more evolved heuristics that, through a strategy that guides and modifies other heuristics, yield better and more efficient solutions (Glover & Laguna, 1997).

3. Practical application

The practical application of the proposed methodology has been carried out in a theme park specializing in wild flora and fauna, which offers a wide variety of species to see and also multiple activities to pursue.

As shown in Tables 1 and 2, first, it is necessary to identify, for each of the different activities in the park, a series of characteristics: location, type, duration, maximum number of times that the activity can be enjoyed, utility, price, and visit schedule (not

Table 1. Species of flora and fauna that can be seen in the theme park.

ANIMALS (Opening hours: open all days)			
BIRDS	**MAMMALS**	**MAMMALS**	**REPTILES**
Griffon Vulture	Aquatic Antelope	Bobcat	Yellow Anaconda
Ground Hornbill	Chapman Zebra	Macaque of Gibraltar	Cuban Boa
Trumpeter Hornbill	Black and white colobus monkey	Mara	Common Iguana
Cassowary	Dromedary	Patas monkey	Piton of Sebas
Abdim Stork	Eland	Egyptian Fruit Bat	
Black-faced Spoonbill	Asian Elephant	White-tailed Gnu	
Lesser Flamingo	Cuvieri Gazelle	Short-nailed Asian Otter	
Crowned Crane	White-handed Gibbon	White Oryx	
Hermit Ibis	Cheetah	Red Panda	
Scarlet Ibis	Spotted Hyena	White Rhino	
Sacred Ibis	Common Hippopotamus	Meerkat	
Black-crowned night heron	Impala	Emperor Tamarin	
African tantalum	Giraffe	Grivet	
	Ring-Tailed Lemur	Wallaby	
	Lion		
	Northern Lynx		
PLANTS (Opening hours: open all day)			
Honey locust	Indian shot	Jerusalem thorn	European fan palm
Carob tree	Krantz aloe	River Red gum	Silk floss tree
Bottle tree	Catalpa	False pepper	Elephant's foot
Ombú	Dwarf Umbrella Tree	Benjamin's fig	Brazilian orchid tree
Rubber fig	Japanese sago palm	Heart-leaf philodendron	Banana tree
Coral tree	Queen palm	Velvet groundsel	Southern silky oak
Queensland umbrella tree	Swan's neck	Hibiscus	Tree germander
Bird of Paradise	Drago	Moreton Bay fig	Mexican Washingtonia
Bamboo	Oak	Mango	Spanish bayonet
	Christ thorn	Date Palm	Staghorn sumac

Table 2. Activities that can be carried out at the theme park.

Type of activity	Timetable (week)	Timetable (Saturdays, Sundays and national holidays)
Adventure activities		
Hanging bridges	Open throughout the day	Open throughout the day
Zip line		
Dromedary ride		
Archery		
Encounters with keepers		
Encounter with HYENA keeper	11:00	11:30
Encounter with LEMUR keeper	11:30	11:30
Encounter with LION keeper	12:10	12:10
Encounter with ELEPHANT keeper	15:50	15:50
Encounter with CHEETAH keeper	17:10	18:00
Exhibits		
Birds of prey exhibit	12:30	12:30/15:15
Safari	12:00/13:00/14:00/15:45/16:30	12:00/12:30/13:00/13:30/14:00/14:30/15:45/16:15/16:45/17:15
Restaurants		
BBQ	12:30–17.30	12:30–17:30
Pizzeria	12:30–17:30	12:30–17:30
Snack	10:00–18:00	10:00–18:00

all the information gathered has been included in the tables, to conserve space and avoid complications).

Regarding the usefulness of activities, we have considered calculating it according to the activities' own relevance and the tourist's preferences, normalizing these values on a scale of 0 to 10 and adding them with equal weight.

Table 3. Example of matrix of distances between activities.

	Animal, mammal: Cheetah	Animal, reptile: Yellow Anaconda	Pizza restaurant	Archery
Animal, mammal: cheetah	–	10	15	15
Animal, reptile: yellow anaconda	10	–	5	15
Pizza restaurant	15	5	–	10
Archery	15	15	10	–

Note: Distances are measured in minutes.

When referring to the relevance of an activity, we try to measure its importance in itself, independently of the tourist's preferences. For each type of activity and each subtype of visit, relevance is calculated in a different way. To obtain this data, park visitors' managers were directly polled.

The tourists will not be able to indicate their preference for each of the activities, since they do not know all of them. Therefore, they are asked to give their preference for the type and subtype of visit and, in the case of restaurants (food), their preferences for type of cuisine are considered.

With regard to the duration of activities, the average duration is used. However, the same activity can be performed for a longer or shorter time, depending on the preferences of the decision-maker. For example, people who really enjoy watching reptiles will want a longer visit than those who simply wish to see them out of curiosity (Botti et al., 2008). Therefore, the minimum and a maximum period for each activity will be collected, and the tourists may indicate if they want it to stay for a longer or shorter time.

To set the duration for each activity in the model, as well as to account for tourists' preferences for the duration of each type of activity, their preferences regarding tour pace must also be considered. Depending on the pace desired by the tourists, a percentage of the actual duration of the activity will be applied, which will be factored in as a rest period between one activity and another. In cases where the tourists want a relaxed tour, a 20% increase will be applied; likewise, it would be 10% for an average tour and 0% for a quick tour.

With regard to the maximum number of times an activity can be performed by visitors, a combination of the park manager's recommendation and information garnered from visitor surveys is used initially, although the final decision is left in the hands of the visitors.

Table 3 shows an example of the 'distances (measured in minutes) between activities' matrix, which will be symmetrical, since the trips are made on foot.

Now let us have a look at an example of a visitor who decided to use our application. First, we collect information regarding his preferences; this is shown in Table 4, which indicates only what is most relevant. Regarding the time he/she wants to devote to each type of visit, a percentage of the total time will be considered. However, precisely fitting a set time can be very complicated, and so the visitor will provide approximate percentages; thus, 100% may be exceeded or may not be reached and shall be adjusted automatically. He/she will be able to enter data for the subtype of activity or for the type in general.

This information is incorporated in the model previously developed, so that the restrictions are defined and adjusted with the objective functions of this model. After the resolution of the model is obtained, the route that best suits the needs and preferences of the visitor is determined, taking into account each of the observations he/she indicated.

Table 4. Distribution of timing, according to information provided by the tourist.

Time of arrival at the park	11.00 h
Day of visit	Friday
Desired time for types of visits:	
Observation of animals:	
Birds	20%
Mammals	10%
Reptiles	–
Observation of plants	5%
Leisure:	50%
Adventure activities	
Encounters with keepers	
Exhibitions	
Safari	
Restaurants	10%
Free time	5%
Usefulness: preference (within each type, rate the subtypes)	Specified for each desired type and subtype
Maximum, minimum or average time by activities:	Specified for each desired type and subtype
Maximum time in the park	6 h 30 min
Eating at the park	Yes
Activity to be carried out	Encounter with LION keeper
	Encounter with ELEPHANT keeper
	Cheetah
Activity not to be carried out	Animals: REPTILES Hanging Bridges
Pace of the visit	Relaxed

Table 5. Ideal route for the tourist in the example.

Time	Activity to be carried out	Identification in Map 1
11.00	Arrival at the park	
11.05	Lesser Flamingo	1
	Lion	
	Cocos Palm	
	False Pepper	
	Dromedary	
	Patas monkey	
11.40	Bird of Paradise	2
	Bamboo	
	Crowned Crane	
	Giraffe	
	Cheetah	
	White-tailed Gnu	
12.10	Encounter with LION keeper	3
13.05	Archery	4
14.00	BBQ restaurant	5
15.00	Free Time	6
15.50	Encounter with ELEPHANT keeper	7
16.45	Oak	8
	Date Palm	
	Abdim Stork	
	African tantalum	
	Ring-Tailed Lemur	
	Red Eucalyptus	
	Brazilian orchid tree	
17.30	Departure	

This route shows the visitor a plan in detail, indicating the schedule and activities to be carried at all times, and the duration of each and their price. Table 5 and Figure 1 show the ideal route, which the visitor will follow.

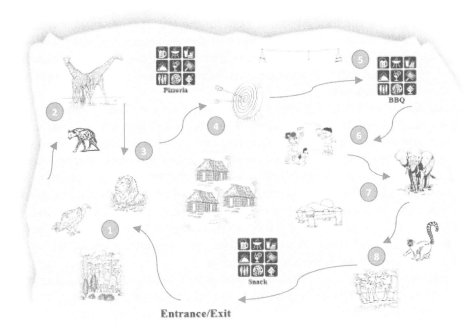

Figure 1. Ideal route for the tourist in the example: Source: Own material.

Owing to the incorporation of the objective functions and the restrictions, it has been possible to offer the tourist a route according to his/her needs. If this model was not available, in many cases, the tourist would not have been able to visit his/her desired attraction during his/her time of stay in the park.

4. Conclusions

In a world where tourist information is expanding and becoming ever simpler to obtain, it is now far easier for tourists to plan their own trips. However, this entails a substantial cost in terms of effort and time, due to the wide range of existing tourism products available in the market and the conflicts between the traveler's objectives; the tourists would like to minimize costs of the activities, and maximize their utility.

In theme parks, which have had a growing number of activities to carry out, visitors are faced with a problem of choosing from a wide variety of activities to pursue in a short time and as per a schedule. The proposed tool offers a personalized route, according to the tourist' preferences; it allows a visitor to a theme park to optimize the time available during their visit, so that they can enjoy the maximum number of attractions possible based on their preferences and needs, in terms of time, price, preferred activities, and so on. For this, a web-page-based system to help visitors will be implemented; it can be used from home through or directly at the park facilities.

Considering that it has been proven that personalized service and system quality affect users' satisfaction, the tool developed is especially significant to managers. The proposal that has been made is applicable for widespread use in any other type of space (natural park, historic center of a city, routes between cities, etc.). Notably, it is a truly efficient tool for the tourism sector, both for the tourist themselves and for travel agencies or public administrations. It helps the former because it aids the decision-making process, also offering the alternative that best fits their needs. It is useful for the latter as they can offer an additional services to the tourists, thus increasing the added value of the product.

We can also highlight the contribution that this tool can have in the field of the management of tourist flows. In a situation like the present one, where an exponential increase of visitors is taking place in many tourism sites and destinations, having tools of this type greatly facilitates both the work of tourism managers and the decision-making process of tourists. If each tourist consider a different route according to his or her needs, it is possible that the problem of congestion will improve. The proposed model, with the corresponding adjustments, can be applied for the management of tourist flows in different tourism places and destinations, so we encourage other researchers to use and apply this tool in their own research, facilitating with their research the real implementation of this proposal.

Applying tools of this type, cities like Amsterdam, Venice, Barcelona, or sites like Macchu Pichu, Chichen Itza or Angkor Wat (and, of course, any other), will be able to make a more adequate management of their tourist flows, improving the quality of the tourist experience, as well as favoring a more positive relationship between visitors and residents. In this way, it is possible to strengthen the role of tourism as an instrument of sustainable development.

One limitation of this work is that it does not take into account the environment and the situation in real time in the park with respect to other visitors, which would help to manage queues and other aspects of management. This could be remedied by combining this technique with some others in the literature.

Disclosure statement

No potential conflict of interest was reported by the authors.

ORCID

Beatriz Rodríguez-Díaz http://orcid.org/0000-0002-1778-7773
Juan Ignacio Pulido-Fernández http://orcid.org/0000-0002-9019-726X

References

Ausiello, G., Bonifaci, V., & Laura, L. (2008). The online prize-collecting traveling salesman problem. *Information Processing Letters*, *107*, 199–204. http://doi.org/10.1016/j.ipl.2008.03.002

Balas, E. (1989). The prize collecting travelling salesman problem. *Networks*, *19*, 621–636. http://doi.org/10.1002/net.3230190602

Bar-Yehuda, R., Even, G., & Shahar, S. (2005). On approximating a geometric prize-collecting traveling salesman problem with time windows. *Journal of Algorithms*, *55*(1), 76–92. http://doi.org/10.1016/j.jalgor.2003.11.002

Bérubé, J-F., Gendreau, M., & Potvin, J-Y. (2007). An exact ε-constraint method for bi-objective combinatorial optimization problems: Application to the traveling salesman problem with profits. *European Journal of Operational Research*, *194*, 39–50. http://doi.org/10.1016/j.ejor.2007.12.014

Birenboim, A., Antón-Clavé, S., Russo, A. P., & Shoval, N. (2013). Temporal activity patterns of theme park visitors. *Tourism Geographies*, *15*, 601–619. http://doi.org/10.1080/14616688.2012.762540

Botti, L., Peypoch, N., & Solonandrasana, B. (2008). Time and tourism attraction. *Tourism Management*, *29*, 594–596. http://doi.org/10.1016/j.tourman.2007.02.011

Brzeski, P. (2017). Viacom Breaks Ground on First Nickelodeon Resort in China. *The Hollywood Reporter*. http://doi.org/https://www.hollywoodreporter.com/news/viacom-breaks-ground-first-nickelodeon-resort-china-960677

Camacho, D., Borrajo, D., & Molina, J.M. (2001). Intelligent travel planning: A multiagent planning system to solve web problems in the e-tourism domain. *Autonomous Agents and Multi-Agent Systems*, *4*, 387–392. http://doi.org/10.1023/A:1012767210241

Castillo, L., Armengol, E., Onaindía, E., Sebastiá, L., González-Boticario, J., Rodríguez, A., Fernández, S., Arias, J. D., & Borrajo, D. (2008). SAMAP: An user-oriented adaptive system for planning tourist visits. *Expert Systems with Applications*, *34*, 1318–1332. http://doi.org/10.1016/j.eswa.2006.12.029

Chao, I., Golden, B., & Wasil, E. (1996). The team orienteering problem. *European Journal of Operational Research*, *88*, 464–474. http://doi.org/10.1016/0377-2217(94)00289-4

Colineau, N., & Wan S. (2001). Mobile delivery of customised information using Natural Language Generation. *Monitor*, *26*, 27–31. http://doi.org/http://citeseerx.ist.psu.edu/viewdoc/download?doi=10.1.1.117.4292&rep=rep1&type=pdf

Feillet, D., Dejax, P., & Gendreau, M. (2005). Traveling salesman problems with profits. *Transportation Science*, *39*, 188–205. http://doi.org/10.1287/trsc.1030.0079

Focacci, F., Milano, M., & Lodi, A. (1999). *Solving TSP with time Windows with constraints*. Proceedings of the 1999 international conference on Logic programming (pp. 515–529), Las Cruces, New Mexico.

Glover, F., & Laguna, M. (1997). *Tabu Search*. Boston: Kluwer Academic Publishers.

Glover, F. (1986). Future paths for integer programming and links to artificial intelligence. *Computers and Operations Research*, *13*, 533–549. http://doi.org/10.1016/0305-0548(86)90048-1

Godart, J. M. (2003). *Beyond the trip planning problem for effective computer-assisted customization of sightseeing tours*. In A. J. Frew, M. Hitz, & P. O'Connor (Eds.), Information and communication technologies in Tourism, 2003, proceedings (pp. 163–172). Austria: Springer.

Grinberger, A. Y., Shoval, N., & McKercher, B. (2014). Typologies of tourists' time-space consumption: A new approach using GPS data and GIS tools. *Tourism Geographies*, *16*(1), 105–123. http://doi.org/10.1080/14616688.2013.869249

Jozefowiez, N., Glover, F., & Laguna, M. (2008). Multi-objective meta-heuristics for the traveling salesman problem with profits. *Journal of Mathematical Modelling and Algorithms*, *7*, 177–195. http://doi.org/10.1007/s10852-008-9080-2

Jung, T., Chung, N., & Leue, M.C. (2015). The determinants of recommendations to use augmented reality technologies: The case of a Korean theme park. *Tourism Management*, *49*, 75–86. http://doi.org/10.1016/j.tourman.2015.02.013

Kantor, M., & Rosenwein, M. (1992). The orienteering problem with time windows. *Journal of the Operational Research Society, 43*, 629–635. http://doi.org/10.2307/2583018

Kemperman, A., Borgers, A., Oppewal, H., & Timmermans, H. (2003). Predicting the duration of theme park visitors' activities: An ordered logit model using conjoint choice data. *Journal of Travel Research, 41*, 375–384. http://doi.org/10.1177/0047287503041004006

Laporte, G., & Martello, S. (1990). The selective travelling salesman problem. *Discrete Applied Mathematics, 26*, 193–207. http://doi.org/10.1016/0166-218X(90)90100-Q

Leifer, A., & Rosenwein, M. (1994). Strong linear programming relaxations for the orienteering problem. *European Journal of Operational Research, 73*, 517–523. http://doi.org/10.1016/0377-2217(94)90247-X

Mahmood, T., Ricci, F., Venturini, A., & Höpken, W. (2008). *Adaptative recommender systems for travel planning*. In P. O'Connors, W. Höpken, & U. Gretzel (Eds.), *Information and Communication Technologies in Tourism* (pp. 1–11). Innsbruck, Austria: Springer-Verlag.

Meijles, E. W., de Bakker, M., Groote, P. D., & Barske, R. (2014). Analysing hiker movement patterns using GPS data: Implications for park management. *Computers, Environment and Urban Systems, 47*, 44–57. http://doi.org/10.1016/j.compenvurbsys.2013.07.005

Muñuzuri, J., Grosso, R., Cortés, P., & Guadix, J. (2013). Estimating the extra costs imposed on delivery vehicles using access time windows in a city. *Computers, Environment and Urban Systems, 41*, 262–275. http://doi.org/10.1016/j.compenvurbsys.2012.05.005

Paris, C. (2002). Information delivery for tourism: from information filtering to effective communication tools. *IEEE Intelligent Systems for Tourism*, 9–11.

Ricci, F. (2002). Travel recommender systems. *IEEE Intelligent Systems for Tourism*, 3–5.

Schmidt-Belz, B., Laamanen, H., Poslad, S., & Zipf, A. (2003). *Location-based mobile tourist services-first user experiences*. In A. Frew (Ed.), *Information and communication technologies in tourism*. New York: Springer Computer Science.

Schrijver, A. (2005). On the history of combinatorial optimization (till 1960). In K. Aardal, G. L. Nemhauser, & R. Weismantel, (Eds.), *Handbook of Discrete Optimization* (pp. 1–68). Amsterdam: Elsevier.

Shoval, N., & Isaacson, M. (2010). *Tourist mobility and advanced tracking technologies*. New York: Routledge.

Sun, Y., Fan, H., Bakillah, M., & Zipf, A. (2015). Road-based travel recommendation using geo-tagged images. *Computers, Environment and Urban Systems, 53*, 110–122. http://doi.org/10.1016/j.compenvurbsys.2013.07.006

Ten Hagen K., Modsching, M., & Krarner, R. (2005). A city guide agent creating and adapting individual sightseeing tours. In *Proceedings of the 5th International Conference on Intelligent Systems Design and Applications* (pp. 148–153). Warsaw. http://doi.org/10.1109/ISDA.2005.5

Thornton, P. R., Williams A. M., & Shaw, G. (1997). Revisiting time-space diaries: An exploratory case study of tourist behavior in Cornwall, England. *Environment and Planning A, 29*, 1847–1867. http://doi.org/10.1068/a291847

Tsai, C. Y., & Lai, B. H. (2015). A location-item-time sequential pattern mining algorithm for route recommendation. *Knowledge-Based Systems, 73*, 97–110. http://doi.org/10.1016/j.knosys.2014.09.012

Tsai, C. Y., & Chung, S. H. (2012). A personalized route recommendation service for theme parks using RFID information and tourist behavior. *Decision Support Systems, 52*, 514–527. https://doi.org/10.1016/j.dss.2011.10.013

Xiang, Z., Wang, D., O'Leary, J. T., & Fesenmaier, D. R. (2014). Adapting to the Internet: Trends in travelers' use of the web for trip planning. *Journal of Travel Research. 54*(4): 511–527, DOI:10.1177/0047287514522883

Xu, H., Li, Q., Chen, X., Chen, J., Guo, J., & Wang, Y. (2015). Logistical routing of park tours with waiting times: case of Beijing Zoo. *Tourism Geographies, 17*, 208–222. http://doi.org/10.1080/14616688.2014.997281

Yu, S., Spaccapietra, S., Cullot, N., & Aufaure, M. A. (2003). User profiles in location-based services: Make humans more nomadic and personalised. In *Proceedings of the International Workshopon Next Generation Geospatial Information*, NG2I, 2003, Cambridge.

Zanakis, S. H., & Evans, J. R. (1981). Heuristic optimization: Why, when and how to use it. *Interfaces, 11*, 84–91. http://doi.org/10.2307/25060151

Zipf, A. (2002). Adaptive context-aware mobility support for tourists. *IEEE Intelligent Systems for Tourism, 17*, 57–59.

Pattern of Chinese tourist flows in Japan: a Social Network Analysis perspective

Bindan Zeng

ABSTRACT

Social Network Analysis (SNA) has been introduced into tourism and hospitality research. However, little research has specifically addressed the structural pattern of tourist flow network. Chinese travelers to Japan keep increasing and become the largest market for Japan's inbound tourism. In order to understand the pattern of Chinese tourist flows in Japan, 430 itineraries from travel services and 458 itineraries from free independent tourists' trip dairies were collected and SNA with evaluation indicators was employed to identify the nodes' structure and the structural characteristics of Chinese tourist flows. The empirical analysis shows that distribution of Chinese tourist flows is disequilibrium and it mainly concentrates in the central Japan (Kanto, Chubu and Kinki region). Through node structure analysis by means of node centrality indicators, the roles and functions of destinations in the tourist flow network are recognized: core node, secondary core node, important node, common node and attached node. Moreover, empirical results indicate that 232 nodes and 981 ties constitute the Chinese tourist flow network and the structure of this network is complex. Overall it can be divided into five sub-regions with different patterns, which are summarized as: multi-center agglomeration structure, single center equilibrium structure, single center agglomeration structure, single center dispersion structure and multi-center equilibrium structure.

摘要：
社会网络分析已经在旅游研究中得到运用，然而很少有研究聚焦于旅游流网络的结构模式。中国赴日旅游持续增长且中国已成为日本入境旅游第一大市场。为理解赴日中国旅游流的结构特征，本文从中国的旅行社企业搜集了430条包价旅游线路，并基于在线网络游记搜集了458条自由行游客线路，利用社会网络分析相关指标研究了中国赴日旅游流的节点结构和网络结构特征。研究结果表明：赴日旅游流主要集中在日本中部（包括关东、中部和近畿地区）。通过节点结构和功能分析可以将目的地分为核心节点、次核心节点、重要节点、普通节点和附属节点。此外中国赴日旅游流总体网络由232个节点和981个连接组成并形成复杂网络结构。总体可分为五个子区域，并具有不同的结构模式：多中心集聚结构、单中心均衡结构、单中心集聚结构、单中心分散结构和多中心均衡结构。

Supplemental data for this article can be accessed https://doi.org/10.1080/14616688.2018.1496470.

Introduction

A tourist flow is a projection of the tourists' itinerary and related activities in geographical space and is composed of three basic elements: direction, rate and link mode (Bowden, 2003). International tourist flow has been one of the most important topics in tourism and geography research fields. In addition to the studies on the types, characteristics and influential factors of tourist flow, the spatial patterns (Pearce, 1987), seasonal concentration (Antonio, 2003) and forecast of tourist flows (Song & Li, 2008) are the major topics in this field. Tourist flow involves the movement among destinations of people through time and space. Lew and McKercher (2006) illustrated that understanding how tourists move through time and space has important implications for infrastructure and transportation development, product development, destination planning and the planning of new attractions, as well as management of the social, environmental and cultural impacts of tourism. Therefore, a detailed understanding of spatial distribution and agglomeration of tourist flow as well as role and function of destination have theoretical and practical significance.

Chinese outbound tourism keeps increasing and the number of Chinese travelers to Japan reached 4.994 million in 2015. This figure accounted for 25.3% of all foreign visitors to Japan, moving China up from second in 2014 to first in the rankings of numbers of foreign visitors by country of origin (Japan Tourism Agency [JTA], 2016). Meanwhile, Chinese visitor spent exceeded 1 trillion yen in 2015 for the first time which accounting for 40% of all foreign visitors' tourism consumption. The *Tourism Vision to Support the Future of Japan* announced by the Japanese government on 30 March 2016 made tourism one of the major pillars of the growth strategy of Japan. It includes new goals such as 40 million foreign tourists and 8 trillion yen in spending by foreign tourists in 2020, both twice the results for 2015. China still will be the driver due to recent sharp increase in number of travelers to Japan and size of consumption. In recent years, Chinese tourists are interested in not only traditional destinations such as Tokyo and Kyoto, but also other destinations such as Tokachigawa and Kushiro in East Hokkaido. Against this background, for the future tourism planning and marketing, it is very important to understand the Chinese tourist flows in Japan.

In spite of its significant contribution to Japan's tourism industry, Chinese travel has not yet been comprehensively analyzed. Recent studies of Chinese travel to Japan focus on motivation of Chinese tourists to Japan and the patterns and characteristics of Chinese tourists' behaviors (Guo, Chen, Huang, & Su, 2015; Jin, 2015; Ye, 2013). Some scholars have studied Chinese tourist's behavior change and its regional differences (Hishida, Hibino, & Morichi, 2012; Shimizu, 2007), sightseeing routes and spatial characteristics of Chinese package tours (Cui, 2011; Jin, 2009), travel behavior and expenditures of Chinese (Shi et al., 2012). Overall, few research has specifically addressed the structural pattern associated with the Chinese tourist flow in Japan. Without this realization, it is difficult for government departments, destination planners and tourism service providers to develop appropriate facilities at a particular destination.

The aim of this study is to identify the characteristics and network patterns of Chinese tourist flows in Japan at inter destination level. Specifically, geographical distribution of Chinese tourist flows, spatial structure and pattern of the whole network and roles of destinations in this network will be analyzed from a perspective of Social Network Analysis (SNA). The results will yield planning implications for future development of Japan's inbound tourism.

Before the analysis, delimiting some concepts is necessary due to their ambiguity. Based on the definition of UNWTO (2002) and the discussion of Lew and McKercher (2006), the 'destination' in this study is defined as the area that includes tourism products such as support services, attractions and tourism resources. Basically, it has administrative boundaries on a city/district level and could normally be consumed in a daytrip from the heart of the destination. The services and attractions are normally promoted by the travel services as part of its overall suite of products so they share integrated image and perception defining its market competitiveness. In this sense, there are some exceptions of destination crossing the administrative boundaries. For instance, the Fujisan (Mountain Fuji) is viewed as one destination although the attractions are located in different cities. In addition, tourist flows are defined by touring routes in this study. Tourist flow network in this research is defined as a network constituted by the destinations and the tourist flows among them while the destinations are viewed as nodes.

Literature review

Tourist flow and patterns

Since Williams and Zelinsky (1970) initially attempted at uncovering a few major patterns of tourist flows among a selected group of countries which dominated the international tourist market, patterns of tourist flows have received a great amount of attention from scholars. It can be explaining at different spatial scales, such as global, national, regional and local destination.

At the macro level, tourists travel from the generating region to destinations or between destination regions. Gunn (1972) is one of the first to discuss different forms of trips: the 'Destination' trip and the 'Touring' trip. Pearce (1987) studied spatial patterns of package tourism in Europe which include intra-ECAC patterns of ITC traffic and sub-national patterns of package tourism.

At inter destination level, Mings and McHugh (1992) identified four types of trip configurations: Direct Route, Partial Orbit, Full Orbit and Fly/Drive. Lue, Crompton, and Fesenmaier (1993) proposed five distinctive spatial patterns that may be adopted by pleasure travelers: single destination, en route, base camp, regional tour and trip chaining (LCF-Model). This trip pattern conceptualization put forth in LCF was proved to be a useful method for classifying, analyzing and describing the travel patterns (Susan & Christine, 1997). Oppermann (1995) proposed a more specific framework to exploring intra national and international travel itineraries, which distinguishes five main types of travel patterns: single-destination trip S1, base camp S2, destination area loop M3, open jaw loop M4 and multiple destination area loopM5. Flogenfeldt (1999) identified four types of patterns taken by Norwegians: day trip, resort trip, based holiday and round trip. Chris and Gu (2007) conducted a study of a desired itinerary among students in New Zealand and China and identified two ideal itinerary patterns: open-jaw route and overlaying triangular route. Lau and McKercher (2007) summarized the movement patterns into six categories: single point, base site, stop-over, chaining loop, destination region loop and complex neighborhood.

At the intra destination level, Lew and McKercher (2006) developed the intra destination movement patterns deductively in two dimensions: four types of territorial patterns (no movement, convenience-based movement, concentric exploration and unrestricted destination-wide movement) and three types of linear path patterns (point-to-point patterns, circular patterns and complex patterns). McKercher and Lau (2008) examined the daily movements of tourists in Hong Kong and identified total 78 discrete movement patterns which can be categorized into 11 movement styles. Leung, Wang, and Wu (2012) used content analysis and SNA methods to analyze overseas tourist movement patterns in Beijing during the Olympics. Smallwood, Beckley, and Moore (2012) described and quantified within destination movement patterns of visitors travelling for recreation throughout Ningaloo Marine Park, in northwestern Australia, using various modes of travel.

The literatures reviewed above provide a good starting point for understanding of tourist flow. However, most previous articles were limited to isolated routes and linear pattern. They did not consider the positioning of various destinations in whole region so they are limited in their ability to analyze the tourist flows from the perspective of network. Furthermore, the studies did not provide quantitative indicators for evaluating the roles and functions of destinations, link mode and spatial pattern. Thus, it is necessary to construct tourist flow network to reveal characteristics of tourist flow through quantitative methods.

Measurement of tourist flow

A variety of techniques have been applied in analysis of tourist flow. Traditional methods of tracking tourist flow relied on observations, interviews, post-visit questionnaires, recall maps or movement diaries (East, Osborne, Kemp, & Woodfine, 2017; Leung et al., 2012). These methods need are burdensome to both tourists and researchers, and they often lack needed accuracy (Hallo et al., 2012).Global positioning system (GPS) provides new ways for collecting information about travel behavior (Draijer, Kalfs, & Perdok, 2000). It offers advantages over traditional methods for tracking visitors, including more reliable, accurate and precise data (Hallo et al., 2012). GPS data can used to identify spatial and temporal travel patterns and distribution of visitors (Beeco et al., 2013). Recently, studies have shown GPS is mainly viable in large attractions such as theme parks but has difficulties in gaining a large sample size (East et al., 2017). In addition, when more and more tourists use internet to obtain travel information, share travel diaries and photographs, the online user-generated content is used by researchers. For example, Leung, Wang, and Wu (2012) examined 500 online trip diaries for identifying tourist movement pattern. Vu, Li, Law, and Ye (2015) introduced a framework for extracting geographical information from geo tagged photos posted online to identify the travel behaviors of tourists and travel route.

As for methodological techniques, network analysis (Hwang, Gretzel, & Fesenmaier, 2006), cluster analysis (Asakura & Iryo, 2007), Markov chains (Xia, Zeephongsekul, & Arrowsmith, 2009), logistic-regression and general log-linear models (Xia et al., 2010) have been employed to analyze the tourist flow. Regional economics, physics theory, metering statistics and other related methods also have been adopted. Geographic Information System (GIS) analysis has been a very powerful tool to map tourist flow data and movement patterns (Connell & Page, 2008; East et al., 2017; Lau & Mckercher, 2007; Palomares, Gutiérrez, & Mínguez, 2015). In recent years, scholars have begun to apply the SNA method in research regarding tourism planning, marketing, stakeholders and online networks (Peng, Zhang, & Liu, 2016).

SNA of tourist flow

SNA is a method used to map and measure relationships and flows between people, groups, organizations and other connected information/knowledge entities (Wasserman & Faust, 1994). Based on graph theory, SNA can describe the structure of relations (displayed by links) between given entities (displayed by nodes), and applies quantitative techniques to produce relevant indicators and results for studying the characteristics of a whole network and the position of individuals in the network structure (Shih, 2006). Although SNA is most applied in sociological research, it has been introduced into tourism and hospitality research. Three research streams could be identified with studies applying SNA in the tourism contexts: network analysis on tourism research collaboration and knowledge creation; network analysis on the tourism supply, destination and policy systems; and network analysis based on tourist movements and behavioral patterns (Liu, Huang, & Fu, 2017).

In the specific context of destination network and tourist flow, if destinations are viewed as nodes of a network and tourism routes as links among destinations or nodes, SNA methodological tools can be used to classify destinations by a set of metrics, measure relationships among tourism destinations and to describe their network features (Rosario, Simona, & Venera, 2013). Based on this, Shih (2006) investigated network characteristics of drive tourism destinations in Nantou, Taiwan. Hwang et al. et al. (2006) studied multicity trip patterns within the US by international tourists. Liu et al. (2012) revealed the roles and functions of destinations from tourist flow network's perspective by using centrality indicators and structural equivalence model. Rosario et al. et al. (2013) proposed an application of Network Analysis to study tourism mobility from individual routes, examining effects both on the single destinations and the whole tourism system in Sicily, Italy. Asero, Gozzo, and Tomaselli (2016) constructed a tourism network through tourist mobility and explored the network characteristics using centrality measures, ego-networks and structural equivalence indicators; the results show that the tourists' choice defined the role of a destination as 'central' or 'peripheral' within a network.

There are also several related studies conducted in China in recent years. Some topics are studied from the SNA perspective: Urban tourism in Nanjing city (Yang, Gu, & Wang, 2007), inbound tourists flow in Beijing and Shanghai (Wu & Pan, 2010), inbound tourist flows in Guangzhou city (Wang, Wu, Tang, & Yang, 2013), inbound European tourist flow network in China (Wang et al., 2013), the rules and roles of the destination cities in China's inbound foreigner tourist flow network (Wu, 2014). Furthermore, Liu et al. (2017) explored how the tourist attractions network in a regional tourism destination was formed using relationship as a mechanism by applying Quadratic Assignment Procedure in SNA.

The studies have shown its advantages in tourism research. Firstly, when applied in studies on tourist flow patterns, SNA has function to visualize travel flow data which can reflect destinations (nodes) themselves and the relationships in and among them. Secondly, SNA can offer numerous techniques and indicators (Centrality, Structural holes, Cliques, etc.) to measure the links among nodes and demonstrate the structural patterns of connected systems. For instance, this methodology is useful for investigating the network features of multiple destinations and thereby, to specify both the relevant and the marginal destinations by their centrality within the routes. (Rosario et al., 2013). Although SNA method has unique advantages, studies regarding tourist flows that utilized the SNA method are scarce, and direct analyses that systematically employ SNA indicators to study the spatial structures and network characteristics of tourist flows and the roles of nodes are lacking (Peng, Zhang, Liu, Lu, & Yang, 2016). In addition, a summary of the tourism network patterns based on SNA is still insufficient. Based on this discussion, and according to the literature reviewed, this study focuses on the Chinese tourist flows within Japan in order to define the pattern of tourist flow network.

Data and methodology

Data collection

One critical problem that restricts the generalizability of tourist flow research lies on the deficiency in detailed, standard and accurate data, since each tourist's spatial movement cannot be recorded thoroughly and accurately (Noam & Michal, 2007). Although some scholars collected precise tourists spatial data by passive mobile positioning methods (Ahas, Aasa, Roose, Mark, & Silm, 2008), it is not applicable to the inter destination tourist flow research.

At the inter destination level, majority of the data for existing studies come from investigations with tourists and panel data. However, both panel data from the supply-side and from the demand-side do not take multi-destination trip phenomenon into account adequately. As for the investigations with tourists, sample size becomes a sensitive issue with trip itinerary data because of the great diversity of routes and destinations that travelers take (Lew & Mckercher, 2002).

Although group tour is still the main selection for Chinese outbound tourists, there are more and more tourists traveling independently to Japan. In 2016, the number of personal tour visa for Chinese citizens issued by Japanese government reached 1.63 million while number of group tour visa issuance was 1.75 million. Therefore, this study was designed to collect tourist flow data of both Group Package Tourists (GPTs) and Free Independent Tourist (FITs).

The tourist flow data of GPTs was collected through a leading online travel group (one of the top three online tourism groups in China, it is not only a travel agency but also an online platform so travel services in China can sell their tourism products *via* this group's website) and based on two aspects: travel itineraries and sales data. The travel itineraries sold by travel services provide many information guidance (product ID, length of trip, airline, hotel, transport, destinations and attractions), which involve the directionality characteristic of tourist flows. Through content analysis of travel itinerary brochures, the number of destinations and their sequence and length of stay of each itinerary are identified. On the other hand, the sales data provide more detailed information about the price, departure time, source region of tourist and number of tourists who brought the itineraries, which is important because it includes the quantitative characteristic of tourist flows. By means of descriptive statistics of sales data, tourists' sources and their choices for itineraries are analyzed. At last, a total of 430 itineraries from 52 travel services for a full year 2016, were collected. All itineraries are multi destination itineraries which excluded the situation of 'airline ticket' or 'hotel + airline ticket' product.

The original data of FITs were collected from 458 trip diaries on two websites, which were posted by mainland Chinese tourists who traveled to Japan in 2016. The two websites used are Mafengwo and Ctrip. Mafengwo (http://www.mafengwo.cn) is the most famous Chinese travel SNS website that enables users to share travel experiences with each other. Ctrip (http://www.ctrip.com) is the biggest provider of travel services including accommodation reservation, transportation ticketing and also the trip diaries sharing in China. Tourists who wrote diaries on these websites were independent tourists, as a result their movements in Japan were of their free will. The tourists visited more than one destination in one trip so that their trip itineraries are multi-destination itineraries. Besides, the diaries contain detailed and accurate information about travel purposes, trip arrangement, daily movements, attractions visited, activities at each destination and transport mode among destinations.

As displayed in Table 1, both GPTs and FITs were mainly from East China (64.6% and 42.4% respectively), which is the most developed region in China. Majority of GPTs (73.1%) stayed for 6 days 5 nights while FITs stayed 8 days 7 nights and more (61.9%). Most GPTs (82.3%) chose a trip with 4–7 destinations, and the average number of destinations visited by GPTs per trip is 5.7 while that of FITs is 6.8. The majority of tourists' cost of per package trip was 5001–7000 RMB (43.3%) and 3001–5000 RMB (37.9%) while majority of FITs (65.0%) spend more than 9000 RMB per trip. Overall, comparing to GPTs, FITs visit more destinations, stay longer and spend more accordingly.

Social network analysis

Process of analysis

SNA method is employed to analyze structural characteristics and pattern of Chinese tourist flows in Japan, where the destinations are treated as nodes and the tourist routes between destinations are regarded as a series of links.

First, the scope and nodes of Chinese tourist flow are determined. The activity space of travel itineraries is the network scope and the related destinations are the nodes. Particularly, Okinawa is not considered in this research since it is far away from Japan's home islands and it is often a single destination for Chinese tourists. Based on the analysis of travel itineraries, a map is constructed to get an overview of geographical distribution of Chinese tourist flow in Japan.

Second, this article constructs asymmetric valued matrix in which a row stands for the starting node of the destinations and a column for the terminal node. The number of tourists moving from one destination to another is recorded in the relative cell. In other words, a n in the (i, j)th cell (row i, column j) indicates n tourists traveled from

Table 1. Profile of the sample.

	Group package tourist (%)	Free independent tourist (%)
Source regions of tourists		
East China	64.6	42.4
North China	13.6	20.7
South China	7.6	16.7
Central China	6.4	2.8
Southwest China	3.7	13.5
Northeast China	2.9	1.5
Northwest China	1.2	2.4
Length of trip		
4 days 3 nights and less	0.5	3.6
5 days 4 nights	11.3	10.2
6 days 5 nights	73.1	12.1
7 days 6 nights	11.7	12.2
8 days 7 nights and more	3.4	61.9
Number of destinations per trip		
2–3	5.9	11.5
4–5	41.9	28.8
6–7	40.4	27.4
8–9	9.2	18.1
10 and more	2.6	14.2
Average cost of each itinerary (RMB)		
≤3000	5.0	2.2
3001–5000	37.9	4.3
5001–7000	43.3	12.7
7001–9000	10.2	15.8
≥9001	3.5	65.0

Note:
East China: Shanghai, Zhejiang, Jiangsu, Shandong, Anhui;
North China: Beijing, Hebei, Tianjin, Shanxi, Inner Mongolia;
South China: Guangdong, Guangxi, Fujian, Hainan;
Central China: Hunan, Hubei, Henan, Jiangxi;
Southwest China: Chongqing, Sichuan, Yunnan, Guizhou;
Northeast China: Heilongjiang, Jilin, Liaoning;
Northwest China: Gansu, Shannxi, Ningxia.

node i to node j, and a 0 in the cell indicates that the tourist flow does not exist between i and j. Valued matrices for whole tourist flow network, GPT network and FIT network are constructed, respectively.

Finally, based on the valued matrix, an appropriate cut-off value (the cut-off value is 1 in this study) is selected to dichotomize the cells of the valued matrix. To analyze the characteristics of the tourist-flow network, the numerical matrix (valued matrix) must be translated into a dichotomized matrix by selecting an appropriate cutoff value after repeated testing and selection (Peng et al., 2016). Lastly we get three dichotomized matrices and apply the binary data to the indicators and graphs of the network analysis.

Indicators of SNA

The following paragraphs present the techniques and indicators of the SNA which are appropriate for examining the network characteristics of Chinese tourist flows in this study. The indicators include two aspects: the nodes structure and the network structure. Among them, the node centrality is the main indicator to evaluate structural characteristics of nodes. The indicators of whole network structure include: size, density, diameter and centralization of the network. The formulas of these indicators have been used and explained frequently (Hwang et al., 2006; Peng et al., 2016; Shih, 2006), so here is just to introduce its implication and significance in tourist flow study (Table 2).

Node centrality is used to measure the prominence of certain nodes in a network (Wasserman & Faust, 1994). Three of these centrality concepts have been identified as particularly relevant in the context of multicity trip networks: degree centrality, betweenness centrality and closeness centrality (Hwang et al., 2006).

Degree centrality, which is the simplest and most intuitive, refers to the number of links that a node connects to all other nodes in the network. In directional networks, degree centrality can be divided into out-degree and in-degree centrality. The out-degree centrality of a destination is the indicator of the effects of tourist flow divergence to others in the region. The higher out-degree means better performance as the gateway with more tourists taking this destination as the entrance to the region. On the contrary, the in-degree centrality reflects the gathering ability of tourist flows. By examining and comparing the two indices, we can judge the function of a particular destination as a gateway, egress or hub (Liu et al., 2012). Generally degree centrality allows for recognition of central destinations in the tourism networks (Asero et al., 2016).

Closeness centrality focuses on how close a destination is to all the other destinations in the network. It is defined as the inverse of the sum of the geodesic distances from a node to all the other nodes in the network. In a directional network, closeness centrality can be divided into in-closeness and out-closeness, respectively, based on inward and outward connections, even so both formulas are the same (Shih, 2006). In the context of tourist flow network, the higher closeness centrality one destination has, the more reachable other destinations it possesses and it is more central and closer to all of the other destinations, and *vice versa*.

Betweenness centrality measures the extent to which a particular node lies between the various other nodes in the network (Shih, 2006). Betweenness centrality of a node is the sum of this node's estimated probabilities of standing along any geodesic that all pairs of nodes in the network have selected. Higher betweenness centrality means more powerful control of tourist flows and more structural advantages, which indicates a destination will be depended by other destinations in a more intensive way (Liu et al., 2012).

Network centralization is a measure used to describe the structural characteristics of the network as a whole. It is determined by calculating the difference between the centrality scores of the most central node and those of all other nodes in the network. It is usually expressed as a ratio of the actual sum of the differences to the maximal possible sum of them (Hwang et al., 2006). It can be classified into three levels: degree centralization, closeness centralization and betweenness centralization.

The network size is a measure of the number of nodes or elements that compose the network (Asero et al., 2016). The diameter of the network is the longest geodesic distance between two nodes (Casanueva, Gallego, & Garcia-Sanchez, 2016). The density of a network is the proportion of possible lines that are actually present in the network. It is the ratio of the number of lines present, L, to the maximum possible (Wasserman & Faust, 1994). In the analysis of tourist flow network, density is the

Table 2. Explanation of indicators used in Social Network Analysis process.

	Indicator	Explanation	Function	
Node	Degree centrality	The number of links that a node connects to all other nodes in the network	Out-degree centrality of a destination is the indicator of the effects of tourist flow divergence to others in the region. The in-degree centrality reflects the gathering ability of tourist flows	$C_D(n_i) = \sum_{j=1}^{I} r_{ij}$
	Closeness centrality	The inverse of the sum of the geodesic distances from a node to all the other nodes in the network	It reflects how many reachable other destinations one destination has, the more it possesses and it is more central and closer to all of the other destinations, and *vice versa*	$C_C(n_i) = \sum_{j=1}^{I} \frac{1}{d(n_i, n_j)}$
	Betweenness centrality	The sum of the node's estimated probabilities of standing along any geodesic that all pairs of nodes in the network have selected	It measures the extent to which a particular destination lies between the various other destinations in the network. A destination with high betweenness scores can be conceptualized as hub that control flows between other destinations	$C_B(n_i) = \sum_j \sum_k \frac{g_{jk}(n_i)}{g_{jk}}$
Network	Degree centralization	The ratio of the actual sum of differences between the centrality scores of the most central point and those of all other points, to the maximum possible sum of differences	It measures the variability in the degree centrality scores of all nodes in the network. A high degree centralization of the entire network indicates that a small number of destinations accounts for a large number of the connections made within the network	$C_D = \frac{\sum_{i=1}^{g}[C_D(n^*) - C_D(n_i)]}{(g-2)(g-1)}$
	Closeness centralization		It measures the variability in the closeness centrality scores of all nodes in the network	$C_C = \frac{\sum_{i=1}^{g}[C_C(n^*) - C_C(n_i)]/(g-1)}{(g-2)(g-1)/(2g-3)}$
	Betweenness centralization		It measures the heterogeneity of the betweenness scores of the individual nodes. In a network with high centralization, all travel occurs through a small number of hubs	$C_B = \frac{2\sum_{i=1}^{g}[C_B(n^*) - C_B(n_i)]}{(g-1)^2(g-2)}$
	Network size	The number of nodes or elements that compose the network	It indicates the number of destinations visited by tourists and reflects the scope of a network	
	Diameter	The longest geodesic distance between two nodes	The diameter is representative of the linear size of a network	
	Density	Proportion between the existing number of links (L), or routes connecting tourist destinations, and the maximum number of potential ties $[g(g-1)/2]$	It describes the level of linkages among the destinations	$\Delta = 2L/g(g-1)$

Source: Asero et al., (2016), Casanueva et al. (2016), Peng et al. (2016), Hwang et al. (2006) and Shih (2006).

Figure 1. Geographical distribution of Chinese tourist flows in Japan.

proportion between the existing number of links, or routes connecting tourist destinations, and the maximum number of potential ties (Asero et al., 2016).

Results and discussion

Distribution of tourist flow

Based on the analysis of tourist itineraries, the map of general geographical distribution of Chinese tourist flow in Japan is constructed. As displayed in Figure 1, the size of the line represents the relative volume of the tourist flows. The distribution of Chinese tourist flows is disequilibrium, characterized by an extensive dispersion with localized concentrations from an overall perspective. Both GPT flows and FIT flow are mainly concentrated in the central Japan (including Kanto, Chubu and Kinki region) and then the Hokkaido and Kyushu region. Two hundred and thirty-two (232) destinations are visited, including 102 for GPTs and 203 for FITs. 'Osaka–Kyoto' and 'Tokyo–Fujisan' are the destination pairs with most tourist flows.

However, comparing to GPTs, the FIT flows show different characteristics. Firstly, the spatial distribution of FIT flows is more extensive. FITs not only travel to more destinations around gateway cities, but also visit more regions, such as Tohoku region, Chugoku region and Shikoku region where there are very few destinations for GPTs (Figure 2). Secondly, FITs have more inter regional movement. More domestic airlines in Japan have been used by FITs, such as air routes of Fukuoka–Tokyo, Nagoya–Sapporo and Osaka–Hakodate. Thirdly, FITs show diversity in transportation choice. Tour bus is the main transportation way for GPTs although there are some

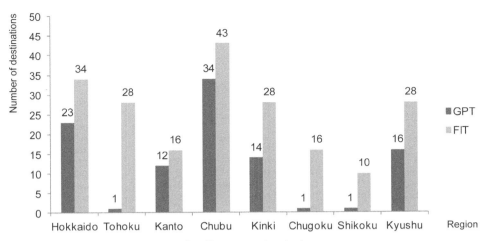

Figure 2. Distribution of destinations for Chinese tourists in Japan.

ferry routes in Seto Inland Sea and airline routes between Hokkaido region and other regions are used. The transportation choice for FITs is obviously freer and diverse. When electric train and public bus are mainly used within regions by FITs, Bullet train (Shinkansen) and airplanes are used for their inter region movement.

Tourism resources can be found as a key factor affecting distribution of tourist flow. Of the 20 World Heritage Sites of Japan, 10 sites are located in central Japan, which constitute an important part of tourism attractions. In addition, the biggest cities such as Tokyo, Osaka, Nagoya, etc., are also concentrated in central Japan, which provide the urban landscape, services and facilities (especially the popular theme parks and shopping malls/outlets for Chinese tourists). Itineraries of GPTs are usually arranged by travel services so the tourist flows are concentrated in popular destination with traditional tourism resources. FITs like to customize their travel itineraries and seek different resources. For example, Setouchi art exhibition is a very key element to attract Chinese FITs visiting Takamatsu, Naoshima and Shodoshima.

Accessibility is another important factor in terms of distribution of tourist flows. Although there exist direct air routes between 22 cities in Japan and 38 cities in China, there are only 12 cities can be found as gateway destinations for Chinese tourists in the study. Osaka (Kansai airport), Tokyo (Narita airport) and Nagoya (Chubu airport) are the main egress and gateway destinations which are located in central Japan. Sapporo, Shizuoka and Fukuoka are the secondary. Omitama (Ibaraki airport) is also an important egress destination since the non-stop flight route linking Shanghai with Ibaraki was launched. In addition, Asahikawa, Takamatsu, Saga, Okayama and Komatsu play a role of regional gateway destinations as well.

Node structure

Based on the dichotomized matrix, the indicators of network analysis for the whole tourist flow network are calculated by UCINET 6.6 and the results are shown in Table 3.

Table 3. The structural indicators of nodes in whole tourist flow network.

		Degree centrality			Closeness centrality			
		Out	In		Out	In	Betweenness centrality	
	Tokyo	52	54	Tokyo	0.44	0.49	Tokyo	21184
	Osaka	46	47	Osaka	0.45	0.47	Osaka	17501
	Kyoto	49	39	Kyoto	0.43	0.42	Kyoto	8613
	Fujisan	26	33	Nagoya	0.39	0.41	Fukuoka	6521
	Nagoya	22	24	Fujisan	0.38	0.40	Fujisan	4340
	Sapporo	21	23	Sapporo	0.37	0.40	Sapporo	4293
	Fukuoka	20	17	Noboribetsu	0.36	0.39	Sendai	4086
	Nara	17	16	Nara	0.37	0.39	Kanazawa	2856
	Sendai	15	17	Hakone	0.36	0.38	Aomori	2480
	Noboribetsu	13	14	Shizuoka	0.36	0.38	Kagoshima	2454
	Kanazawa	12	13	Kagoshima	0.36	0.38	Nagoya	2434
	Hakodate	11	13	Fukuoka	0.38	0.36	Beppu	2283
	Hiroshima	9	15	Kamakura	0.36	0.37	Takamatsu	2236
	Otaru	11	12	Kobe	0.38	0.36	Hiroshima	2183
	Takayama	10	13	Kanazawa	0.35	0.38	Kumamoto	1910
	Aomori	11	11	Sendai	0.36	0.37	Nara	1789
	Kobe	12	10	Yokohama	0.36	0.37	Noboribetsu	1575
	Chitose	10	11	Himeji	0.34	0.38	Asahikawa	1360
	Asahikawa	11	10	Hamamatsu	0.33	0.38	Chitose	1325
	Hakone	12	9	Hakodate	0.33	0.39	Kamakura	1321
Mean		4.22	4.22		0.29	0.29		547.10
S.D.		6.56	6.57		0.05	0.06		2007.47

Note:
(1) Only first 20 nodes are list here.
(2) The value to assign undefined distances was defined as the max observed distance plus 1 when the closeness centrality was calculated.

The indicator of degree centrality indicates that Tokyo, as the capital city and brand of Japan tourism, is the tourist flow distribution center in the network which has the highest degree centrality. It keeps most connections with other tourist destinations and has the strongest aggregation function. Osaka and Kyoto, as the most famous urban tourism destination and cultural and historical destination in Japan respectively, both have very high degree centrality just behind Tokyo.

Closeness centrality reveals the extent to which a particular destination is reachable from and to other destinations (Shih, 2006). Destinations Tokyo and Osaka have the highest in-closeness centrality because of their network position as gateway destination for tourists. In addition, destinations around Tokyo and Osaka such as Fujisan and Kyoto also possess high in-closeness. As for out-closeness centrality, Osaka still has the highest value. Nagoya and Sapporo, resulting from its function as gateway destination, also possess high out-closeness.

The rating of betweenness centrality in the tourist flow network ranges between 0 and 21,184, causing the standard deviation to be 2007, exceeding the mean value 547 greatly. Therefore, considerable variation exists in the betweenness centrality of this network. Still Tokyo has the highest betweenness centrality and act as an irreplaceable mediator among different regions. In addition, Osaka, Kyoto, Fujisan and regional key cities such as Fukuoka, Sapporo and Sendai also have high betweenness centrality.

In the light of previous studies (Lew & Mckercher, 2002; Liu et al., 2012) and according to centralities of nodes (Table 3), a preliminary categorization on 232 nodes in Chinese tourist flow network is proposed. Destinations can be generalized into five types: core node, secondary core node, important node, common node and attached

Table 4. Types and characteristics of nodes in Chinese tourist flow network

Type	Nodes	Centrality characteristics	Role and function
Core node	Tokyo, Osaka, Kyoto, Fujisan	Highest and balanced centralities	Tourist distribution center of whole network Most important gateway and egress destination of Japan Agglomeration of comprehensive facilities and world class tourist attractions
Secondary core node	Nagoya, Sapporo, Fukuoka, Nara, Sendai	Centralities are second only to core node	Most important gateway and egress destination of Japan Information and transport center Agglomeration of diversified attractions and tourist facilities
Important node	Noboribetsu, Kanazawa, Hakodate, etc. (16 destinations)	All centralities are relatively higher	Regional hub of the network Important gateway and egressway or destination of region Important touring destination
Common node	Yokohama, Shizuoka, Himeji etc. (38 destinations)	All centralities are relatively lower	Common touring destination Agglomeration of attractions with regional characteristics Single function destination
Attached node	Kyogoku, Muroran, Toyama etc. (169 destinations)	Centralities are the lowest and only one or two tourist flow that was appended to a certain destination	Touring destination or small gateway and egress destination Single function destination (for only sightseeing, accommodation, shopping or transportation)

node. Depending on their location within the overall trip itinerary, places can exhibit characteristics of one or more destination types: gateway destination, egress destination, touring destination and hub destination (Lew & McKercher, 2002). From the perspective of function, some of nodes are destinations with single function (only for sightseeing, shopping, accommodation or transportation) and some are destinations with comprehensive functions. Types and characteristics of nodes are summarized in Table 4.

Tokyo, Osaka, Kyoto and Fujisan are the core nodes. Although Fujisan and Kyoto are not exclusively traffic hubs, they are tourists' hubs and distribution centers of whole network, which control the transferability of relative tourist flows extensively. They are great attractions to tourists who come to Japan for the first time. Nagoya, Sapporo, Fukuoka, Nara and Sendai are the secondary core nodes. These destinations also own gateway and egress functions, which control the entrance and exit of tourist flows and have potential to be the tourists' hub and distribution center.

The important nodes include 16 destinations, which are regional hubs of the network or important touring destinations. Their tourist flow linkages concentrate in limited number of destinations with a certain distance and resource types and the hub functions they carried are confined. Among them Hiroshima and Takamatsu are important gateway and egress destinations of the Chugoku and Shikoku region, respectively. Common nodes include 38 destinations which mainly depended on core or important nodes and their roles are limited as touring destinations. Attached nodes include 169 destinations. They are attached to one or two destinations and act as single function destinations. For instance, Omitama and Saga are gateway destinations with small airports. Toyota and Jozankei are places just for tourists' accommodation.

Table 5. Comparison of node degree centrality for GPT and FIT network.

	GPT			FIT	
	Out-deg	In-deg		Out-deg	In-deg
Fujisan	23	31	Tokyo	45	49
Kyoto	28	21	Osaka	39	39
Tokyo	24	20	Kyoto	36	28
Osaka	19	18	Sapporo	19	22
Nagoya	15	14	Nagoya	19	19
Sapporo	13	13	Fukuoka	20	17
Nara	13	9	Sendai	15	16
Toyako	7	11	Fujisan	11	15
Otaru	7	10	Kanazawa	12	12
Hamamatsu	7	10	Hiroshima	9	15
Shizuoka	9	8	Noboribetsu	11	12
Noboribetsu	8	8	Hakodate	10	13
Hakone	8	7	Aomori	11	11
Chitose	6	8	Kobe	11	10
Shirakawa	6	6	Kamakura	11	8
Ise	6	6	Takayama	9	10
Asahikawa	7	4	Nara	9	10
Toyohashi	5	6	Takamatsu	11	8
Nakatsugawa	5	6	Kumamoto	9	10
Furano	6	4	Asahikawa	9	9

Note: Only first 20 nodes are list here.

For comparison, the values of node degree centrality of GPTs and FITs network are calculated and present in Table 5, which are based on the 102 × 102 GPT dichotomized matrix and 203 × 203 FIT dichotomized matrix. The similarity and differences are summarized as follows: Firstly, in terms of the absolute value of degree centrality, most nodes in FIT network have higher degree centrality than the nodes in GPT network. Secondly, from a relative importance perspective, the node Tokyo, Kyoto and Osaka are the most important destinations for both the GPTs and FITs. However, the destination Fujisan is not ranked within the most important destinations for FITs. In addition, regional key cities such as Fukuoka (Kyushu Region), Sendai (Tohoku Region), Hiroshima (Chugoku Region), and the cities with small international airports such as Hakodate, Aomori, Takamatsu and Asahikawa are more important to FITs.

Network pattern

In terms of the structural characteristics of the whole network (Table 6), there are 232 nodes in the whole tourist flow network and the diameter of this network is 8. The density of the tourist flow network is 0.018. Theoretically, a network with 232 nodes should possess 53,824 link relationships. However, only 981 link relationships exist and thus, the network density is considerable low.

Table 6 also shows the main results of comparative analysis for GPT and FIT network. The comparison clearly reveals a larger size, longer diameter and lower density for the FIT network which means the FIT network is looser compared to GPT network overall. Notably, analysis of the structure of network indicates the higher degree centralization of the GPT network compared to FIT network. The result confirms that GPTs appear to visit and combine a smaller number of destinations. However, the FIT network shows a higher betweenness centralization which means FITs are more

Table 6. Indicators of network.

	Size	Diameter	Density	Degree centralization		Betweenness centralization (%)
				Out	In	
Whole network	232	8	0.018	0.208	0.216	39.01
GPT	102	8	0.037	0.242	0.272	32.86
FIT	203	9	0.019	0.205	0.225	40.31

dependent on some hubs. It is probably because the different transportation way for FITs and GPTs. For GPTs, the tour bus arranged by travel services is the main way so that they do not need to consider the transfer hubs while the traffic hubs are more used by FITs since they rely heavily on local public transportation system.

For more in-depth analysis of the structure of the whole network, it can be divided into five sub-regions according to the nodes' structure and position: Sub-region 1 (Kanto-Chubu-Kinki), Sub-region 2 (Hokkaido), Sub-region 3 (Kyushu), Sub-region 4 (Tohoku) and Sub-region 5 (Chugoku-Shikoku). This breakdown allows for a more detailed picture of the sub-patterns comprising the overall tourist flow pattern created. A comparison of indicators of five sub-regions is present in Table 7. A comparison of closeness centralization is not possible in this research as a number of isolates appeared in the network. Closeness is a distance measure and, thus, cannot be calculated if a network is not connected (Hwang et al., 2006).

In Hokkaido and Kyushu region, FIT networks have higher degree centralization and betweenness centralization, indicating that a small number of nodes account for a large number of the connections and all travel occurs through a small number of hubs within these FIT sub networks. Sapporo and Fukuoka are the centers for FIT network in Hokkaido and Kyushu regions respectively. In contrast, the degree and betweenness centralization in Sub-region 1 (Kanto-Chubu-Kinki) are lower for FIT network. This region owns the most popular tourist destinations and most highly developed transportation systems therefore FITs have more choices for destinations and transportation ways. In sub-region Tohoku and Chugoku-Shikoku region, only FIT networks exist since only Sendai, Okayama and Takamatsu in these regions became the destinations for GPTs and cannot form the network.

When combining the result of distribution of tourist flow, the structure of nodes and the characteristics of sub-regions, the spatial pattern of whole network can be summarized. We judge the sub-network structure (agglomeration, equilibrium or dispersion) according to the result whether the difference between in-degree centralization and out-degree centralization is less than 10%. As present in Figure 3 (a schematic diagram for network structure), the tourist flow network pattern is characterized by followings:

(1) The sub-networks for GPT and FIT present different patterns. The GPT network comprises three sub-regions: Sub-region 1 owns four centers: Tokyo, Osaka, Fujisan and Kyoto, showing a multi-center agglomeration structure. Sub-region 2 shows characteristic of agglomeration structure with only one center (Sapporo) in the network. Sub-region 3 has two nodes (Beppu and Fukuoka) as its centers, showing multi-center agglomeration structure. Comparatively, the FIT network

Table 7. Comparison of network indicators for GPT and FIT network.

	Size	Density	Degree centralization Out	Degree centralization In	Type of network	Center
GPT network						
Sub-region 1 Kanto-Chubu-Kinki	60	0.067	0.398	0.467	Agglomeration	Fujisan, Tokyo, Osaka, Kyoto
Sub-region 2 Hokkaido	23	0.166	0.302	0.349	Agglomeration	Sapporo
Sub-region 3 Kyushu	16	0.171	0.173	0.244	Agglomeration	Beppu, Fukuoka
FIT network						
Sub-region 1 Kanto-Chubu-Kinki	87	0.042	0.287	0.264	Equilibrium	Tokyo, Osaka, Kyoto
Sub-region 2 Hokkaido	34	0.111	0.386	0.417	Equilibrium	Sapporo
Sub-region 3 Kyushu	28	0.107	0.427	0.388	Dispersion	Fukuoka
Sub-region 4 Tohoku	28	0.090	0.329	0.368	Agglomeration	Sendai
Sub-region 5 Chugoku-Shikoku	26	0.108	0.221	0.346	Agglomeration	Hiroshima, Takamatsu

comprises five sub-regions and different patterns. Sub-region 1, 2 and 3 reveal multi-center equilibrium, single center equilibrium and single center dispersion structure, respectively. Sub-region 4 has one center (Sendai), presenting a single center agglomeration structure due to greater in-degree centralization. Sub-region 5 still display an agglomeration structure but with two important nodes as its centers (Hiroshima and Takamatsu).

(2) Tourism flows with different intensity present hierarchical characteristic. This applies both to GPT and FIT networks. A large number of tourist flows are confined to nodes within the sub-region. Strong flows mainly exist between core nodes and secondary core nodes or surrounding nodes. The tourist flow between Tokyo and Fujisan has the largest size. Common flows exist mainly among secondary core nodes, important nodes and common nodes. Weak flows are comparative dispersion, existing among nodes with different levels.

(3) The tourism connections between sub-regions are considerable weak. The connections within FIT network are stronger than GPT network. As discussed previously, FITs have more inter regional movement and more transportation choices. It can be found that FIT flows between adjacent regions rely on the Shinkansen such as the Tohoku Shinkansen between Kanto Region and Tohoku Region, the Sanyo Shinkansen between Chugoku Region and Kinki Region. The connection between remote regions relies on airlines such as the air routes between Sapporo and Osaka or Sapporo and Tokyo. In addition, in GPT network some ferry routes exist between Sub-region 1 and Sub-region 3 (ferry route from Beppu to Osaka), Sub-region 2 and Sub-region 4 (ferry route from Tomakomai to Sendai). Generally, the weak connection is not only because traffic links between regions are insufficient, but also the travel time and cost restrict the long haul travel in Japan.

Different patterns are formed within different sub-regions due to kinds of factors. Destination characteristics (such as the hierarchy of tourism resources, touring reputation) have basic effect on tourist flow network. The higher hierarchy a destination has the more likely it become a center in the tourist flow network. As preceding paragraphs stated, both Fujisan and Kyoto own world class tourism resources, making them easier to become centers. Transportation network has a profound effect on

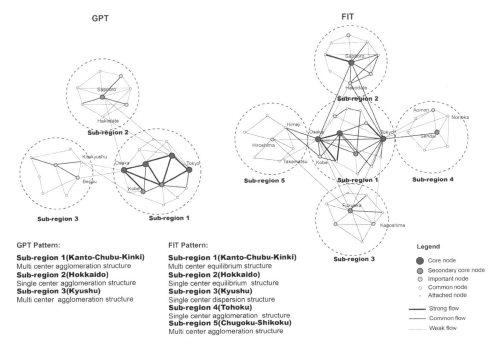

Figure 3. Pattern of Chinese tourist flow network in Japan.

tourist flow network. For example, although Hiroshima is the largest city in Chugoku region and owns Hiroshima international airport, it cannot become a single center for Chinese tourists probably because it lacks enough direct airline routes connecting China. Contrary, Beppu, as a mediator between Kyushu region and Kinki region, shows its high betweenness centrality as an important node. Itinerary patterns also have an effect on tourist flow network. Sub-region 1 has lowest density probably because the travel itineraries in this region are mainly linear (such as the golden route: Tokyo–Fujisan–Nagoya–Kyoto–Osaka) rather than loop or complex pattern. On the other hand, the base camp travel pattern is more adopted in Hokkaido region which make the tourist flow network shows a single center structure (tourists usually take Sapporo as a primary destination and 'base camp' from which visit other destinations).

Overall, this network structure of Chinese tourist flows seems rather consistent with the model of Chained Destination Region model (Dredge, 1999) and destination systems and flow patterns in Nanjing (Jin, Xu, Huang, & Cao, 2014). However, the results in this study are more focused on the inter destination level and network perspective and integrated the results of literatures about tourist flow patterns. Theoretically, there maybe one other model: multi-center dispersion structure. The tourist flows from other countries maybe display different structures from the results of this study.

Conclusion

This research analyzed Chinese tourist flows in Japan at inter destination level using SNA, constructed an evaluation indicators system and identified the nodes' structure and the spatial pattern of the network. It enriches tourist flow research from a social network perspective and verifies the applicability of SNA method. Since tourists choose several destinations to visit and present many different itineraries, this study contributes to the literatures by providing insights into multi-destination travel patterns.

From a theoretical point of view, this study constructs tourist flow network and try to understand tourist flow from three levels utilizing SNA: node, itinerary and network. Besides a general description of the structural characteristics of the network presented, we made a comparison between the GPT network and FIT network. By means of node centrality indicators, the roles and functions of destinations in the tourist flow network are identified and they are classified into five types: core node, secondary core node, important node, common node and attached node. Through descriptive measurements, it can be found that the distribution of tourist flows is disequilibrium, characterized by an extensive dispersion with localized concentrations from an overall perspective. In terms of network, in contrast with other studies where tourist flow network characteristics are not summarized, this study indicates that there may be six theoretical types of network pattern at inter destinations level: multi-center agglomeration structure, multi-center dispersion structure, multi-center equilibrium structure, single center equilibrium structure, single center dispersion structure and single center agglomeration structure, and five of them have been found in Chinese tourist flow network.

The empirical analysis in this study shows that:

(1) Chinese tourist flows are mainly concentrated in the central Japan (including Kanto, Chubu and Kinki Region). Compared to GPTs, spatial distribution of FIT flows is more extensive, FITs visit more regions including Tohoku region, Chugoku region and Shikoku region and have more inter regional movements.
(2) Destinations with higher hierarchy are more likely to have comprehensive functions while destinations with lower hierarchy own single function. Most nodes in FIT network have higher degree centrality than the nodes in GPT network. The node Tokyo, Kyoto, Osaka are the most important destinations for both the GPTs and FITs. However, the destination Fujisan is not ranked within the most important destinations for FITs. In addition, regional key cities and the cities with small international airports are more important to FITs.
(3) Moreover, empirical results indicate that 232 nodes and 981 ties constitute the Chinese tourist flow network and the pattern of this network is complex. Overall, it can be divided into five sub-regions with different patterns, which are affected by destination characteristics, transportation network and itinerary patterns. FIT network has larger size, longer diameter and lower density, showing a looser structure compared to GPT network. FIT network comprises five sub-regions while GPT network comprises three. Tourist flows with different intensity present hierarchical characteristic for both GPT and FIT network. Tourism connections between sub-regions are considerable weak but the connections within FIT network are stronger than GPT network.

As a practical implication, the recognition of structural characteristic and pattern of Chinese tourist flow network can be useful for planning tourism facilities in Japan and defining marketing strategies. Firstly, tourist flows are concentrated in the major destinations such as Tokyo, Fujisan, Kyoto and Osaka currently, suggesting a significant opportunity for locations outside of top destination areas to attract more tourists. Especially, since demand simulations for 2020 indicate that the country may face up to a 50% shortage in accommodation in Tokyo/Kyoto/Osaka, and up to 30% overflow in air capacity for Haneda and Narita airports (Andre, Tasuku, & Naomi, 2016), the development for accommodations and infrastructure in local destinations (especially the common nodes and attached nodes in this study) is more necessary. Secondly, there are very few GPT flows distributed in Tohoku, Chugoku and Shikoku Region, suggesting that more promoting campaigns about these regions should be conducted targeting at the tourists and travel industry in China. Thirdly, considering the growth trend of FITs to Japan and high betweenness centralization of FIT network, it is necessary to promote the convenience of transportation between destinations within sub-regions and reduce the language barrier for FITs. For example, enhancing the connections between Takamatsu and other destinations in Shikoku Region may help to strength tourism development of this region. Additionally, it is necessary to strengthen the direct linkage between the sub-regions and China due to the weak connections among sub-regions. For instance, since China Eastern Airlines introduced its flights from Shanghai Pudong to Asahikawa in 2014, Chinese travel to East Hokkaido increased. The direct airlines between Takamatsu and Shanghai promoted the Chinese travel to Shikoku and Chugoku Region to some extent.

This study has some limitations. The data in this study are based on itineraries collected from travel agencies and tourists' trip diaries in one year. It may neglect the tourists who do not like to express their views on internet. In addition, it could not reflect the formation and evolution of network. The formation mechanism or factors influencing tourist flow network needs be studied in the future. For example, how travel agencies make the travel itineraries so the structure can be influenced? Such studies will help to understand tourist flow network deeply.

Disclosure statement

No potential conflict of interest was reported by the author.

References

Ahas, R., Aasa A., Roose, A., Mark, U., & Silm, S. (2008). Evaluating passive mobile positioning data for tourism surveys: An Estonian case study. *Tourism Management*, 29, 469–486.
Andre, A., Tasuku, K., & Naomi, Y. (2016). The future of Japan's tourism: Path for sustainable growth towards 2020. Retrieved from http://www.mckinsey.com

Antonio, F. M. (2003). Decomposing seasonal concentration. *Annals of Tourism Research*, 30, 942–956.

Asakura, Y., Iryo, T. (2007). Analysis of tourist behavior based on the tracking data collected using a mobile communication instrument. *Transportation Research Part A*, 41, 684–690.

Asero, V., Gozzo, S., & Tomaselli, V. (2016). Building tourism networks through tourist mobility. *Journal of Travel Research*, 55, 751–763.

Beeco, J. A., Huang, W. J., Hallo, J. C., Norman, W. C., McGehee, N. G., McGee, J., & Goetcheus, C. (2013). GPS tracking of travel routes of Wanderers and planners. *Tourism Geographies*, 5, 551–573.

Bowden, J. (2003). A cross-national analysis of international tourist flows in China. *Tourism Geographies*, 5, 257–279.

Casanueva, C., Gallego, A., & Garcia-Sanchez, M. R. (2016). Social network analysis in tourism. *Current Issues in Tourism*, 19, 1190–1209.

Chris, R., & Gu, H. (2007). Spatial planning, mobilities and culture: Chinese and New Zealand student preferences for Californian travel. *International Journal of Tourism Research*, 9, 189–203.

Connell, J., & Page, S. J. (2008). Exploring the spatial patterns of car-based tourist travel in Loch Lomond and Trossachs national park, Scotland. *Tourism Management*, 29, 561–580.

Cui, L. W. (2011). About the sightseeing activities of Chinese visitors to Japan – A case study of the group package tours. *Tourism Science Studies*, 4, 39–52 (in Japanese).

Draijer, G., Kalfs, N., & Perdok, J. (2000). Global positioning system as data collection method for travel research. *Transportation Research Record*, 1719, 147–153.

Dredge, D. (1999). Destination place planning and design. *Annals of Tourism Research*, 26, 772–791.

East, D., Osborne, P., Kemp, S., &Woodfine, T. (2017). Combining GPS & survey data improves understanding of visitor behavior. *Tourism Management*, 61, 307–320.

Flogenfeldt, T. (1999). Traveler geographic origin and market segmentation: The multi trips destination case. *Journal of Travel and Tourism Marketing*, 8, 111–118.

Gunn, C. A. (1972). *Vacationscape: Designing tourist regions*. Austin, TX: Bureau of Business Research.

Guo, Y. Z., Chen, Y., Huang, J.F., & Su, Y. (2015). Travel intentions of Chinese residents to Japan based on a multidimensional interactive decision tree model. *Tourism Tribune*, 30, 42–52 (in Chinese).

Hallo, J. C., Beeco, J. A., Goetcheus, C., McGee, J., McGehee, N. G., & Norman, W. C.(2012). GPS as a method for assessing spatial and temporal use distributions of nature-based tourists. *Journal of Travel Research*, 51, 591–606.

Hishida, N., Hibino, N., & Morichi, S. (2012). Chinese tourists in China: Time-series analysis in their destination choices and its multiplicities. *Infrastructure Planning Review*, 68, 1667–1677 (in Japanese).

Hwang, Y., Gretzel, U., & Fesenmaier, D. R. (2006). Multicity trip patterns: Tourists to the United States. *Annals of Tourism Research*, 33(4), 1057–1078.

Japan Tourism Agency (JTA). (2016). White paper on tourism in Japan the tourism situation in FY2015. Retrieved from http://www.mlit.go.jp/kankocho/en/siryou/whitepaper.html

Jin, C., Xu, J., Huang, Z., & Cao, F. (2014). Analyzing the characteristics of tourist flows between the scenic spots in inner city based on tourism strategies: A case study in Nanjing. *Acta Geographica Sinica*, 69, 1858–1870 (in Chinese).

Jin, Y. S. (2009). Spatial characteristics of Chinese tourist activities in Japan. *Geographical Review of Japan*, 82, 332–345 (in Japanese).

Jin, Y. S. (2015). Film-induced tourism focusing on Chinese visits to East Hokkaido, Japan: Case study of the Chinese movie if you are the one. *Geographical Review of Japan*, 88, 514–530 (in Japanese).

Lau, G., & Mckercher, B. (2007). Understanding tourist movement patterns in a destination: A GIS approach. *Tourism and Hospitality Research*, 7(1), 39–49.

Leung, X. Y., Wang, F., Wu, B., Bai, B., Stahura, K. A., & Xie, Z. (2012). A social network analysis of overseas tourist movement patterns in Beijing: The impact of the Olympic Games. *International Journal of Tourism Research*, 14, 469–484.

Lew, A., & Mckercher, B. (2002). Trip destinations, gateways and itineraries: The example of Hong Kong. *Tourism Management*, 23, 609–621.

Lew, A., & Mckercher, B. (2006). Modeling tourist movements: A local destination analysis. *Annals of Tourism Research*, 33, 403–423.

Liu, B., Huang, S. & Fu, H. (2017). An application of network analysis on tourist attractions: The case of Xinjiang, China. *Tourism Management*, 58, 132–141.

Liu, F., Zhang, J., Zhang, J., Chen, D., Liu, Z., & Lu, S. (2012). Roles and functions of tourism destinations in tourism region of South Anhui: A tourist flow network perspective. *Chinese Geographical Science*, 22, 755–764.

Lue, C., Crompton, J. L., & Fesenmaier, D. R. (1993). Conceptualization of multidimension pleasure trips. *Annals of Tourism Research*, 20, 289–301.

Mckercher, B., & Lau, G. (2008). Movement patterns of tourists within a destination. *Tourism Geographies*, 10, 355–374.

Mings, R. C., & McHugh, K. E. (1992). The spatial configuration of travel to Yellowstone National Park. *Journal of Travel Research*, 30, 38–46.

Noam, S., & Michal, I. (2007). Tracking tourists in the digital age. *Annals of Tourism Research*, 34, 141–159.

Oppermann, M. (1995). A model of travel itineraries. *Journal of Travel Research*, 33, 57–61.

Palomares, J. C. G., Gutiérrez, J., & Mínguez, C. (2015). Identification of tourist hot spots based on social networks: A comparative analysis of European metropolises using photo-sharing services and GIS. *Applied Geography*, 63, 408–417.

Pearce, D. G. (1987). Spatial patterns of package tourism in Europe. *Annals of Tourism Research*, 14(1), 183–201.

Peng, H., Zhang, J., Liu, Z., Lu, L., & Yang, L. (2016). Network analysis of tourist flows: A cross-provincial boundary perspective, *Tourism Geographies*, 18, 561–586.

Rosario, D'A., Simona, G., & Venera, T. (2013). Network analysis approach to map tourism mobility. *Quality & Quantity*, 47, 3167–3184.

Shi, Y. X., Sun, H., Yoshida, Y., & Yamamoto, Y. (2012). Travel behavior and expenditure of Chinese visitors in Japan: A case study of visiting relative's family. *The Review of Agricultural Economics*, 67, 1–6 (in Japanese).

Shih, H. (2006). Network characteristics of drive tourism destinations: An application of network analysis in tourism. *Tourism Management*, 27, 1029–1039.

Shimizu, I. (2007). Changes in the patterns of Chinese tourism to Japan. *Geographical Studies*, 82, 37–52 (in Japanese).

Smallwood, C. B., Beckley, L. E., & Moore, S. A. (2012). An analysis of visitor movement patterns using travel networks in a large marine park, north-western Australia. *Tourism Management*, 33, 517–528.

Song, H., & Li, G. (2008). Tourism demand modelling and forecasting – A review of recent research. *Tourism Management*, 29, 203–220.

Susan, I. S., & Christine, A. V. (1997). Multi-destination trip patterns. *Annals of Tourism Research*, 24, 458–461.

UNWTO. (2002). *Think tank enthusiastically reaches consensus on frameworks for tourism destination success*. Madrid: World Tourism Organization.

Vu, H. Q., Li, G., Law, R., & Ye, B. H. (2015). Exploring the travel behaviors of inbound tourists to Hong Kong using geotagged photos. *Tourism Management*, 46, 222–232.

Wang, J. Y., Wu, J. F., Tang, L., & Yang, X. (2013). Research on the properties and structural characteristics of inbound European tourist flows network in China based on SNA. *Human Geography*, 28, 147–153 (in Chinese).

Wang, Y. Q., Wu, J. F., & Ren, R. P. (2013). Geographical distribution and network structure characteristics of inbound tourist flows from Guangzhou city. *Journal of Shaanxi Normal University (Natural Science Edition)*, 41, 91–97 (in Chinese).

Wasserman, S., & Faust, K. (1994). *Social network analysis: Methods and applications*. Cambridge: Cambridge University Press.

Williams, A. V., & Zelinsky, W. (1970). On some patterns in international tourist flows. *Economics Geography*, 46, 549–567.

Wu, J. F. (2014). Distribution of inbound foreigner tourist flows and its property and structure characters in China. *Journal of Arid Land Resources and Environment*, 28, 177–182 (in Chinese).

Wu, J. F., & Pan, X. L. (2010). Characteristic of Beijing and Shanghai inbound tourists flow network. *Scientia Geographica Sinica*, 30, 370–376 (in Chinese).

Xia, J., Zeephongsekul, P., & Arrowsmith, C. (2009). Modelling spatio-temporal movement of tourists using finite Markov chains. *Mathematics and Computers in Simulation*, 79, 1544–1553.

Xia, J., Evans F. H., Spilsbury, K., Ciesielski, V., Arrowsmith, C., & Wright, G. (2010). Market segments based on the dominant movement patterns of tourists. *Tourism Management*, 31, 464–469.

Yang, X. Z., Gu, C. L., & Wang, Q. (2007). Urban tourism flow network structure construction in Nanjing. *Acta Geographica Sinca*, 62, 609–620 (in Chinese).

Ye, W. (2013). *Travel decision influencing factors of Shanghai residents to Japan*. Shanghai, China: Fudan University (in Chinese).

Understanding visitors' spatial behavior: a review of spatial applications in parks

Geoffrey K. Riungu, Brian A. Peterson, John A. Beeco and Greg Brown

ABSTRACT
The integration of spatial concepts with social science data in natural resource management has progressed rapidly over the past 15 years. There is now a foundational understanding, and supporting empirical work, that recreational use at parks and protected areas (PPAs) is a spatially conditioned process. To better understand visitor's spatial behavior, we present an updated review of the incorporation of space into human dimensions of natural resources research; what it has illuminated about human behavior, human values, and PPA management; how spatially related social science data are being integrated with other resource issues; and identify knowledge gaps and propose future directions for research. Overall, our review suggests that the examination of spatially related social science data are only in their infancy because of rapidly evolving technology which continues to advance the value of this type of research. Additionally, the geographic scope of studies often determines the applicability of the findings. For example, participatory mapping methods are typically used for macro-level PPA management applications such as infrastructure planning while visitor data logging are often used for more localized visitor management applications. Therefore, one significant advancement over the past five years has been the incorporation of multiple methods in single studies.

摘要
在过去15年中，空间概念与自然资源管理中的社会科学数据的整合取得了快速地进展。现在有一个基本的认识，并且有实证工作支持，即在公园和保护区(PPAs)的娱乐利用是一个受空间制约的过程。为了更好地理解游客的空间行为，我们提供了一个更新版的文献综述，将空间纳入自然资源研究的人类维度研究之中。该综述阐述了人类行为、人类价值观和公园及保护地管理；空间相关的社会科学数据如何与其他资源问题进行整合；该综述识别了知识缺口，并提出未来的研究方向。总的来说，我们的综述表明，对空间相关社会科学数据的研究还处于起步阶段，这是因为快速发展的技术不断提升了这类研究的价值。此外，研究的地理范围常常决定了研究结果的适用性。例如，参与式绘图方法通常用于基础设施规划等宏观尺度的公园及保护地管理，而访问者记录数据通常用于更小范围的游客管理领域。因此, 在过去的五年里, 一个重要的进步是将多种方法结合到单个的研究中。

Introduction

Recreation in parks and protected areas (PPAs) is a spatially conditioned process that affects visitors' experiences and impacts to biophysical resources (Beeco & Brown, 2013; Beeco, Hallo, English, & Giumetti, 2013). A spatially conditioned process is a relationship between space and a human-related phenomena. Beeco and Brown (2013) identified how nature-based recreation is a spatially conditioned process because of the visitor interaction with space within a PPA. Specifically, the physical terrain structure, along with anthropogenic infrastructures, affects the spatial trajectory of visitors leading to spatial diffusion—where visitors concentrate in specific areas. Beyond the physical behavioral aspect of PPA visitors, their spatial behavior is manifested from a complex psychological dynamic that includes values, motivations, beliefs, attitudes, and norms. Visitor use distribution impacts experiential factors, natural resources, and cultural resources, which are all directly related to where visitors travel. Finally, managers also use space to segment visitor use through management zones and spatial segmentation practices.

Spatial behavior is also strongly connected to time, hence the jargon term 'spatiotemporal' (Birenboim, Anton-Clavé, Russo, & Shoval, 2013). Hägerstrand (1970, 1973) stated that time is an essential aspect of spatial behavior, because time-budgets affect spatial movements. Spatiotemporal data are important for managers of PPAs to understand: how much time visitors spend in specific locations, the distribution of visitors, the identification, evaluation and evolution of possible resource impacts, and where and when mitigation of problems may be prevented (D'Antonio & Monz, 2016). Consequently, this information can help managers effectively manage for social, environmental, cultural, and managerial impacts. This knowledge can reduce PPA management spending and staff time. Hence, it is critical to assess not only the spatial component of visitors' travel patterns, but to investigate the temporal factor in conjunction with spatial data, hence the importance of spatiotemporal research in PPAs.

The advances of the integration of spatial concepts with social science data in natural resources management has progressed rapidly over the past 15 years. Thus, the purpose of this article is to review spatial applications in PPAs that conducted research within the scope of understanding visitors' spatial behavior. This state of knowledge review serves as a concise consolidation of research conducted to explain visitors' spatial behaviors and the methods employed. Beeco and Brown (2013) conducted a similar review, although not congruent, in which the incorporation of space into PPA research was reviewed, along with concepts, methods, gap analyses, and lastly proposals for future research were provided. This article builds on the review of Beeco and Brown (2013) and primarily focuses on research done since 2013, which includes research that explored a single method and the affiliated outcomes, along with how researchers have ingeniously combined multiple methods to gain a rich understanding into visitors' spatial behavior. The Beeco and Brown (2013) paper found that research had mostly described spatial behavior instead of explaining spatial behavior and therefore focused largely on methodical approaches.

A framework for spatial research in PPAs

This review begins with an organizing framework for describing spatial research conducted in PPAs (Figure 1). Row 1 of Figure 1 displays four general spatial processes—diffusion, interaction, impacts, and segmentation—that are presented as organizing categories for understanding how space is applied to measuring, predicting, and managing visitor use in PPAs. Spatial diffusion describes where visitors go, spatial interaction describes why visitors go there, spatial impacts identity resources that may be affected, and spatial segmentation identifies how space can be managed. Row 2 provides examples of spatial operations that have been performed on visitor spatial data including cluster, density, proximity, overlay, and network analyses. The spatial operations are a means to examine and assess spatial data to inform a range of PPA applications (Row 3) such as physical infrastructure design and management (facilities, roads, trails, and information services), the management of visitor social behavior (experiences, conflict, crowding), and the management of PPA areas and features (levels of service, zoning).

The framework is intended to be organizational and illustrative, not exhaustive of all categories and relationships. Multiple spatial processes and operations are typically used when analyzing spatial data for a given PPA management application. For simplicity, the framework depicts a one-to-one relational hierarchy, however, a more accurate graphical representation would show multiple arrows connecting spatial operations to multiple PPA management applications. For example, at its most basic Global Positioning System (GPS), data are used to understand where visitor's travel

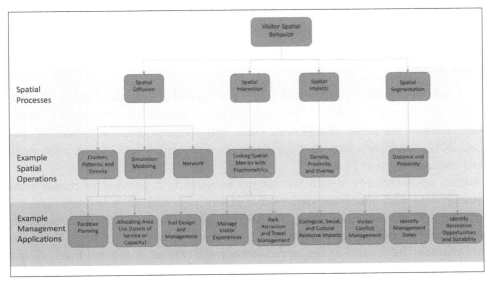

Figure 1. A framework for understanding spatial behavior in parks and protected areas management. Source: Authors.

(spatial diffusion) and often analyzed using a density measure. However, that same data could be linked with survey data to understand why visitors are traveling to certain places at certain times (spatial interaction). Further, the findings from this analysis could then inform management zones, a spatial/temporal zoning regime, trail design and management, and facilities planning.

Spatial data—data logging versus user-generated content

Locational data for visitor activities and behaviors in PPAs fall into two general categories—data that is captured through GPS loggers or remote-sensing equipment (e.g. cameras, aerial imagery) and data provided directly by visitors who identify locations on a map, either hardcopy or digital. This latter method is typically described as public participation Geographic Information Systems (PPGIS) or volunteered geographic information (VGI) systems. Data loggers can provide accurate locations of visitor use over time using GPS tracks while remote-sensing equipment can provide location information about PPA use at a single point in time. PPGIS and VGI systems typically capture PPA spatial data from users during or after their visits and have the advantage of providing greater context for the spatial data generated from user descriptions.

Over the past five years the greatest advances in methodology have come from innovatively combining and cross validating spatial methods rather than the development of new approaches. The use of GPS data loggers solely for descriptive analysis is rarely sufficient to help managers of PPAs, but as described below, combining GPS data loggers with questionnaires, using GPS to cross-validate other data, and using GPS data to determine assessment indicators are three examples of creatively achieving results. Similarly, PPGIS and VGI systems alone may not generate sufficient spatial data at a scale that is adequate for the management of specific features or areas within a PPA. The combination of spatial data collection methods can generate spatial information to inform PPA management at multiple scales, from park feature and trail management, to larger area zoning for visitor experience and resource protection.

Spatial diffusion

Spatial diffusion is the geographical pattern of spatial distribution (Beeco & Brown, 2013). The locations people visit, their travel routes, and the amount of time spent at these locations are some of the most basic, but relevant, data on recreation (Hallo et al., 2012). Multiple methods have been used to better understand how visitors travel through space in PPAs.

Recent advancements in GPS technology have made it possible to collect spatio-temporal data with affordable devices that collect high-resolution and accurate time-space data (Birenboim et al., 2013). The GPS data loggers are an effective device that record waypoint position at regular time intervals in its internal memory. These devices are small (some models are approximately the size of a thumb drive), typically waterproof, can be carried in a pocket, and purchased at an affordable price. Accordingly, GPS data loggers have regularly been featured as a tool to further gain knowledge about visitor use management in PPAs (Beeco & Hallo, 2014; Beeco, Hallo,

& Brownlee, 2014; D'Antonio & Monz, 2016; D'Antonio et al., 2010; Kidd et al., 2015). Even though GPS data loggers are commonly used as one method for understanding visitors' behavior, the methods of analysis are underdeveloped (Beeco & Brown, 2013; Beeco & Hallo, 2014), and can gain richness by being combined with social data.

Most of the GPS studies in PPAs have largely focused on the utility of GPS technology and mapping visitor travel patterns. These studies are usually limited to visual analyses such as mapping, point densities, or overlays and descriptions of clustering and pattern analysis (Beeco & Hallo, 2014; Zheng, Huang, & Li, 2017). Fortunately, there is high potentiality to investigate inventive research questions that categorize GPS attribute data into specific classifications that help describe a fuller understanding of visitor travel patterns, and the implications visitor travel patterns have on other knowledge and on management implications. More recent studies have done just that—used GPS to better understand human behavior.

A popular setting that draws researchers to use GPS data loggers is recreational trail activity. Taczanowska et al. (2014) combined graph theory with GPS data to assess the functionality of a trail network in Austria. Graph theory, which has marginally been applied to PPAs, is applicable for understanding properties and functions of networks, and is useful for evaluating overall trail connectivity and the relative importance of trail intersections (Gross & Yellen, 2006). This two-pronged approach, utilized by Taczanowska et al. (2014), determined that the official trail network does not strongly correspond with hikers' behavior, that a network of informal trails encourages hikers to leave official trails, and connectivity indices produced from graph theory are an efficient method to measure change to a trail network.

Another study coupled GPS data loggers and questionnaires to analyze how visitors travel within and through a complex trail network (Beeco & Hallo, 2014). The study operationalized travel patterns into three distinct (but overlapping) measures: total distance traveled, number of zones (areas) encountered, distance (Euclidean) from start, and time spent using the trail system. This study generally found (in a more-to-less order) that mountain bikers, horseback riders, runners, and then hikers travel the most miles, encountered the most zones, and traveled the furthest from the starting point. These results also suggest that horseback riders stayed significantly longer on the trails than all other groups.

GPS tracking of visitor use in PPAs has challenged some theoretical assumptions in visitor use. Studies performing simulation modeling assume the temporal or spatial distribution of visitor use remains constant even as use levels rise in the study areas modeled (Lawson, Hallo, & Manning, 2008). Using GPS to measure visitor dispersion patterns, D'Antonio and Monz (2016) indicated that this assumption is only valid for some recreational settings. Visitor spatial behavior (i.e., dispersal away from hardened surfaces) varied with use level in areas that had a single attraction point or feature for visitors to view (i.e. 'view sites').

Innovative application of analyses have also taught us more about how visitors are distributed through time and space in PPAs. Point density analysis has become a popular tool to determine where visitors are 'dense' within a PPA. Point density analysis is possible because GPS data loggers are programmed to take a waypoint at a pre-determined interval, such as recording a waypoint every five seconds. These

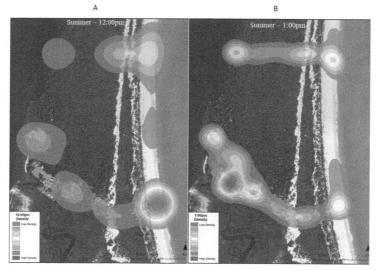

Figure 2. Point density display of 12 noon (A) and 1:00 PM. (B) waypoints collected during the summer of 2016 at Cumberland Island National Seashore (Peterson, Brownlee, & Sharp, 2017).

waypoints recorded by the GPS data logger are connected to form tracks using GIS software, such as ArcGIS. The waypoint data can be used to analyze point data density. Density analysis can be assessed at numerous scales, such as by season or by hour. Point density analysis by season will display seasonal densities of point data gathered by GPS data loggers. Hourly point density analysis is a smaller scale that can display density patterns for each hour of the day. For example, using point density analysis it is possible to assess the density of summer visitors at each hour of each day. This would result in a density display for spring data for 9:00 am, 10:00 am, 11:00 am, etc., for each day of the week for each season. This would show managers where visitors are dense within the PPA for each hour of the day for each day of the week for summer data. Figure 2 illustrates point density maps at 12:00 noon and 1:00 pm for data collected during the summer of 2016 with GPS data loggers at Cumberland Island National Seashore. Stratifying data are useful for managers to gain enhanced understanding of the visitor population. Similarly, kernel density estimation could also be used and has other advantages, including it has a smoothing effect that produces a clean display and is a non-parametric process on which each point is looked at uniquely and no underlying distribution is assumed.

Line density is a tool that can be employed to analyze the density of tracks. Line density is similar to point density, but instead of being applied to point features, line density is applied to linear features, such as a travel routes. Line density is a tool that has not been employed as often as point density. Point density has become more popular due to its analysis of individual waypoints and thus resulting in a more detailed analysis versus analyzing all the waypoints together that form a continuous track. A line density analysis was conducted of trail users that was segmented by user groups (Beeco et al., 2013). The line density analysis revealed drastically different travel

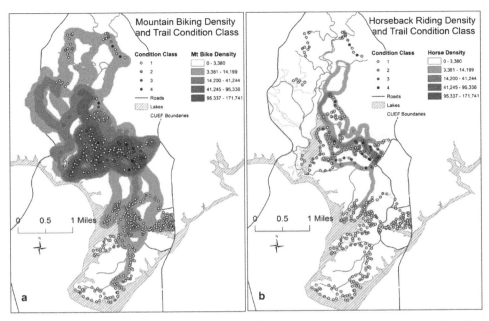

Figure 3. Line density analysis of travel patterns of mountain bikers and horseback riders (Beeco et al., 2013).

patterns for mountain bikers versus horseback users (Figure 3; Beeco et al., 2013; note that this is the same overall project cited as Beeco & Hallo, 2014).

Another approach to understanding visitor use patterns has been to examine phenomena at different scales. Balmford et al., (2015) analyzed visitor spatial behavior at a macro level to model predicted visitation variation of international PPAs. The researchers built several variables into their model schema: visitation rates, local population size, PPA remoteness, PPA natural attractiveness, and national income. Generalized linear models were constructed to predict variation in PPA visitation. The model data were used to make inferences about visitation and economic significance. This research was the first of its type to illuminate the scale of PPA visitation and the economic significance. The pinnacle inference that was revealed is that for the amount of visitation to PPAs, they are insufficiently funded, which suggest that if PPAs were substantially more funded, there would consequently be higher economic expansion at PPAs and their surrounding local areas.

As opposed to macro level analyses, micro-level analyses have also been conducted. GPS data loggers are a worthy tool for also analyzing walking speed of visitors at PPAs. Bauder (2015) analyzed tourists' velocity to interpret tourists' behavior. This study analyzed various groups that may have different walking speeds, such as age, gender, and traveling with children. This study coupled GPS data loggers with questionnaires to identify and isolate some of the factors that influence tourists' spatial behavior. These methods are valuable for comparing visitors' spatial behavior before, after, and during managerial actions. Analyzing visitors' velocities enable researchers to determine what spatial areas are causing visitors to slow their walking velocity and what areas are causing visitors to increase their walking velocity. Bauder (2015) created three meter circles of the study area, and mean speed for all points within each three meter circle was calculated. This type of analysis can be combined with questionnaire data to obtain differences in visitor groups and to investigate factors that underpin visitors' spatial behavior. Additionally, this type of analysis can be implemented before and after management actions. Speed analysis is a strong method to assess the attractiveness of a site within a PPA.

Additionally, while the vast majority of these studies have employed GPS data loggers, we would be remiss if we did not mention advances in tracking using mobile phones. Mobile positioning data can be used to measure visitor flows at a destination. Raun, Ahas, and Tiru (2016) used log files consisting of the location coordinates of mobile phones from Estonia's largest mobile network operator to measure visitor flows. Passive mobile positioning data files are stored automatically in the memory of mobile network operators and contains roaming data. 'Roaming' refers to situations where mobile phones registered in a particular country can be used outside that country (e.g. a mobile phone registered in the US being used in Canada) for outgoing and incoming calls, sending and receiving short message services (SMSs) and using internet data services (Ahas, Aasa, Mark, Pae, & Kull, 2007). This method of tracking visitors can analyze the behavior of international tourists at the country level at relatively low cost and is suitable for macro-scale research. However, sole use of mobile positioning data fails to provide additional information about the visitor besides the country of origin and travel patterns.

Another emerging line of research to understand visitor travel patterns is the use of social media. Researchers have utilized geo-tagged social media data to analyze tourist flows in Italy. Chua, Servillo, Marcheggiani, and Moere (2016) used geo-tagged Twitter data that was collected from Twitter's application programming interfaces (API). The researchers organized tweets by account and by time to create a time-ordered collection of geotagged tweets. The researchers applied this data to a visualization tool they developed called Flowsampler (Chua, Marcheggiani, Servillo, & Moere, 2014). This tool produces flow maps that can be filtered across four variables: time, direction of travel, number of trips, and demographic group. Although tourist flow knowledge is derived from numerous sources, the authors concluded that geo-tagged social media data are a valuable source that contributes to knowledge of tourist flow patterns. However, when using data acquired from social media, it is important to be strongly aware of the limitation of this data. For example, this type of data is not validated by ground truth verification, which means biases may be present in the data. Additionally, not all tourists use social media, nor are tourists providing geo-tagged data to social media at all times to fully understand tourists' itineraries.

The use of PPGIS for land use planning and management has grown significantly over the last two decades (Brown & Kyttä, 2018). These systems provide user-generated spatial data for a wide range of PPA attributes ranging from recreational activities to place values and management preferences. The majority of PPGIS studies involve sampling of households and/or on-site visitors to PPAs where participants place markers on a map identifying attribute locations. PPGIS systems have been implemented for different types of PPAs including national parks (Brown & Weber, 2013;

Engen et al., 2017; Pietilä & Kangas, 2015; van Riper, Kyle, Sutton, Barnes, & Sherrouse, 2012; Wolf, Wohlfart, Brown, & Lasa, 2015), national forests (Brown, 2013; Brown & Reed, 2009; Clement & Cheng, 2011), and conservation areas (Brown & Weber, 2013). PPGIS data are analyzed to show the diffusion of spatial attributes within the PPA, identifying areas of intensity and clustering of activities and place values. Unlike GPS systems, PPGIS data indirectly measure visitor spatial behavior through marker locations. At a PPA-wide scale, these spatial patterns of use, values, and preferences can be used to identify facility needs, the spatial locations of potential user conflict, and to delineate areas for more specific uses (management zones).

Volunteered Geographic Information (VGI) systems are becoming popular to study the movement of people engaged in recreation. Using tracking applications installed on mobile devices and webshare services (e.g. sports tracker, Strava, GPSies.com, and wikiloc), people share routes, experiences and georeferenced photos in online platforms (Campelo & Mendes, 2016; Heesch & Langdon, 2017; Oksanen, Bergman, Sainio, & Westerholm, 2015; Santos, Mendes, & Vasco, 2016). Korpilo, Virtanen, and Lehvävirta (2017) demonstrate the utility of available and voluntarily collected smartphone GPS self-tracking data for applications in urban forest management by locating spatial clustering of off-trail movement in intensively used areas—'hotspot analysis'. This low-cost participatory data collection approach using smartphone GPS tracking is relatively accurate (Haddad, Kelly, Leinonen, & Saarinen, 2014; Korpilo et al., 2017), and mitigates possible concerns affecting participants' spatial behavior due to their awareness of researcher supplied GPS data loggers (Wolf et al., 2015). Overlaying user-generated maps with official land record datasets, roads, and habitat charts help PPA managers identify where trespassing occurs, where informal/illegal trails exist and where ecological impacts may happen (Campelo & Mendes, 2016). However, VGI may be limited to only collecting information related to visitors' movement patterns. PPA managers also need to understand visitors' route choice motives. Therefore, VGI data needs to be linked with other instruments (e.g. survey data) to gain more knowledge of the visitors' profiles and environmental features that may influence their spatial behavior in PPAs (Korpilo et al., 2017).

Korpilo, Virtanen, Saukkonen, and Lehvävirta (2018) advanced the research conducted by Korpilo et al. (2017) by combining smartphone GPS tracking and questionnaires to study visitor behavior at an urban park in Helsinki, Finland. The researchers utilized public PPGIS from 'MyDynamicForest' to gather spatiotemporal data. The researchers determined that different activity types were associated with distinctive travel patterns. Runners and cyclists predominantly stayed on formal trails. Mountain bikers were found to concentrate around a few informal trails when traveling away from formal trails. Walkers and dog walkers were found to travel off-trail the most frequently. Off-trail behavior was found to be caused by an affinity for scenic views, exploration, and viewing flora and fauna.

GPS tracking has also been used as a cross-validation tool for other spatial methods of measuring visitor distribution. Wolf et al. (2015), used PPGIS mapping and GPS data loggers to monitor mountain bikers in Australia. Participants identified and marked locations on a map (either online or paper map) about perceived place attributes like riding frequency, popularity and issues on specific trail tracks. The collected GPS data were then used to cross-validate the results from PPGIS mapping. The study revealed a strong positive correlation between the ranked tracks from the PPGIS mapping and GPS tracking, thereby implying the validity of the PPGIS method for estimating future use at specific locations (Wolf et al., 2015).

Spatial interactions

Spatial interaction processes are evident when one area of space affects other areas of space (Beeco & Brown, 2013). Another way of considering this is how do visitors affect their own travel patterns and other's travel patterns? This is essentially the 'why' visitors are traveling the way they travel. Because this question directly addresses visitor behavior, early research suggests complicated answers. Logically, there are two approaches here. First, what is it about visitors' characteristics, motivations, and goals that affect spatial behavior? Second, how do certain visitor behaviors affect other visitors' behaviors? Connected to both of these approaches is how does time affect visitor use patterns?

The use of typologies was one way Beeco and Brown (2013) identified how researchers had approached this first question. At that time, there had been some theoretical and qualitative approaches (non-spatial), but few that assessed visitor behavior spatially. Two types of approaches to assess visitor typologies have emerged: non-spatial and spatial approaches (Beeco et al., 2013). Non-spatial approaches group visitors using psychological measures, such as values, attitudes, and motivations, and then use spatial data to determine whether these psychological measures reflect differences in spatial behaviors. The second method is to group visitors according to how they travel through space (Beeco et al., 2013; McKercher, Wong, & Lau, 2006), and then use measures (e.g. psychological) to try and understand those patterns.

Beeco et al. (2013) matched non-spatial tourist characteristics with spatial movement patterns. The study linked self-reported travel style of two visitor typologies identified in the literature, wanderers and planners (McKercher et al., 2006), with visitor travel patterns at Blue Ridge Parkway in Virginia. The study revealed that travel style (of wanderers and planners) had no significant effect on actual travel patterns. This means that regardless of whether participants were wanderers, planners, or a little of both, they used the same routes and visited the same locations for approximately the same time duration.

Presently, there is growing interest in categorizing visitors by relying on visitors' spatial patterns. For example, Kidd et al. (2018) classified visitors based on vehicular behavior along the Moose-Wilson corridor of Grand Teton National Park. Vehicle behavior variables (e.g. trip start and end time, location and duration of stops along the corridor etc.) were extracted from the GPS tracks and exploratory factor analysis conducted (Kidd et al., 2018). Cluster analysis was then performed to determine the factors that were deemed important for specific visitor types. By incorporating survey data, the study suggested three types of visitors: opportunistic commuters, wildlife/scenery viewers, and hikers. At the same site, by tracking visitors' vehicular patterns, Newton, Newman, Taff, D'Antonio, and Monz (2017) simultaneously examined space and time statistics to better understand visitor flow. The space-time cube tool was used to create bins representing a location and time, and correlated stopped points within the study area. Hot spot analysis was then conducted to identify significant hot and cold spots. The study found four categories of statistically significant cold spots. They were likely influenced by the presence of wildlife along the road, the number of pull offs, the number of cars on the road, and availability of parking. Also, the study found that there was a significant decrease in stopping point counts over time.

Another approach to use is to analyze how motivations and visitor use characteristics influence visitor use patterns. One study used GPS data loggers and questionnaires to analyze how visitors traveled within and throughout a complex trail network (Beeco & Hallo, 2014). This is the same study that operationalized travel patterns into three distinct (but overlapping) measures: total distance traveled, number of zones (areas) encountered, distance (Euclidean) from start, and time spent using the trail system. The study surveyed mountain bikers, horseback riders, runners, and hikers. This study measured self-report ability/skill, finding that the more ability/skill reported, the more miles they traveled, zones they encountered, further they ventured from the trailhead, and the longer they stayed. The researchers also determined factors that displayed a positive relationship with trip time (number of years visiting, group size, and motivations to develop skills), and factors that displayed a negative relationship with trip time (number of visits over the past 12 months, gender, and motivations for physical exercise).

Secondly, an assumption in recreation ecology is that as visitor use increases and places become crowded, visitors will disperse leading to potentially greater resource changes (Hammitt & Cole, 1998). GPS studies that tracked visitor use indicated that visitor dispersion in response to use level may remain unchanged and conversely in some cases decreasing use levels may result in increased visitor dispersal (D'Antonio & Monz, 2016). Therefore, a better understanding of the relationship between visitor use level and visitor spatial behavior will help managers better predict the potential for resource change under changing use levels.

Another assumption that has been both challenged and supported is that repeat visitors travel differently than other visitors. This was found not to be supported for visitors traveling for recreation throughout a marine park, in northwestern Australia. In the study, visitors were intercepted and asked to identify beach access points, their length of stay, and the location of their furthest traveled site from a place of accommodation for recreation purposes. Visitor responses were mapped and analyzed. The study found no significant differences between first time and repeat visitors on distances traveled by foot from beach access locations to shore recreation sites. However, when vehicles were used as mode of travel from a place of accommodation to beach access locations differences were observed between them. Also, first time visitors who stay for 1–3 days were reported to travel further (Smallwood, Beckley, & Moore, 2012). Also, the Beeco and Hallo's (2014) paper previously cited found that self-reported knowledge of the destination resulted in greater use distribution across an entire trail system regardless of group type (hikers, runners, mountain bikers, and horseback riders).

Lastly, an approach to the third question (how does time interact with behavior) examines the travel patterns of visitors based on demographic characteristics such as age or group composition. Space has been a popular research focus, however, the temporal attribute has not received as much attention. The space-time budget concept has received the most attention (Fennel, 1996). The concept suggests that the amount of time visitors have allotted to their recreational experience will determine the amount of space they can travel through. Research in PPAs have focused more nominally on time-budgets and more specifically on other time-related variables. Schamel and Job (2017) modeled the walking times of different hiker groups in reaching different zones at Germany's alpine Berchtesgaden National Park (BNP). This study focused more directly on walking speeds by age. The park is geographically divided into two zones: the core zone and the buffer zone. The study matched visitor surveys and GPS-loggers information to identify the travel patterns of different hikers from access areas such as parking areas to the buffer and core zones (i.e. intra-area accessibility). The results suggest that day use groups with children and groups of older visitors may access fewer trails. For example, at an average hiking time of about three hours, visitors aged 60 may need to stay overnight to access the core zone that is further away from parking areas. Therefore, if older visitors do not extend their time-budgets, the buffer zone may experience significant levels of use. The concentration of visitors in this zone may lead to crowding and diminished recreational experiences. Another study (Beeco & Hallo, 2014) found that recreational trail users differed in the time they spent recreating depending upon group type—specifically, horseback riders spent significantly longer at the destination than hikers, runners, and mountain bikers.

Spatial impacts

Understanding the relationship between visitor movements and various impacts offers tremendous potential for managers to efficiently remedy potential problems. Currently, examining the relationship between visitor use with impacts to trails and wildlife have seen the most attention. However, examining economic impacts (mostly from tourists) and social interactions (e.g. crowding and conflict) are currently under explored topics.

One study examined the relationship between amount of use, type of use, and trail conditions by tracking visitor use using GPS (Beeco et al., 2013). A total of 396 trail conditions points were measured on 76-trail segments throughout the trail system. The number of routes that crossed each point (including the user type) were counted. This allowed the researchers to link amount of use, type of use, and trail conditions at 396 points throughout the trail system. While controlling for trail design (e.g. trail slope), results suggest that horseback riders created the most impacts, while mountain bikers, trail runners, and hikers had minimal effects. This finding supported prior findings (Hammitt & Cole, 1998; Pickering, Hill, Newsome, & Leung, 2010), but used a vastly different method. Additionally, this study also identified how spatial-nested data (also called spatial auto-correlation) can bias results, and provides one method for dealing with this type of data.

Coppes and Braunisch (2013) used spatial modeling for research done in the Black Forest of Germany to predict where recreationalists were most likely to travel off trail, and determined what environmental factors were the most likely to trigger this off-trail behavior. The researchers investigated three types of factors influencing off-trail behavior: topography, forest structure, and infrastructure needs (such as signage) across three types of winter recreationists: cross-country skiers, hikers, and snowshoe users. Trail signage was found to be the most influential trigger that led to off-trail behavior. The research revealed that if a summer trail, which was closed for winter, had visibly posted signage, then recreationists were likely to leave the winter trail and follow the closed summer trail. The steepness of the terrain (slope) was the second most influential factor triggering off-trail behavior, and proved to be a deterrent. The researchers used MAXENT software program to model environmental conditions, including trail infrastructure, location, direction, and types of tracks that led off trail for the three types of winter recreationists analyzed in the study. MAXENT enabled the researchers to plot the probability of off-trail behavior as a function of each variable. The models were overlaid with sensitive wildlife areas to determine conflict areas. The primary implication of this research is that it reduces the locations managers need to monitor recreationists from entering sensitive wildlife areas.

GPS tracking was employed by Kidd et al. (2015) to investigate whether educational strategies were effective at compelling hikers to stay on formal trails. Spatial analysis revealed statistically significant differences among educational treatments that encouraged hikers to stay on formal trails. The treatments included the following educational strategies: personal contact educational message, an ecological-based message, and an amenity-based message. Both the ecological-based message and the amenity-based message were posted on signs. Spatial behavior was analyzed in ArcGIS by creating a four meter buffer around each trail. Visitor's tracks that went beyond the four meter buffer were deemed to display off-trail behavior. The distance traveled from formal trails was calculated using Euclidean distance for tracks that displayed off-trail behavior. Euclidean distances were compared for the educational treatments using ANOVA calculations. The researchers determined that trail markings and trail directional signage were persuasive at encouraging hikers to stay on formal trails. The ecological-based message and the amenity-based message were found to be ineffective, and that the trail markings and trail directional signage was adequate. Personal contact was found to be the most effective for resource impact education. The researchers also analyzed a summit area to see if hikers were hiking off trail around the summit area to assess the effectiveness of each educational treatment. The researchers employed the Directional Distribution tool in ArcGIS to calculate the spatial extent of distribution of off-trail behavior for the summit area. This tool determines a distribution center and creates standard deviational ellipses around the distribution center. The researchers chose to employ an ellipse constructed from one standard deviation, which depicted 68% of all off-trail waypoints for the summit area. The researchers constructed an ellipse for each educational treatment and then calculated the total spatial area of each ellipse to enable direct comparison.

GPS technology has also provided increased insights into how wildlife respond to human activity. In order to understand recreational conflict between visitors and wildlife, GPS tracking of visitor use was used at a key marine turtle rookery island in Greece (Katselidis, Schofield, Stamou, Dimopoulos, & Pantis, 2013). Employing GPS, the study recorded turtle nesting locations, locations of all anthropogenic features (e.g.

permanent beach umbrellas), and beach locations that had high visitor use. The overlap in the distribution of nests with the area used by beach visitors was determined by measuring the number of nests located in areas of recorded beach visitor use and then overlaying the GPS data for the two data sets. The study also calculated the probability of nests occurring in designated beach furniture zones (Katselidis et al., 2013).

D'Antonio and Monz (2016) examined the relationship between visitor use levels and spatial behavior at multiple backcountry recreation destinations. This research illuminated two primary conclusions: (1) instead of visitors dispersing more as visitor use levels increase, dispersion was more likely when low use periods were prominent; and (2) visitor use levels may be a less important influence of ecological change than visitor behavior (as mentioned previously in this article). The researchers employed infrared trail counters and GPS data loggers. The infrared trail counters determined visitor use levels. The waypoints produced by the GPS data loggers were analyzed for dispersion. The GPS waypoints were grouped into high use and low use as determined by the infrared trail counters. The GPS waypoints were then used to calculate a median center. The median center was used to produce a standard deviational ellipse around each median center that was fit to one standard deviation. The standard deviational ellipses were compared for the two groupings of use level across multiple backcountry destinations. The researchers also calculated average Euclidean distance from the median center for the two use level groupings (high use and low use levels) at each backcountry site analyzed. These averages were compared using two-sample t tests. The average Euclidean distances were then standardized for comparison across sites.

Wolf, Brown, and Wohlfart (2017) used both PPGIS and GPS methods in a study to identify visitor conflict potential between different trail users, with a specific focus on mountain bikers and horse riders. The PPGIS data mapped concurrent trail usage intensity (validated by GPS data) to predict potential conflict locations over a large study area to identity trails of greatest concern. The responses to survey questions that accompanied spatial mapping revealed that the trail conflict was somewhat asymmetrical, with horse riders expressing more conflict than mountain bikers. The conflict was based on differences in visitor behavior characteristics such as intensity of activity styles and personal attachment to specific trails. The largest number of intra-activity conflicts (i.e. conflict within the same trail user group) was also mapped along high-usage horse and mountain bike trails. The results indicated that intra-activity conflicts were localized and many high-usage trails were not identified for conflict. Thus, high trail usage was not necessarily a good predictor of intra-activity trail conflict given the infrequent and localized nature of the conflict. The authors noted that PPGIS methods functions as a diagnostic to identify trail segments that would benefit from more site-specific investigation and management.

Tracking visitors in PPAs has also been extended to hunting. Hunting in public lands or private leased forestland remains a popular recreational activity in the US (Mingie, Poudyal, Bowker, Mengak & Siry, 2017). It is necessary to provide spatial data on the behavior of hunters and their impact on the hunted population (Brøseth & Pedersen, 2000). Understanding how hunters behave while hunting and their spatial distribution across different habitats may aid PPA managers to more efficiently achieve management objectives. For example, Gross, Cohen, Prebyl, and Chamberlain (2015), tracked the movements of wild turkey hunters at Tunica Hills Wildlife Management Area in Louisiana, and found that hunting locations were centered near access points such as roads and parking lots. The study also estimated that 75% of hunting activity occurred on less than 10% of the study area. Therefore, spatial-temporal data can be used by PPA managers to make decisions about creating hunter access and opportunities while attempting to maintain high-quality hunting experiences (Gross et al., 2015). Likewise, managers may be able to identify habitats where wildlife species are at greater risk and adjust their management accordingly (Stedman et al., 2004). GPS tracking also provides opportunities to measure hunter behavior in public lands that have different management restrictions. For example, hunter movement in public areas managed with lottery hunting as opposed to areas with open-access hunting.

The spatial movement of wildlife has been tracked to compare the relative effect of different recreational activities. Marchand et al. (2014) contrasted the behavioral metrics of the Mediterranean mouflon in three contiguous areas in southern France that had varying levels of hunting and hiking pressures. Specifically, the researchers tracked movement sinuosity, habitat use, and activity pattern of 66 collared mouflon between 2003 and 2012. Study findings showed that mouflon that were less disturbed did not display any direct or indirect response to the presence of hikers. Contrastingly, hunting was highly disruptive. There were immediate responses in terms of less sinuous movements and decreased daytime activities, and a delayed compensatory response in terms of increased movement sinuosity, use of foraging areas, and activity level during nighttime. The effects of hunting were extended to animals living in the wildlife reserve, where no hunting occurred. Animals displayed modified daily activity budget during hunting period, though less pronounced than in the hunted areas. The study suggests that non-lethal forms of recreation may have less impact on wildlife. Further, during breeding periods and in adverse climatic seasons, recreational activities in protected areas should be restricted to reduce ecological impacts.

Spatial segmentation

Spatial segmentation is the partitioning of a formerly homogenous region into two or more sub-regions. This is a common management practice in PPA where management may have many different zones for managing visitor use. Additionally, recreation specific activities are often zoned to prevent recreational conflict by only allowing certain users to access certain areas.

Visitors' movement patterns may be used to define ecological and recreation zones. Miller, Vaske, Squires, Olson, and Roberts (2017) used GPS to track motorized and non-motorized use to demonstrate the complexity of recreation zoning and conflict in the Vail Pass Winter Recreation Area in Colorado. GPS data collected in the study identified areas of mixed non-motorized and motorized use. The study concluded that there was higher interpersonal conflict among respondents who traveled in areas of mixed-use, compared with those traveling outside mixed-use areas. Therefore, PPA managers may use spatiotemporal visitor flow information to develop indicators and thresholds for recreation conflict based on historical use patterns for the area, topographic features, and access routes for different visitor groups (Miller et al., 2017).

To reduce socio-ecological impacts, backcountry management plans often encourage the dispersal of visitors. However, by tracking backcountry recreationists in Denali, Stamberger, van Riper, Keller, Brownlee, and Rose (2018) suggest that visitors tend to be clustered and highly concentrated along the park road. Land cover analysis indicated that only a few (18%) of overnight backpackers camped on durable surfaces. Also, despite Denali's Backcountry Management Plan prohibiting campsites within the viewshed of the park road, a large proportion of campsites were visible. Therefore, to preserve the wilderness experience, managers at Denali may use the study findings to prioritize actions such as developing backcountry education programs to minimize socio-ecological impacts.

Recreation Suitability Mapping (RSM) is a GIS approach that seeks to inform visitor use or recreation zoning regimes. RSM often couples terrain conditions with social data, which determines the areas most suitable for specific recreational activities, and the relationships that exist between terrain attributes and social preferences (Kliskey, 2000). RSM methods quantify areas of recreational worth through weighting social preferences for terrain conditions, and coupling those weightings with measurements of physical conditions for the area that is being studied (Kliskey, 2000). Using RSM, it is possible to couple social data with such terrain features as percent of tree cover, or miles of single-track trail, which can then be coupled with social preferences determined through questionnaires that quantify the relationships between social preferences and terrain conditions, and to produce maps of these relationships (Beeco et al., 2014). For example, a hiker might prefer an area that has vistas, proximity to water, trails that are steep, and proximity to known wildlife habitats. The degree that these physical conditions exist is measured in the field and then coupled with the social preference weightings resulting in quantified relationships between social preferences and terrain conditions. Ultimately, RSM techniques can be used to map areas of recreation value in accordance to visitors' preferences. The implications of RSM help managers to zone PPAs, assess the suitability of an area for specific activities, and to understand the relationships between resource conditions and experiential outcomes (Aklıbaşında & Bulut, 2014; Beeco et al., 2013). Additionally, using RSM techniques, researchers can map place-experience interactions for multiple user groups. Each user group can be mapped as a layer, and then researchers can combine all the layers together to determine where there are overlapping attributes (Goodchild, Anselin, Appelbaum, & Harthorn, 2000).

Beeco et al. (2014) integrated GPS visitor tracking and RSM. The researchers mapped visitor use preferences to determine recreational suitability models for competing recreational groups (hikers, trail runners, mountain bikers, and horseback riders). The researchers produced suitability maps of the North Forest of the Clemson Experimental Forest in South Carolina. The maps displayed which areas of the forest were most suitable for recreational groups. The suitability zones were constructed through quantifying suitability values for each recreational group. Examples of the variables used to calculate the suitability values were questionnaire preference ratings of trail slope, proximity to water, length of trail, land cover type, trail width, trail surface, and condition of trail.

RSM has been employed to map experiential elements along the northern Appalachian Trail for long-distance hikers (Peterson, Brownlee, & Marion, 2018). The relationships between trail-tread conditions and specific experiential elements of long-distance hiking were weighted and quantified from questionnaire data. These data were combined with the extent that trail-tread conditions were present along five-kilometer sections of the northern Appalachian Trail. The researchers produced maps of where specific experiences were likely to occur along the northern Appalachian Trail. This was the first time that RSM had been applied to a restricted recreational corridor, and was efficient in comparing experiential elements of various trail sections along the Appalachian Trail, and quantifying the relationships between trail-tread conditions and experiential elements of long-distance hikers of the Appalachian Trail. The pinnacle management implication of this technique is that it provides managers with data to manage for trail sustainability and a quality hiking experience. Additionally, this research can be used in the future as a method to design sustainable trail networks that produce intentional experiential outcomes, such as level of challenge.

At a PPA-wide scale, PPGIS methods can be used to determine whether spatial segmentation occurs among different PPA visitor groups. For example, Muñoz, Hausner, Brown, Runge, and Fauchald (in press) found that local, domestic, and international visitors to Jotunheimen National Park and Utladalen Protected Landscape in Norway spatially self-segregate to some degree with local users emphasizing harvesting and cultural identity park uses compared to tourists. These results can help inform strategies to avoid visitor conflict or reduce overuse through spatial zoning or information and marketing aimed at the different visitor groups. The authors suggested that given the spatial self-segregation results, increased tourism in PPAs may be possible without degrading the values and experiences desired by local users.

Conclusions

This state of knowledge review discussed many articles which all contributed to the advancement of knowledge of understanding visitors' spatial behavior. Some research illuminated specific findings, while other research revealed effective techniques and broad outcomes. The geographic scope of the research often determines the applicability of the findings. Participatory mapping methods are typically used for macro-level PPA management applications such as infrastructure planning and zoning while visitor data logging are typically used for more localized visitor management applications such as modifying visitor behavior in specific areas of the PPA. One of the largest advancements over the past five years has been the incorporation of multiple methods in single studies. Generally, these types of studies used some form of tracking in combination with another method. Moreover, some studies employed GPS technology to validate research findings of previous studies that did not utilize GPS technology or to validate other methods such as PPGIS or VGI. It is important for research of visitors' spatial behavior to combine multiple approaches to gain a robustness of insight. Mapping visitor travel patterns is not sufficient without context as it does not provide comprehensive information to managers. Researchers need to combine several types of analyses to develop thorough knowledge of visitors' spatial behavior. Data from

GPS data loggers supply enough data to map visitor travel patterns, conduct time allocation analysis, conduct sequence analysis, conduct speed analysis, and conduct density analyses at various temporal scale (such as hourly point density analysis). Additionally, this information is useful for managers to assess crowding, the impact intensity of visitors, and creation of use-zones. Furthermore, the potential of more methods is high as more innovative research questions are generated, and as techniques are combined in which social data are also utilized.

Another general finding is that spatial research with respect to visitor use management is being conducted world-wide. While most studies were conducted in the United States and Australia, studies have been conducted Asia and Europe as well. Despite the steady growth in nature-based tourism in developing economies such as countries in Africa and South America, there is little evidence of spatial research for visitor use management purposes (Shoval & Ahas, 2016). Spatial research in protected areas in this part of the world has been limited to wildlife monitoring (e.g. Abrahms et al., 2016; O'Connor, Butt, & Foufopoulos, 2016). Therefore, recreation managers may largely be unaware of where visitors go, how much time they spend, what activities they undertake, and the how they interact with resources. To better manage visitor experiences, recreation managers need to track visitors' movements.

Understanding human behavior, values, and management

There are many site-specific conditions and characteristics that influence visitors' spatial behavior. Coupling any spatial method with social data is a necessity towards understanding visitors' spatial behavior when visiting a PPA. Questionnaire data provide a contextual tool for determining the 'why' behind spatial behavior, such as group type, motivations, and familiarity with the site.

Specific findings about human spatial behavior in PPAs have seen rapid development. Many of these findings depend on a single study and warrant more research, while some other findings have coalesced through multiple studies. Below is a list of findings that have been derived from studies cited above:

- The connectivity of a trail network influences visitors' off trail behavior
- Trails should lead to attractions, such as scenic vistas, to reduce off trail behavior
- Educational approaches to influencing visitors' spatial behavior have a range of effectiveness
- Visitor dispersion is likely influenced by the concentration of visitor use and may have an inverse relationship
- Visitor's familiarity with a site influences travel patterns—visiting different locations and having higher distribution across an area
- Grouping by non-spatial typologies may not predict spatial behavior
- Activity type influences visitor spatial behavior
- Visitor characteristics, such as motivations or abilities, can influence visitor spatial behavior
- Visitor use levels may be a weaker predictor of ecological change compared to visitor behavior

- Visitor spatial/temporal segmentation continues to be an appropriate management technique to reduce conflict

Integration with other resource issues

As mentioned in Beeco and Brown (2013), space is an excellent platform for integrating different aspects of natural resource management. One example of this was the study related to turtle nesting, where researchers overlapped the distribution of nests with visitor use areas to better protect turtle nesting. However, the studies identified here generally revealed a lack of combining spatially related social science data with other natural resources issues.

One area ripe for development in this application is soundscapes in natural areas. A reported increase in visitation densities at many US parks (National Park Service, 2016) and discussions on managing visitor experiences (Kim & Shelby, 2011) has led to calls to manage the noise generated by visitors. Mennitt and Fristup (2016), constructed a regression model that predicted sound levels across the continental United States, based upon both natural (e.g. land cover type) and non-natural (e.g. roads) considerations. This model also used an algorithm for removing anthropogenic contributions of noise so that estimated natural conditions could be compared to existing conditions. This model was developed by researchers in and partners of the Natural Sounds and Night Skies Division of the US National Park Service to assist in park planning efforts. Further, standardized modeling tools such as Aviation Environmental Design Tool (2017) and Federal Highway Traffic Noise Model (Menge, Rossano, Anderson, & Bajdek, 1998) used by the US Department of Transportation have regularly been used to model the noise from overflights and road traffic, many times at National Park Service units. Both of these models produce spatial or temporal-spatial models of noise, which can be used to inform visitor use planning or determine if management actions (such as public shuttles) are having the desired benefits in noise reduction for visitors. While these models are now beginning to be used to inform visitor use management, the visitor, space, and noise line of research is only just beginning. One of the reasons for this delay is likely the level of expertise and software to run these models.

Gaps and future directions of research

This review illustrates that the theme of understanding visitors' spatial behavior still has growth to make. As technology continues to develop, easier field methods, and more intuitive computer programs will make this toolset available and efficient for more researchers, even if they are not trained to use GIS. This means that spatiotemporal models of visitors' travel patterns are going to become more exact, more available, and thus more useful for managers to correctly comprehend how visitors are behaving and what is causing those behaviors.

First, there should not be an over reliance on GPS data to track visitors. While GPS data provide a rich data source, researchers should also be looking to camera data, infrared trail counter data, and remote sensing imagery, when GPS may not prove practical. All researchers should be looking towards conducting comprehensive visitor behavior investigations, which will further validate the findings and provide a more accurate description of visitors' spatial behavior for PPA managers. For example, the use of macro-level PPGIS and VGI methods, in combination with tracking data, can illuminate visitor motivations by identifying the specific values and experiences that visitors seek.

Second, most of the tracking studies have heavily relied on the assumption that group behavior is dependent on whomever fills out the questionnaire. Most of these studies used methods to address this assumption, such as asking the person in the group with the 'nearest birthday' to complete the questionnaire. However, it is likely that the group as a whole influence spatial travel patterns, whether that includes resting at a scenic vista while hiking or choices in which attractions to visit. Therefore, future research efforts should seek to determine the effects of group dynamics and decision making on travel behavior.

Third, a better understanding of how time relates to space is needed. Currently, space-time budgets have been the focal point of this research (Beeco & Brown, 2013; Fennel, 1996). In space-time budgets, visitors must make decisions about what to see and where to visit based upon the time they have allotted. While space-time budgets continue to be a line of research in tourism, few studies have applied this concept to PPAs with respect to travel patterns. Further, because this has really been the only approach to understanding time, other approaches may prove fruitful.

Fourth, many of the studies listed above also contributed to theoretical, statistical, or methodological advances. Graph theory, spatial nesting (spatial autocorrelation), and tracking use through cell phones are specific examples of this type of progress. More focus on these contributions is needed. Specifically, the tracking of mobile positioning data enviably leads to a discussion about 'big data'. Future research efforts will likely be addressing how big data can assist visitor use management and understanding visitor travel patterns. This area of research is currently very limited, but has vast opportunities. Application of spatial theory is worthy to form valid scientific hypotheses, yet the employment of spatial theory has been under-stated.

Fifth, there are research dimensions where spatial analysis are still lacking, yet may be truly beneficial. For example, recreational boating (RB) is one of the major water-based activities in the United States. Participation in RB is considered to be substantial, with 36% of US households participating in it annually (National Marine Manufacturers Association [NMMA], 2017). In water-based recreation, such as lakes and rivers, recreational use is extremely contained by the physical presence of water, yet like other recreational activities, high level of participation in RB may lead to undesirable conditions. Overcrowding in public waterways may result in displacement with boaters and other recreationists dispersing to other lakes or locations (Gyllenskog, 1996; Kuentzel & Heberlein, 2003; Robertson & Regula, 1994; Tseng et al., 2009). Recreation managers should therefore strive to understand visitor experiences so as to decide on appropriate management responses like where to establish new boating facilities and crafting policy that minimizes conflict between RB and other waterway users. RB spatial information provides baseline information important for managing public lands and waters. Information such as total distance traveled, furthest distance from shore, vessel speed, and turning angle can be recorded using GPS devices to classify RB typologies. This can help to simulate recreational boats' trajectory in a GIS model for boating traffic analysis (Pelot & Wu, 2007).

Therefore, in closing, spatial research related to visitor use management in PPAs is expanding rapidly and contributing to our knowledge about visitors' spatial behavior. Perhaps, more importantly, we believe that this rapidly developing line of research is only in its infancy because of quickly evolving technology and the continued demonstrated value this line of research is providing.

Disclosure statement

No potential conflict of interest was reported by the authors.

References

Abrahms, B., Jordan, N. R., Golabek, K. A., McNutt, J. W., Wilson, A. M., & Brashares, J. S. (2016). Lessons from integrating behaviour and resource selection: Activity-specific responses of African wild dogs to roads. *Animal Conservation*, *19*, 247–255. doi: 10.1111/acv.12235

Ahas, R., Aasa, A., Mark, Ü., Pae, T., & Kull, A. (2007). Seasonal tourism spaces in Estonia: Case study with mobile positioning data. *Tourism Management*, *28*, 898-910. doi: 10.1016/j.tourman.2006.05.010

Aklıbaşında, M., & Bulut, Y. (2014). Analysis of terrains suitable for tourism and recreation by using geographic information system (GIS). *Environmental Monitoring and Assessment*, *186*, 5711–5719. doi: 10.1007/s10661-014-3814-6

Aviation Environmental Design Tool (AEDT). (2017). *Technical manual version 2d, Report No. DOT-VNTSC-FAA-17-16*. Washington, D.C.: Federal Aviation Administration, September 2017. Retrieved from https://aedt.faa.gov/documents/aedt2d_techmanual.pdf

Balmford, A., Green, J. M., Anderson, M., Beresford, J., Huang, C., Naidoo, R., …, & Manica, A. (2015). Walk on the wild side: Estimating the global magnitude of visits to protected areas. *PLoS Biology*, *13*, e1002074. doi: 10.1371/journal.pbio.1002074

Bauder, M. (2015). Using GPS supported speed analysis to determine spatial visitor behaviour. *International Journal of Tourism Research*, *17*, 337–346. doi: 10.1002/jtr.1991

Beeco, J. A., & Brown, G. (2013). Integrating space, spatial tools, and spatial analysis into the human dimensions of parks and outdoor recreation. *Applied Geography*, *38*, 76–85. doi: 10.1016/j.apgeog.2012.11.013

Beeco, J. A., & Hallo, J. C. (2014). GPS tracking of visitor use: Factors influencing visitor spatial behavior on a complex trail system. *Journal of Park and Recreation Administration, 32*, 43–61. Retrieved from https://js.sagamorepub.com/jpra/article/view/5725

Beeco, J. A., Hallo, J. C., & Brownlee, M. T. (2014). GPS visitor tracking and recreation suitability mapping: Tools for understanding and managing visitor use. *Landscape and Urban Planning, 127*, 136–145. doi: 10.1016/j.landurbplan.2014.04.002

Beeco, J. A., Hallo, J. C., English, W. R., & Giumetti, G. W. (2013). The importance of spatial nested data in understanding the relationship between visitor use and landscape impacts. *Applied Geography, 45*, 147–157. doi: 10.1016/j.apgeog.2013.09.001

Beeco, J. A., Huang, W. J., Hallo, J. C., Norman, W. C., McGehee, N. G., McGee, J., & Goetcheus, C. (2013). GPS tracking of travel routes of wanderers and planners. *Tourism Geographies, 15*, 551–573. doi: 10.1080/14616688.2012.726267

Birenboim, A., Anton-Clavé, S., Russo, A. P., & Shoval, N. (2013). Temporal activity patterns of theme park visitors. *Tourism Geographies, 15*, 601–619. doi: 10.1080/14616688.2012.762540

Brøseth, H., & Pedersen, H. C. (2000). Hunting effort and game vulnerability studies on a small scale: A new technique combining radio-telemetry, GPS and GIS. *Journal of Applied Ecology, 37*, 182–190. doi: 10.1046/j.1365-2664.2000.00477.x

Brown, G. (2013). Relationships between spatial and non-spatial preferences and place-based values in national forests. *Applied Geography, 44*, 1–11. doi: 10.1016/j.apgeog.2013.07.008

Brown, G., & Kyttä, M. (2018). Key issues and priorities in participatory mapping: Toward integration or increased specialization? *Applied Geography, 95*, 1–8. doi: 10.1016/j.apgeog.2018.04.002

Brown, G. G., & Reed, P. (2009). Public participation GIS: A new method for use in national forest planning. *Forest Science, 55*, 166–182. doi: 10.1093/forestscience/55.2.166

Brown, G., & Weber, D. (2013). A place-based approach to conservation management using public participation GIS (PPGIS). *Journal of Environmental Planning and Management, 56*, 455–473. doi: 10.1080/09640568.2012.685628

Campelo, M. B., & Mendes, R. M. N. (2016). Comparing webshare services to assess mountain bike use in protected areas. *Journal of Outdoor Recreation and Tourism, 15*, 82–88. doi: 10.1016/j.jort.2016.08.001

Chua, A., Marcheggiani, E., Servillo, L., & Moere, A. V. (2014). FlowSampler: Visual analysis of urban flows in geolocated social media data. In L. M. Aiello & D. McFarland (Eds.), *International Conference on Social Informatics* (pp. 5–17). Cham: Springer. doi: 10.1007/978-3-319-15168-7_2

Chua, A., Servillo, L., Marcheggiani, E., & Moere, A. V. (2016). Mapping Cilento: Using geotagged social media data to characterize tourist flows in southern Italy. *Tourism Management, 57*, 295–310. doi: 10.1016/j.tourman.2016.06.013

Clement, J. M., & Cheng, A. S. (2011). Using analyses of public value orientations, attitudes and preferences to inform national forest planning in Colorado and Wyoming. *Applied Geography, 31*, 393–400. doi: 10.1016/j.apgeog.2010.10.001

Coppes, J., & Braunisch, V. (2013). Managing visitors in nature areas: Where do they leave the trails? A spatial model. *Wildlife Biology, 19*(1), 1–11. doi: 10.2981/12-054

D'Antonio, A., & Monz, C. (2016). The influence of visitor use levels on visitor spatial behavior in off-trail areas of dispersed recreation use. *Journal of Environmental Management, 170*, 79–87. doi: 10.1016/j.jenvman.2016.01.011

D'Antonio, A., Monz, C., Lawson, S., Newman, P., Pettebone, D., & Courtemanch, A. (2010). GPS-based measurements of backcountry visitors in parks and protected areas: Examples of methods and applications from three case studies. *Journal of Park and Recreation Administration, 28*, 42–60. Retrieved from https://js.sagamorepub.com/jpra/article/view/1373

Engen, S., Runge, C., Brown, G., Fauchald, P., Nilsen, L., & Hausner, V. (2017). Assessing local acceptance of protected area management using public participation GIS (PPGIS). *Journal for Nature Conservation, 43*, 27–34. doi: 10.1016/j.jnc.2017.12.002

Fennel, D. A. (1996). A tourist space-time budget in the Shetland Islands. *Annals of Tourism Research, 23*, 811–829. doi: 10.1016/0160-7383(96)00008-4

Goodchild, M. F., Anselin, L., Appelbaum, R. P., & Harthorn, B. H. (2000). Toward spatially integrated social science. *International Regional Science Review, 23*, 139–159. doi: 10.1177/016001760002300201

Gross, J. T., Cohen, B. S., Prebyl, T. J., & Chamberlain, M. J. (2015). Movements of wild turkey hunters during spring in Louisiana. *Journal of the Southeastern Association of Fish and Wildlife Agencies, 2*, 130. Retrieved from http://www.seafwa.org/

Gross, J. L., & Yellen, J. (2006). *Graph theory and its applications*. Boca Raton, FL: Chapman & Hall/CRC. doi: 10.1201/9781420057140

Gyllenskog, L. (1996). *Utah division of parks and recreation incident/accident report*. Salt Lake City, UT: Utah Parks and Recreation.

Haddad, R., Kelly, T., Leinonen, T., & Saarinen, V. (2014). *Using locational data from mobile phones to enhance the science of delivery*. World Bank report ACS9644, World Bank Group. Retrieved from http://documents.worldbank.org/curated/en/687441468313509206/pdf/ACS96440REVISE0very00final0Digital0.pdf

Hägerstrand, T. (1970). What about people in regional space? *Papers of the Regional Science Association, 24*, 7–21. doi: 10.1007/bf01936872

Hägerstrand, T. (1973). The Domain of Human Geography. In R. J. Chorley (Ed.)., *Directions in Geography* (pp. 67–87). London: Methuen and Co. Ltd. doi: 10.7202/021205ar

Hallo, J. C., Beeco, J. A., Goetcheus, C., McGee, J., McGehee, N. G., & Norman, W. C. (2012). GPS as a method for assessing spatial and temporal use distributions of nature-based tourists. *Journal of Travel Research, 51*, 591–606. doi: 10.1177/0047287511431325

Hammitt, W. E., & Cole, D. N. (1998). *Wildland recreation: Ecology and management* (2nd ed.). New York: Wiley.

Heesch, K. C., & Langdon, M. (2017). The usefulness of GPS bicycle tracking data for evaluating the impact of infrastructure change on cycling behaviour. *Health Promotion Journal of Australia, 27*, 222–229. doi: 10.1071/HE16032

Katselidis, K. A., Schofield, G., Stamou, G., Dimopoulos, P., & Pantis, J. D. (2013). Evidence-based management to regulate the impact of tourism at a key marine turtle rookery on Zakynthos Island, Greece. *Oryx, 47*, 584–594. doi: 10.1017/S0030605312000385

Kidd, A. M., D'Antonio, A., Monz, C., Heaslip, K., Taff, D., & Newman, P. (2018). A GPS-based classification of visitors' vehicular behavior in a protected area setting. *Journal of Park & Recreation Administration, 36*, 69–89. doi: 10.18666/JPRA-2018-V36-I1-8287

Kidd, A. M., Monz, C., D'Antonio, A., Manning, R. E., Reigner, N., Goonan, K. A., & Jacobi, C. (2015). The effect of minimum impact education on visitor spatial behavior in parks and protected areas: An experimental investigation using GPS-based tracking. *Journal of Environmental Management, 162*, 53–62. doi: 10.1016/j.jenvman.2015.07.007

Kim, S. O., & Shelby, B. (2011). Effects of soundscapes on perceived crowding and encounter norms. *Environmental Management, 48*, 89–97. doi: 10.1007/s00267-011-9680-x

Kliskey, A. D. (2000). Recreation terrain suitability mapping: A spatially explicit methodology for determining recreation potential for resource use assessment. *Landscape and Urban Planning, 52*, 33–43. doi: 10.1016/S0169-2046(00)00111-0

Korpilo, S., Virtanen, T., & Lehvävirta, S. (2017). Smartphone GPS tracking—Inexpensive and efficient data collection on recreational movement. *Landscape and Urban Planning, 157*, 608–617. doi: 10.1016/j.landurbplan.2016.08.005

Korpilo, S., Virtanen, T., Saukkonen, T., & Lehvävirta, S. (2018). More than A to B: Understanding and managing visitor spatial behaviour in urban forests using public participation GIS. *Journal of Environmental Management, 207*, 124–133. doi: 10.1016/j.jenvman.2017.11.020

Kuentzel, W. F., & Heberlein, T. A. (2003). More visitors, less crowding: Change and stability of norms over time at the apostle islands. *Journal of Leisure Research, 35*, 349. doi: 10.1080/00222216.2003.11950001

Lawson, S., Hallo, J., & Manning, R. (2008). Measuring, monitoring, and managing visitor use in parks and protected areas using computer-based simulation modeling. In R. Gimblett & H. Skov-Peterson (Eds.), *Monitoring, simulation, and management of visitor landscapes* (pp. 175–188). Tucson, AZ: University of Arizona Press.

Marchand, P., Garel, M., Bourgoin, G., Dubray, D., Maillard, D., & Loison, A. (2014). Impacts of tourism and hunting on a large herbivore's spatio-temporal behavior in and around a French protected area. *Biological Conservation, 177*, 1–11. doi: 10.1016/j.biocon.2014.05.022

McKercher, B., Wong, C., & Lau, G. (2006). How tourist consume a destination. *Journal of Business Research, 59*, 647–652. doi: 10.1016/j.jbusres.2006.01.009

Menge, C. W., Rossano, C. F., Anderson, G. S., and Bajdek, C. J. (1998). *FHWA Traffic Noise Model, Version 1.0. Technical Manual, Report Nos. FHWA-PD-96-010 and DOT-VNTSC-FHWA-98-2*, Cambridge, MA: John A. Volpe National Transportation Systems Center.

Mennitt, D. J., & Fristrup, K. M. (2016). Influence factors and spatiotemporal patterns of environmental sound levels in the contiguous United States. *Noise Control Engineering Journal, 64*, 342–353. doi: 10.3397/1/376384

Miller, A. D., Vaske, J. J., Squires, J. R., Olson, L. E., & Roberts, E. K. (2017). Does zoning winter recreationists reduce recreation conflict? *Environmental Management, 59*, 50–67. doi: 10.1007/s00267-016-0777-0

Mingie, J. C., Poudyal, N. C., Bowker, J. M., Mengak, M. T., & Siry, J. P. (2017). Big game hunter preferences for hunting club attributes: A choice experiment. *Forest Policy and Economics, 78*, 98–106. doi: 10.1016/j.forpol.2017.01.013

Muñoz, L., Hausner, V. H., Brown, G., Runge, C., and Fauchald, P. (In press). Identifying spatial overlap in the values of locals, domestic- and international tourists to protected areas. *Tourism Management*.

National Park Service. (2016). National Park Service visitor use statistics. Retrieved from https://irma.nps.gov/Stats/

National Marine Manufacturers Association [NMMA]. (2017). *2016 Recreational boating participation study [Press release]*. Retrieved from https://www.nmma.org/press/article/21457

National Park Service. (2016). National Park Service visitor use statistics. Retrieved from https://irma.nps.gov/Stats/

Newton, J. N., Newman, P., Taff, B. D., D'Antonio, A., & Monz, C. (2017). Spatial temporal dynamics of vehicle stopping behavior along a rustic park road. *Applied Geography, 88*, 94–103. doi: 10.1016/j.apgeog.2017.08.007

O'Connor, D. A., Butt, B., & Foufopoulos, J. B. (2016). Mapping the ecological footprint of large livestock overlapping with wildlife in Kenyan pastoralist landscapes. *African Journal of Ecology, 54*, 114–117. doi: 10.1111/aje.12241

Oksanen, J., Bergman, C., Sainio, J., & Westerholm, J. (2015). Methods for deriving and calibrating privacy-preserving heat maps from mobile sports tracking application data. *Journal of Transport Geography, 48*, 135–144. doi: 10.1016/j.jtrangeo.2015.09.001

Pelot, R., & Wu, Y. (2007). Classification of recreational boat types based on trajectory patterns. *Pattern Recognition Letters, 28*, 1987–1994. doi: 10.1016/j.patrec.2007.05.014

Peterson, B., Brownlee, M., & Marion, J. (2018). Mapping the relationships between trail conditions and experiential elements of long-distance hiking. *Landscape and Urban Planning, 180*, 60–75. doi: 10.1016/j.landurbplan.2018.06.010

Peterson, B., Brownlee, M., & Sharp, R. (2017). *Understanding visitor use at Cumberland Island National Seashore: GPS visitor tracking. Technical report submitted to the U.S. National Park Service. Fulfillment of Cooperative Agreement No. P16AC00449*.

Pickering, C. M., Hill, W., Newsome, D., & Leung, Y.-F. (2010). Comparing hiking, mountain biking, and horse riding impacts on vegetation and soils in Australia and the United States of America. *Journal of Environmental Management, 91*, 551–562. doi: 10.1016/j.jenvman.2009.09.025

Pietilä, M., & Kangas, K. (2015). Examining the relationship between recreation settings and experiences in Oulanka National Park – A spatial approach. *Journal of Outdoor Recreation and Tourism, 9*, 26–36. doi: 10.1016/j.jort.2015.03.004

Raun, J., Ahas, R., & Tiru, M. (2016). Measuring tourism destinations using mobile tracking data. *Tourism Management, 57*, 202–212. doi: 10.1016/j.tourman.2016.06.006

Robertson, R. A., & Regula, J. A. (1994). Recreational displacement and overall satisfaction: A study of Central Iowa's licensed boaters. *Journal of Leisure Research*, *26*, 174–181. doi: 10.1080/00222216.1994.11969952

Santos, T., Mendes, R. N., & Vasco, A. (2016). Recreational activities in urban parks: Spatial interactions among users. *Journal of Outdoor Recreation and Tourism*, *15*, 1–9. doi: 10.1016/j.jort.2016.06.001

Schamel, J., & Job, H. (2017). National Parks and demographic change – Modelling the effects of ageing hikers on mountain landscape intra-area accessibility. *Landscape and Urban Planning*, *163*, 32–43. doi: 10.1016/j.landurbplan.2017.03.001

Shoval, N., & Ahas, R. (2016). The use of tracking technologies in tourism research: The first decade. *Tourism Geographies*, *18*, 587–606. doi: 10.1080/14616688.2016.1214977

Smallwood, C. B., Beckley, L. E., & Moore, S. A. (2012). An analysis of visitor movement patterns using travel networks in a large marine park, north-western Australia. *Tourism Management*, *33*, 517–528. doi: 10.1016/j.tourman.2011.06.001

Stamberger, L., van Riper, C. J., Keller, R., Brownlee, M., & Rose, J. (2018). A GPS tracking study of recreationists in an Alaskan protected area. *Applied Geography*, *93*, 92–102. doi: 10.1016/j.apgeog.2018.02.011

Stedman, R., Diefenbach, D. R., Swope, C. B., Finley, J. C., Luloff, A. E., Zinn, H. C., San Julian, G.J., & Wang, G. A. (2004). Integrating wildlife and human-dimensions research methods to study hunters. *Journal of Wildlife Management*, *68*, 762–773. doi: 10.2193/0022-541x(2004)068[0762:iwahrm]2.0.co;2

Taczanowska, K., González, L. M., Garcia-Massó, X., Muhar, A., Brandenburg, C., & Toca-Herrera, J. L. (2014). Evaluating the structure and use of hiking trails in recreational areas using a mixed GPS tracking and graph theory approach. *Applied Geography*, *55*, 184–192. doi: 10.1016/j.apgeog.2014.09.011

Tseng, Y., Kyle, G. T., Shafer, C. S., Graefe, A. R., Bradle, T. A., & Schuett, M. A. (2009). Exploring the crowding – satisfaction relationship in recreational boating. *Environmental Management*, *43*, 496–507. doi: 10.1007/s00267-008-9249-5

van Riper, C. J., Kyle, G. T., Sutton, S. G., Barnes, M., & Sherrouse, B. C. (2012). Mapping outdoor recreationists' perceived social values for ecosystem services at Hinchinbrook Island National Park, Australia. *Applied Geography*, *35*, 164–173. doi: 10.1016/j.apgeog.2012.06.008

Wolf, I. D., Brown, G., & Wohlfart, T. (2017). Applying public participation GIS (PPGIS) to inform and manage visitor conflict along multi-use trails. *Journal of Sustainable Tourism*, *26*, 470–495. doi: 10.1080/09669582.2017.13...15

Wolf, I. D., Wohlfart, T., Brown, G., & Lasa, A. B. (2015). The use of public participation GIS (PPGIS) for park visitor management: A case study of mountain biking. *Tourism Management*, *51*, 112–130. doi: 10.1016/j.tourman.2015.05.003

Zheng, W., Huang, X., & Li, Y. (2017). Understanding the tourist mobility using GPS: Where is the next place? *Tourism Management*, *59*, 267–280. doi: 10.1016/j.tourman.2016.08.009

Leveraging physical and digital liminoidal spaces: the case of the #EATCambridge festival

Michael Duignan, Sally Everett, Lewis Walsh and Nicola Cade

ABSTRACT
This paper conceptualises the way physical and digital spaces associated with festivals are being harnessed to create new spaces of consumption. It focuses on the ways local food businesses leverage opportunities in the tourist-historic city of Cambridge. Data from a survey of 28 food producers (in 2014) followed by 35 in-depth interviews at the EAT Cambridge food festival (in 2015) are used to explain how local producers overcome the challenges of physical peripherality and why they use social media to help support them challenges restrictive political and economic structures. We present a new conceptual framework which suggests the development of place through food festivals in heritage cities can be understood by pulling together the concepts of 'event leveraging', 'liminoid spaces' (physical and digital) and modes of 'creative resistance' which helps the survival of small producers against inner city gentrification and economically enforced peripherality.

摘要
本文总结了利用节日的实体空间和数字空间创造新消费空间的方法。它关注当地美食企业利用剑桥旅游历史城市机遇的方法。本文数据的获取是：2014 年对 28 个美食生产者进行了调查，随后2015年在"吃在剑桥"美食节上进行了35次深度访谈。本文利用这些数据揭示了当地生产商如何克服实体空间偏远的挑战，以及当地生产商如何利用社交媒体的支持帮助他们克服政治与经济体制的制约。我们提出了一个新的概念框架，这个概念框架通过把"事件利用"、"跨实体与数字的中介空间"和"创意性抵抗"这些概念组合在一起可以理解遗产城市通过美食节促进地方的发展， 这种通过美食节促进地方发展的过程有助于理解小生产商在内城绅士化和经济边缘性背景下的生存。

Introduction

Typified as one of Northern Europe's most popular touristic-historic cities, Cambridge has approximately 123,900 permanent residents (ONS, 2011), and attracts approximately four million visitors per year (Tourism South East, 2010) making it the ninth most popular UK city for international tourism (Visit Britain, 2016). Given its size, Cambridge punches above its weight with a visitor to resident ratio of 32:1 and an annual rate of growth of 2.9% gross value added according to the Centre for Economics and Business Research (cited in *The Telegraph*, 2016) and is the sixth fastest growing city in the UK by population (Centre for Cities, 2016). As of 2015, tourism and the wider visitor economy contribute £19,600m (domestic), and £22,072m (overseas) (Tourism South East, 2016) to the south-east region, bolstered by world-leading industries from technology, science, education, right through to retail and having close geographical proximity to London. It is, however, important to note that such growth does not always benefit all stakeholders. The city's central commercial zones have been subject to intense corporate creep since the start of the twenty-first century. Gentrification effects, aided by year or year growth, have served to corporatise central spaces predominantly focused on both retail and hospitality high street offer. According to the latest figures, house prices in Cambridge are rising rapidly, with the Centre for Cities (2016, p. 52) stating that 'nine out of 62 cities were less affordable than the British average, with Oxford, London and Cambridge being the least affordable cities'. With respect to commercial lettings, the National Audit Office (2017) identifies the Cambridgeshire region as having some of the highest business rate growth in the UK with between 4.6% and 9.6%+ increases. Explored and evidenced throughout the paper, we illustrate the challenges this poses for local, smaller stakeholders, namely the 'pricing out' of smaller traders and producers, forcing independent food and drink businesses to occupy peripherally located premises.

Through a study of the EAT Cambridge food and drink festival (#EAT) which started in 2013, this paper explores the role of social media, connected across the life of festivals in providing platforms that bridge the spatial and economic conflict between 'core' versus 'periphery'. We argue that festivals provide a powerful collaborative vehicle for small producers, where one all-encompassing social media identity is built around a physical event ensures alternative food producers are stronger than if they use social media marketing separately and independently. Building on the premise that physical and digital networks help grow and solidify existing networks across an 'in-between' space between core and periphery, we examine this relationship in the context of this tourist-historic city (Ashworth & Tunbridge, 2000). Given that social media and the Internet are relatively inexpensive compared with other advertising media (Standing & Vasudavan, 2000), we explore the #EAT brand to ascertain whether it offers a fairer playing field for smaller producers and companies, thus addressing any deficit that individuals may have in terms of their own 'digital capital'. Consequently, we explore how such media is being utilised to disrupt traditional approaches to place promotion (Kaplan & Haenlein, 2010), and establishing a series a tactical and longer term strategic leverageable event-induced and event-related opportunities (e.g. Chalip, 2004).

The research questions (RQ) for this study were as follows:

RQ1: In what ways do food and drink festivals provide leveragable benefits for participating local and small businesses?
RQ2: How do food and drink festivals act as a vehicle of promotion and enhance marketing communications efforts between producers and consumers - physically and digitally?
RQ3: Why are food and drink festivals and their associated social media activities an important medium for showcasing the 'local' offer?
RQ4: Using EAT Cambridge as a case study, how do food and drink festivals act as key drivers that contribute toward place development?

Literature review

Event leverage: festivals as leverageable opportunities

Events and festivals provide leverageable opportunities for a range of stakeholders and differing levels of urban geographies (Chalip & Leyns, 2002). These include the village, town, city, region, nation as a wider macro-construct, right through to the individuals and small producers within and across targeted localities for which such economic intervention takes place. The act of cultivating and maximising such opportunity is referred to as 'event leveraging' (see Chalip, 2004; Weed, 2008). Events have the potential to provide local business with economic benefits borne by the event visitor economy if the festival and participating traders appropriately leverage them (e.g. Misener, Taks, Chalip, & Green, 2015). Smaller, grassroots festivals are particularly ripe for leverage as they occur annually and are usually bottom-up and locally focused (e.g. Taks, Green, Chalip, Kesenne, & Martyn, 2013). Event managers seek to promote such leverageable opportunities as they can enhance tangible and intangible socio-economic benefits for participants, local host, and regional communities, and promote a strong economic and sustainable tourism outcome (e.g. Schulenkorf & Schlenker, 2017). It has been argued that smaller, locally focused events can be better leveraged to achieve such sustainable outcomes (Ziakas & Boukas, 2016), particularly as such interventions encourage and retain greater expenditure inside the destination and avoids external and economic leakage.

To conceptualise the dynamics of leveraging, Chalip (2004) developed the 'Event Leverage Model' (ELM) (sometimes referred to as the 'Economic Leverage Model' e.g. Weed, 2008). As illustrated by Figure 1, the model is split into four columns to be read from left to right (i.e. Leverageable resource → Means). ELM illustrates how such interventions encompass a range of immediate-term and longer term opportunities and outcomes that characterise and constitute the 'event'. For example, in the context of the Olympics, Duignan (2017) and Pappalepore and Duignan (2016) note these range from the Cultural Olympiad four years prior, Opening and Closing Ceremonies, right through to the longer term cultural projects and events hosted in the preceding years. To extend the application of this model, this paper will outline how a food festival can foster a range immediate-term and longer term opportunities (leverageable resources) – that require targeted strategies and tactics to realise positive tourism and economic developmental benefits (e.g. Chalip & Leyns, 2002). The food and drink industry is a pertinent sector to analyse as such commodities are an essential element of human survival, but in turn, a competitive industry that provides visitors with the freedom to choose what and how they consume (e.g. Taks et al., 2013).

Solberg and Preuss (2007, p. 214) claim the 'pre-event' phase tends to be 'overlooked in discussions of long-term impacts because the focus is on legacy of an event, which by definition occurs post-event period'. Analysis of leverage within smaller scale events is underexplored, specifically the 'immediate' tactics within ELM that have been a neglected focus of this particular. To access 'immediate' bounties borne by the event visitor economy, specifically to 'optimise total trade and revenue', hosts must (1) 'entice visitor spend', (2) 'lengthen visitors' stays', (3) 'retain event expenditures and (4) enhance business relationships' (Chalip, 2004). Chalip notes the festival must seek to avoid 'economic leakage' of event expenditure, which can in turn secure local benefits by retaining spend and sourcing products (and even labour) – locally. The ability for the event to enhance 'business relationships' forms the final vital component of achieving 'immediate' leverage providing access to local and visiting business people (physically and digitally) for those 'associated with event participation, or whose business provide supplies or services to the event' (Chalip, 2004, p. 237). Throughout the application of ELM we argue in the context of Cambridge and #EAT, the pertinent issue is 'why' small traders chose to engage in event leveraging.

Festival tourism: liminal and liminoid spaces and places

Place-specific festivals are said to support and leverage a community's sense of place (Cresswell, 2014), transform spaces and identities, and offer opportunities for tourism revenue generation (Getz, 2005). However, despite the growing body of event literature (Getz & Page, 2016), the call to embrace different dimensions of events tourism remain (Kim, Boo, & Kim, 2013). As the literature has evolved, increasing emphasis has been placed on the complexities and motivations behind what has been simply defined as 'themed, public celebrations' (Getz, 2007, p. 1). One dimension is the adoption of the concept of liminality to describe how festivals might be considered a form of 'social limbo' (Turner, Harris, & Park, 1983). It is perhaps unsurprising that liminality has become a popular concept in tourism literature, given its transformative effects for (re)structuring power and spatial dimensions (Thomassen, 2016).

Picard and Robinson (2006) argue festivals are liminal zones in that the transformation of social space gives way to non-traditional behaviours. The idea of festivals championing subversion and the triumph of non-dominant values in less rigid, prescriptive spaces is certainly well established (Caudwell & Rinehart, 2014). Consequently, liminality in an event context is used to describe a temporary setting which encourages individuals to experience freedom from the mundane existence of everyday life (Shields, 1990), offering transitional dwelling spaces (Shortt, 2015). Festivals sit outside of the everyday structures of life and in turn are useful lenses to view and explore how liminality often refers to the subversion of hierarchy. Where 'festival spaces are arguably locations for both the liminal and the carnivalesque' (Pielichaty, 2015, p. 236) must be examined within a matrix comprising local identity, uniqueness, authenticity and liminality (Ma & Lew, 2012).

However, Pielichaty (2015) argues that liminality is traditionally associated with sacred in-between spaces and the transitional, so suggests the concept of 'liminoidal' may provide a better lens for critical exploration of the transformation of everyday as it is less ritualistic. This builds on Turner (1992, p. 57) who suggests that liminoid phenomena often lie outside the central economic and political processes as they are 'plural, fragmentary and experimental' and 'often subversive, representing radical critiques of the central structures and proposing utopian models'. Although studies have suggested festivals are complex spaces where structures are blurred (Weichselbaumer, 2012), they are perhaps not the temporary release from normative structures traditionally presented. Rather than presenting festivals as inversions of the everyday, the more economic and political urgencies of sustainability, politics and impact have become important, with more social control than might be imagined (Pielichaty, 2015). If this apparent politicisation of the festival space is to be fully explored, we need to move beyond research which prioritises the attendees and event goers, and also examine how local businesses are using such liminoidal opportunities. Perhaps rather than focus on the resistance and social protest undertaken by event goers so often described (Aching, 2010), we need to explore how local people and businesses are using them as platforms for social and economic change, challenge and leverage, both from a physical perspective but also increasingly demonstrating awareness of emergent digital 'liminoid' festival spaces.

Social media in tourism: from the 'what' and 'how', to the 'why'

Social media is said to offer platforms for 'resistance' and 'e-democracy' (Peters, Chen, Kaplan, Ognibeni, & Pauwels, 2013), redefining how businesses communicate across their channels of distribution and with their customers (Rapp, Skinner Beitelspacher, Grewal, & Hughes, 2013). It is what Pechrová, Lohr, and Havlíček (2015) regard as a form of communication which enables niche markets to be served, and to emerge. Given the growth of Internet users (e.g. *The Economist* (2016) states 91.6% of the UK population regularly using the Internet) and the rapid growth of social media adopters, it is little surprise the tourism literature seems to be struggling to keep pace with what it is providing and offering in terms of holistic consumer value and alternative spaces of tourism consumption (Leung, Law, Van Hoof, & Buhalis, 2013).

It is notable that Zeng and Gerritsen (2014) found studies of social media use in tourism were in their infancy, and argued for more studies on community engagement, marketing strategies and differentiated destination management. It is increasingly apparent that the available literature on social media and tourism remains overly developmental and just moving from the 'what' question to the 'how' question' (Minazzi, 2015). It is only recently that the academic community has begun to theorise its role in challenging traditional knowledge and approaches to tourism marketing and consumer engagement (Hudson & Thal, 2013). Tourism studies have to date fallen short on exploring 'how', and for the most part ignored the 'why' and questioned the reasons behind its use and adoption. Social media disrupts the rules of communication with customers, tending to highlight that brands need to be active on social media, but not explaining why (Leung et al., 2013), and what this means for wider urban development and community sustainability of these particular stakeholders.

Tourism literature on social media has tended to be somewhat fragmented and focused on isolated issues rather exploring its holistic impact and value (Felix, Rauschnabel, & Hinsch, 2016). One broader issue which needs attention is how social media fosters links and traceability, shortening the distance between the destination and users, thereby strengthening user involvement and engagement in the innovation process. Undoubtedly, social media has a role in transforming tourism and wider business practices by changing its boundaries and knowledge distances (Afuah & Tucci, 2012; Bogers, Afuah, & Bastian, 2010), but research has been limited on how this effort can bring economic sustainability by challenging the need for physical space, and in turn occupy spaces that were once the domain of those with large marketing budgets.

The concept of social media as creating new spaces of consumption requires further exploration, and indeed is yet to be explored in terms of positive transformation of place. Literature exploring the ways different marketing media open up opportunities for smaller food producers remains in its infancy (Holt, Rumble, Telg, & Lamm, 2015). One idea put forward by Anderson (2007) is the 'long tail' theory which seeks to explain the shift away from a small number of mainstream producers and products towards a huge number of niches 'in the tail', but producer activity is yet to maximise the new market environment afforded by new media. Pechrová et al.'s (2015) study of farmers illustrates this well as they discovered many owners/managers were either unaware of social media tools or lacked the competency to effectively use them. The wider concern that smaller producers may lack the strategic, marketing, and operational skills, capabilities, capital, resources and mindset to access entrepreneurial opportunity is noted by Chalip and Leyns (2002) and Pappalepore and Duignan (2016), in the context of cultural and sporting events. Sturiale and Scuderi (2013) also demonstrate that communication between producer (farmer) and customer is not always being advanced on the three key levels of connection, conversation and construction (co-production). Umbrella (food) organisations and associations, like that of EAT Cambridge, may well offer this competency and opportunity.

Food festivals and the development of new networks and spaces

In exploring the food movement in West Cork in Ireland, Broadway (2017) re-emphasises how important a positive food image is in the selection of a destination by visitors, yet it is clear that local food offerings have taken time to feature at the centre of destination product offerings and marketing campaigns (Tikkanen, 2007). Although the body of work on food-motivated travel has been expanding quickly (Everett, 2016; Getz, Robinson, Andersson, & Vujicic, 2014), much remains unknown about how tourists engage with alternative food providers and local festivals outside of the physical event, i.e. through pre- and post-event online marketing. Online promotion of food and related events remain patchy and overly simplistic (Kim, Yuan, Goh, & Antun, 2009). It is, however, clear from studies of food marketing that marketers and institutions no longer have ultimate control over the image of their destination or product (see Tresidder & Hirst, 2012). Rather, the power of user-generated content through websites is using the Internet to (re)claim market territory from those with generous marketing budgets (Schegg & Fux, 2010).

Although most destination marketing materials now reference some form of culinary offer (Everett, 2016), there is limited literature on the relationship between the adoption of social media marketing communications for food tourism events and their role in supporting local producers and future activities. Few studies have explored how social media linked to food and drink festivals have inspired the growth of food movements, and explored whether food tourism spaces and associated consumer leverage opportunities have become political (Starr, 2010). As food movements grow, Watts, Ilbery, and Maye (2005) has argued that the nature of the alternative(s) is often unclear, fragmented and poorly communicated. Qazi and Selfa (2005, p. 45) further queried whether small producers could effectively initiate alternative reconnections with consumers if they pursued more resistant approaches. Through better online marketing and communication, alternative production and products with an environmental consciousness may be better integrated with each other to create new places. Cultivating aspects of networking, synergies between the local event and business relationship opportunities have been noted as playing a part in long-term economic success of businesses and locations (O'Brien, 2006).

Methodology

An inductive, exploratory and mixed-method approach was employed over two years to explore experiences of traders participating in the annual EAT Cambridge Food and Drink Festival (www.eat-cambridge.co.uk). Primary data generation was undertaken in 2014 with a questionnaire-based survey (28 respondents), followed by 35 in-depth interviews in 2015. The emailed survey asked 15 questions with a mix of open (qualitative) and closed (quantitative) questions covering their customer base, how they build business to business relationships; how they market their business; new marketing techniques and innovation. The 2015 interviews used emergent themes from the previous survey to frame open questions to generate qualitative data on motivation, benefits of the festival, future growth, innovation, social media and marketing, challenges to their business and Cambridge's food culture. Qualitative data generation is sensitive to the social context of the research was employed to unearth more meaningful elements in a multi-layered context (Mason, 2002) which made it a more appropriate approach in the discussion of such subjective topics. To minimise inconsistency, a pre-designed interview open question format was used in every interview. Excel and qualitative data analysis software (NVivo) were used to code data and identify emergent themes, with all four authors independently identifying emergent themes (researcher triangulation), before combining ideas through several data analysis meetings

The sample was purposive, incorporating the perspectives of the local producers involved. The survey used the festival's producers database, and the 2015 interviews were conducted at the event (some participants were the same, others were new and coded appropriately). The festival Director and Chief Executive of the Regional Destination Management Organisation were also interviewed. It was felt these two methods would provide a satisfactory level of 'data saturation' for the four research questions (Morse, 2000). Table 1 summarises the phases of data generation.

Table 1. Summary of methods of data generation.

Method and timing	Process	Sample
Phase 1: Survey (May–August 2014)	Emailed questionnaire to all local producers registered for EAT Cambridge 2014.	28
Phase 2: Interviews (May 2015)	Face-to-face interviews by four authors at EAT Cambridge festival 2015 (33 traders plus Director and Chief Executive)	35

Table 2. Summary of survey respondents (2014).

Survey respondents (2014)	Code used for data analysis and presentation
Artisan 1	AFD1
Artisan 2	AFD2
Bakery 1	B1
Bakery 2	B2
Bakery 3	B3
Bakery 4	B4
Bar/Restaurant 1	BROL1
Bar/Restaurant 2	BROL2
Chilli/Chutney 1	CC1
Chilli/Chutney 2	CC2
Chilli/Chutney 3	CC3
Chocolatier 1	C1
Coffee/Tea 1	CT1
Coffee/Tea 2	CT2
Deli 1	D1
Deli 2	D2
Deli 3	D3
Deli 4	D4
Distillery/Brewery 1	DB1
Distillery/Brewery 2	DB2
Accommodation 1	EA1
Accommodation 2	EA2
Accommodation 3	EA3
Accommodation 4	EA4
Accommodation 5	EA5
Accommodation 6	EA6
Ice cream	IC
Drinks 1	NAD1

Our sample represents 41% for 2014, and 59% for 2015 of the overall population of small traders and local producers who took part, which subsequently helped to enhance the internal, and construct validity of the research. Table 2 summarises details of the 2014 survey respondents, and Table 3 summarises the 2015 interview respondents. All were coded to ensure anonymity and to aid data analysis.

Findings and discussion

The literature review encouraged us to ask not only the 'what?', but more importantly, the 'how' and the 'why' behind the relationship between social media and food festivals. In the context of digital and physical place development, we address these questions and illustrate how festivals manifest, not just as a single socio-economic intervention, but as a series of leveragable resources that serve to foster 'immediate' opportunities for participating producers and provide longer term legacies for place development. In explaining and conceptualising the 'why', a simple framework of relationships between the digital

Table 3. Summary of interviewees (2015).

2015 interview	Code used for data analysis and presentation
Artisan 1	AFD1
Artisan 2	AFD2
Artisan 3	AFD3
Artisan 4	AFD4
Artisan 5	AFD5
Artisan 6	AFD6
Bakery 1	B1
Bakery 2	B2
Bakery 3	B3
Bar/Restaurant 1	BROL1
Bar/Restaurant 2	BROL2
Bar/Restaurant 3	BROL3
Bar/Restaurant 4	BROL4
Chilli/Chutney 1	CC1
Chilli/Chutney 2	CC2
Chilli/Chutney 3	CC3
Chilli/Chutney 4	CC4
Chilli/Chutney 5	CC5
Chocolatier 1	C1
Chocolatier 2	C2
Coffee/Tea 1	CT1
Coffee/Tea 2	CT2
Deli 1	D1
Deli 2	D2
Distillery/Brewery 1	DB1
Distillery/Brewery 2	DB2
Distillery/Brewery 3	DB3
Distillery/Brewery 4	DB4
Accommodation 1	EA1
Accommodation 4	EA4
Accommodation 6	EA6
Ice Cream 2	IC 2
Drinks 1	NAD1
Heidi White (Festival Director, EAT Cambridge)	Heidi
Emma Thornton (CEO, Visit Cambridge and Beyond)	Emma

and physical connected by the concept of 'creative resistance' is proposed and presented just before the conclusion. We start by outlining the Cambridge context before outlining what EAT Cambridge has to offer by presenting the festival as a series of 'leveragable resources'.

What? The Cambridge context and leveraging EAT Cambridge

Local producers have, and continue to face systematic economic challenges associated with the gentrification of core city areas. Cambridge's economic and commercial growth over the past decade serves to explain why urban space emerges valorised. Both residential house prices and business rates continue to increase year on year and are set to rise again in-line with recent government policy to raise business rates by as much as 77% in 2017/18 (National Audit Office, 2017). Within densely occupied, centralised urban topologies like Cambridge, such effects have, and continue to, squeeze and 'price out' smaller, independent traders and producers. Spaces previously accessible are now largely inaccessible. Vulnerable producers of local artefacts operating within low-profit margins are unable to respond to the changing economic conditions. Several respondents alluded to their frustration at the corporatisation of Cambridge's high street, central spaces increasingly being dominated by 'cheap and easy fast-food chains' (AFD1), and 'chain stores that dominate the high street' (AFD4).

> Find me a space! I'll open a deli! Find me a space that doesn't cost three thousand pounds [a month]…we could never afford somewhere in Cambridge city centre. (IC2)

Responses to questions about location suggests producers turn to the cheaper, less trodden path of peripheral and marginal urban districts – out of the way of lucrative centralities. Most respondents claimed they could not operate in the city so were being pushed out away from touristic central zones and associated benefits of its visitor economy. Central areas are largely dominated by corporate high street chains (Independent, 2010). Corporations are physically replacing independents – characteristic of neo-liberal urban conditions and a mindset favouring global forms of cultural production (e.g. food, drink, and retail) over 'locally rooted' culture (e.g. García, 2004). Cambridge is visibly illustrative of such corporatisation effects generally, given it is dubbed the UK's Number 1 'Clone Town' (New Economics Foundation, 2010). Interestingly, the idea of Cambridge as a 'Clone Town' typified views from respondents, claiming '[the] clone town is what Cambridge has become famous for' (BROL2). Conditions described across Cambridge illustrate the varying degrees of conflict between global and local demands whether from a cultural, economic, and physical–spatial perspective between, or as argued in this paper – the 'core' and the 'periphery'.

Evidence reveals that those businesses occupying a permanent central locality reflected a more positive, or at least ambivalent, attitude to the high city centre rents, indicating those businesses who 'have broken down barriers and made it into the centre' (Heidi). Tourism South East (2010) claims over 82% of tourists only visit Cambridge for 3–9 hours, described by one respondent as the '8-hour tourist' (BROL 3) that typically stick to established central zones across the city centre. So, if located peripherally, it would be logical to assume small traders receive less, and limited opportunities to access tourism flows, presenting reasoning to why positive sentiments typify responses from centrally located respondents.

Findings support Chalip's (2004) model which suggested leveragable opportunities are realised through events. The festival has become a spatially dispersed series of 'leverageable resources' focused around 'discovering your local pantry' (Eat Cambridge, 2017). Interviewees were keen to point out it provides an opportunity to engage with central, peripheral, local, regional and national independent traders. As a consequence of its success, other similar cultural initiatives that have sprouted across the region (e.g. FoodPark, Night Markets (www.FoodPark.com) all under the banner of EAT Cambridge) and serve as a critical way to develop new spaces of consumption by connecting the visitor economy with more local, authentic cultural offerings, and attractions which support small traders. The next, arguably more pertinent question is 'how' this is happening.

How? Creating and maintaining digital and physical liminoid spaces

EAT Cambridge provides a strategic array of physical events and reconfigured digital spaces, providing 'immediate opportunities' to secure leverageable benefits. With respect to the 'physical', these include festival event weekends in Cambridge, pop-ups (supper clubs, street food and night markets) and 'fringe events' across surrounding villages. These examples illustrate the wider, physicality of the festival across central and peripheral spaces, highlighting the festival's capacity to divert consumption beyond the core, whilst still drawing producers and consumers together centrally in the middle of the city to develop immediate leveragable short-term and longer term opportunities (e.g. relationship development). These are both important components to what Chalip (2004) refers to as 'effective leverage'.

Physical, face-to-face interaction provided a significant opportunity to enhance brand awareness to directly engage with consumers. Traders were keen to stress that food festivals are 'just awareness, brand awareness. It is much cheaper, and to some extent more effective, to advertise by talking to customers at a stall in a festival than typical advertising [radio, TV]' (AFD1). Such 'conversational' approaches to 1–1 communication was referred to as 'in-person marketing' (AFD1); several respondents made it clear that this was the main reason why the alternative food businesses participate in food festivals. Traders remarked '…you actually get to speak to people, for food and drink, people need to actually see it and they need to try it' (C2) and 'it [EAT food festival] enables us to engage with exactly the right sort of people as well, who we want to talk to, people who are interested in our products' (DB3).

> It's nice having the one-to-one customer interaction, that's definitely what we aim to get from road shows [food festivals], it definitely helps. (AFD1)

These findings partly address the concern expressed by Kim, Kim, Ruetzler, and Taylor (2010), who claimed that little research has been done to examine the relationships between perceived value and intention to revisit, and advocated analysis of small food festivals to properly explain visitors' behaviour and producer engagement. Across the two years of data generation, participants described the engagement they had with consumers at food festivals as an opportunity to 'educate consumers' (DB2), but the momentum had to be retained after the event in order to inspire forms of 'critical consumption' (e.g. Sassatelli & Davolio, 2010) between consumers and producers, and shift consumption preferences to focus on more locally orientate cultural offer.

> … our aim at the events we attended was to educate the public about our business and products, which in turn we hope will broaden our customer base, which should help grow and sustain our long term revenue and future. (D2)

The festival provided a physical place and 'in-person' catalyst to generate more sustainable relationships that were supported and nurtured by social media engagement. Physical components were complemented by a digital spaces created by online social mediums that facilitate customer–producer, customer–festival and producer–festival interactions. These include (i) official #EATCambridge Twitter hashtag, (ii) Facebook, (iii) Instagram, (iv) website and (v) Director's (Heidi) blog: the 'MovingFoodie'. Digital platforms seem to form a major way of fostering and enhancing a festival–producer–consumer tripartite model of interactions. In 2014, 93.1% of survey respondents agreed that the festival 'provided a platform to market their business' (27/29). 86% either agreed (44.8%) or strongly agreed (41.3%) that #EAT provided a much needed collaborative marketing opportunity, echoed by 25 respondents who agreed that social media 'provided an opportunity to expand their customer base' without physical presence in the 'core'. Additionally, it was clear that the festival played a fundamental role as the personal 'check in' to humanise the Twitter messages. This dual marketing strategy of physical presence followed by virtual communication as opposed to a one-off event where messages are lost was welcomed by businesses.

Many felt their social media messages are often received but with little impact, content or reassurance unless they are tied to a more 'central' event. Repeatedly, it was found that the omnipresent physical and digital platforms of #EAT served to champion the 'local' – in terms of producers, products and cultural diversities on offer across Cambridge's region. As suggested later, a greater focus on slower forms of touristic experience, and the overarching critical contribution of EAT Cambridge and wider initiatives play in fostering a 'foodie movement' and resistance against aforementioned economic pressures and spatial disparities serves to underpin 'why' such interventions are important in characteristically neo-liberal contexts like Cambridge city centre.

Many respondents saw the festival and the director (Heidi) as a gatekeeper – a major force in nurturing social networks which foster leveraging opportunities between producers and consumers. This emerged in light of the risks that gentrification can fragment qualitative and quantitative socio-economic dependencies communities rely on (e.g. Raco & Tunney, 2010), thus reducing their competitiveness. Respondents explained how the festival (literally and metaphorically) seems to bridge a spatial geographical–economic divide that physically and subjectively exists – exemplified across the local narratives underpinning these findings. This argument ripples throughout the empirical evidence of this paper, epitomised by a trader who claimed EAT Cambridge participation is all about…

> … gaining exposure to the Cambridge foodie crowd- breaking into a new cross section of local people that we haven't come into contact with much before' (…) '[the festival was a] great opportunity to get ourselves seen by a wide Cambridge (foodie) audience. (AFD 8)

Opportunities now became open, whereas without the festival, they would be closed or at best, more difficult to access. Producers regarded the festival as a promotional catalyst and opportunity to momentarily occupy the 'core', and then follow up with effective digital engagement. This tactical 'oscillation' between temporary physical leverage, and strategic leveraging and development of B2B and B2C relationships via digital platforms typified trader responses.

Twitter (and Facebook) emerged as playing a key role in local promotional strategies, with many relying on '@EatCambridge' official Twitter account as a major conduit between the festival–producers–consumers tripartite relationship. Given their wide networks and 7538 follows (as of 2 May 2017), the impact of the festival team retweeting local traders tweets greatly extended local trader networks. Twitter was the most prominent with respondents who noted it 'helped me gain more respondents to my email marketing' (B2) and 'overall it is very beneficial in promoting our business, increasing awareness of our brand' (AFD6). #EATCambridge was regarded as a vehicle which helped communicate messages they could not themselves, offering amplification, visibility and access to core markets. One trader remarked 'twitter is our main tool, "When @Eat mentioned us or replied etc. we saw an increase in followers" interaction etc…' (BROL4). Most agreed that festivals helped shift consumer focus onto them, and not only provided an alternative, but helped them conduct business in a different way. For example, 50% of the 2014 respondents agreed it 'encouraged them to think about new marketing techniques', further reporting they were considering a deeper involvement with the festival by utilising fringe events linked with the festival. Sixty-two per cent of respondents felt that the festival 'made them think about the possibility of using fringe events in the future to attract custom in the longer-term'. In light of the social media opportunities, evidence indicated traders making a gradual migration towards integrating social media within marketing and communications strategies. Furthermore, some respondents claimed participation in events was driven by their need for interesting content on their Twitter feeds, Facebook posts and Instagram uploads. On the other hand, many were using the events they attended and put on as 'content' (BROL3) for their tweets, posts and uploads.

> I think you really need to understand why people are using it [social media] (…) it [content on Twitter] has to be interesting content and have people that want to read it and be engaged by it… We want to do more events so that we have content [for social media] to talk about. (BROL3)

The 2014 survey found digital networks from the festival helped local producers develop their digital capital and open up new Twitter accounts. These were far more active by 2015, with interviewees suggesting, 'we use Twitter, Instagram and Facebook and the success rate is that Twitter is more successful than Facebook and then Instagram is more of a visual showcase' (BROL 3), and 'so obviously I'm on twitter, so that's been very good' (B3). Almost every respondent stated that they were 'active on Twitter' (B3). Some have thousands of followers illustrating how 'we use Twitter a lot, the general [company] feed has over 2000 followers and our MD [Managing Director] has a 1000 so yeah it is a broad coverage there' (BROL 1). The harmonious balance between the physical and digital interactions between producers–consumers–festival was reiterated repeatedly by traders: 'meeting people at EAT was a really effective way to help us build social media followers and for us get connected with Cambridge foodies' (EA6). In light of this, it is of no surprise to find respondents claimed Twitter handle @EATCambridge and #EATCambridge hashtag emerged vital to 'talk to people' (DB2). And that the 'Twittersphere' landscape was helping to build up 'brand recognition' (DB6). Furthermore, Twitter was seen as an efficient way to communicate to large, and wide pool of potential consumers as 'actively talking face-to-face [to customers] takes up quite a lot of time' (DB2). It was clear that digital engagement offered an opportunity to go beyond the local, region into the global spectrum of potential consumers who may decide to visit Cambridge as a visitor destination for its food and drink tourism scene.

> … everyday people pick up their phones and go on Twitter and Facebook, Instagram, so for people to see our product/brand on there [social media] is going to really get people to recognise it. (AFD1)

The 'follow the food' concept developed by Cook and Harrison (2007) is now an almost literal process via social mediums, like Twitter. Traders would use Twitter to showcase to their network of potential consumers a 'physical' trace indicating when they would pop up at other physical locations. In turn, potential consumers and their 'social networks' become co-producers of knowledge – sharing the geo-locations of the traders, thus using a form of online 'liminoid' space to provide digital clues to the physical locations of producers. Furthermore, the #EATCambridge hashtag provides a suitable platform for valuable content generation to stimulate these conversations. What this may mean, is that following the trader within core spaces, and beyond into the periphery, continues to exemplify leveragable opportunities and helps marginalised producers 'transcend' the core in order to redistribute event related benefits (Ziakas, 2014). What we can see is that 'following' and 'tracing' supply chain components and physicality of trader presence may not just drive consumer value by giving immediate and ongoing reassurance to those visitors wanting to buy locally produced goods, but also provides traders with a virtual alternative to having a fixed trading space. Fixed, permanent, central spaces have, by and large, become inaccessible for the average producer.

> ... the general public started to recognise the brand when they are out and about. And recognise that the brand is local (DB2) (...) and 'the major benefit of the EAT was the coverage really, particularly the all-round coverage on Twitter. Every event has brochures and flyers so you can see what's going on. But Eat Cambridge on Twitter was incredibly good! I was always re-twitting, yeah! (BROL 1)

The paper now shifts its attention to understanding 'why' festivals promote and produce such digital and physical space, and the wider, more conceptual reasons for their existence.

Why? Creative resistance, foodie movement and recapturing space

We have outlined the contextual challenges facing small producers and traders, and the idea that festivals provide a series of leverageable resources provide opportunities for the emergence of physical and digital liminoid spaces. Here we suggest festivals can manifest as a 'critical movement' and be conceptualised as forms of 'resistance'. EAT Cambridge can be seen as creating both physical and digital spaces, across a series of temporal phases, opening up 'lines of flight' for small traders to resist economic pressures and the tension between occupying 'core' versus 'peripheral' commercial and geographical localities. We argue that this can be seen as both a logical outcome of such intervention, and one that emerges dominant in the empirical findings and small business narratives of this paper. Empirically driven, the data presented illustrates the power of festivals to disrupt traditional consumption practices and resist the spectre of the Clone Town effect. Social media, specifically, providing the platforms affording unique opportunities to prolong 'event leverage' – before, during and after the physical aspects of the festival has disappeared and morphed into one of the many other food and drink fringe initiatives.

EAT Cambridge fosters what Deleuze and Guattari (1987) may theorise as modes of 'creative resistance'. Creative, locally rooted cultural products illustrate the plethora of leverageable resources available to resist, and in fact strengthen the emergence of an inclusive, alternative food movement. Direct, in-person contact at physical events provides a powerful catalyst and foundation, for which social media can take over to provide a long-term relationship builder. Evidence here illustrates the pertinence of oscillating between both physical and digital platforms and spaces across varying temporal frames. It has been argued that people and social media can never be detached from each other (Zhuo, Wellman, & Yu, 2015), with Lim (2012, p. 242) suggesting that 'social media may be viewed both as technology and space for expanding and sustaining the networks upon which social movements depend'. What became increasingly apparent was producers saw the adoption of social media as a way they could resist the centre, and challenge the dominant spatial orthodoxies in Cambridge. Social media offers a useful mechanism to transcend from the periphery to the 'core' as it provides a bridge – or – perhaps a 'third space'. Social media overcomes an in/out dualism, creating a space for transgressive discourse and self-affirmative resistance (Soja, 1996). The festival brand seems to have a role in the intersecting geometries of power, identity and meaning associated with the notion of liminality.

Respondents felt the festival was important in establishing an 'in-person' marketing approach, then social media built these relationships beyond the limited timeline of the physical festival. The festival's social media arm of #EATCambridge was regarded by many respondents as a crucial education vehicle and a facilitator of what we could conceptualise as 'liminoid positionality', with a key role to play in the campaign to encourage consumers to buy from alternative food producers – engaging in modes of 'critical consumption'. Through building links across both core and peripheral locations with consumers, other businesses and festival gatekeepers, Twitter and Facebook were helping to traverse liminoidal spaces of the city, and simultaneously reduce the dependency on occupying core touristic urban centres. Festivals could, therefore, be seen as a way of 'democratising' non-traditional opportunities within challenging business environments, with both physical and digital liminoid spaces practically affording plurality of voice in an urban setting dominated by the narratives of corporate enterprise and global expressions of food and drink culture. As a result, festivals have the potential to support the wider redistribution of visitor economy benefits and improve the economic sustainability of peripherally located, and arguably more vulnerable smaller traders and producers (e.g. Ziakas, 2014), through stimulating greater small business positive, planned, unplanned, short-term and longer term event 'legacies' (e.g. Pappalepore & Duignan, 2016; Preuss, 2015).

The festival serves as a major role in stimulating food and drink tourism to the city and developing new sense of place. This was reflected on by several responded illustrating 'we [Cambridge] are becoming more of a foodie destination. People are more and more interested in food, and good quality food as well. There are more and more events, which prove that' (AFD1). It was remarked that the emerging 'foodie movement', could be moving beyond satisfying the demands of the local, regional Cambridgeshire population who have a somewhat protectionist attitude towards 'wanting to support their local traders' (CC2) – towards encouraging wider, national, European and international audiences. Evidence suggests this has, and continues to come to fruition, with the rise of new food and drink initiatives (FoodPark, Night Markets, themed nights and transformation of urban spaces to host ad-hoc and summer long festivals such as the Thirsty River Biergarten):

> We're getting people who are choosing to come to Cambridge and they're doing their foodie research and go, 'Right! I want to eat in these establishments. They're cherry-picking us, and that's exciting! (BROL3)

Almost all respondents interviewed suggested Cambridge's food and drink scene had 'grown dramatically in the last 18 months' (IC2) characterised by the emergence of many new specialist food outlets and new event platforms. Many felt that they were part of a 'new movement', described as a 'revolution' (BROL 3). Director of EAT Cambridge felt that the 'foodie' movement is being driven by 'explosion in food blogging, cookbooks, food and drink on social media by people who treat food and drink experiences as a hobby and a topic to share' (Heidi). As identified earlier, although frustrated with the corporatisation of Cambridge's inner city, seen as a barrier to some, others were more positive and actually claimed that such challenging conditions had in fact promoted a form of local 'revolution':

> I think it has [Cambridge foodie reputation] grown because there's been a frustration at this kind of clone town. Generally that frustration has led to a sort of revolution. I think it's been born out of independents wanting to act like we make a difference in our town. (BROL3)

Arguments presented so far illustrate that the 'new foodie movement' was seen as being financed by the relative economic prosperity of Cambridge's citizens, something that the responding businesses were acutely aware of stating that 'I think the opportunity that Cambridge has is that it has a lot of relatively wealthy people to take advantage of' (B3). Consumers' high level of disposable income was said to be reflected in their 'willingness to be 'experimental' (B1), giving niche food producers, whose offering is premium products that are not found in high street chains – a market to sell. Intimations here illustrate the rather paradoxical nature of urban food movements as being inherently 'middle-class' as indicated previously by Sassatelli and Davoli (2010) and discussed more recently by Duignan and Wilbert (2017) in the context of Cambridge; an interesting qualifier with respect to the study's limited generalisability to different socio-economic contexts:

> Small vendors have recognised there is a financial confidence in Cambridge, therefore, the type of sort of foodie products that they want to sell - there is a market there for it and it is a constant market.(BROL3)

Alongside the growing festival scene, parallel emergence of more street traders and urban food trucks are seizing festival opportunities. What we found was a nascent, but strident resistance from businesses who currently occupy central locations within Cambridge to re-purpose, re-brand and even re-name specific urban zones and streets within the city centre itself – unofficially referred to as 'Meat Street' down Cambridge's Bennett Street (official name). Here, observational evidence illustrates an agglomeration of small, independently owned food and drink outlets attempting to resist and repel corporatisation. Interestingly, whilst accepting that higher rents are part of 'doing business', centrally located businesses of whom occupy permanent central trading space, made it very explicit that they were keen to break down barriers and sought to inspire other alternative food providers to rent a shop in the centre. Furthermore, they expressed the will to prove they could compete with the 'chain' businesses, to set an example to the rest of the foodie movement. There was a clear perception that being physically in the core was advantageous:

> … we are in a really good place, rather than let's say being out in the periphery, where it might have taken longer to prove our business and get recognition from customers and alike' (…) and I think for it to really take a foothold, you have to have permanent locations…so we can actually take on the kind of corporate giants that are in the game. (BROL3)

Narratives of enterprising 'in' businesses were akin to that of an organised resistance group fighting back against the 'clone town that Cambridge has become famous for' (BROL3). They were aware of the need to educate consumers to stimulate modes of critical consumption, actively contesting and avoiding consumption within the city's large chain outlets, therefore contributing to an emerging and revised brand 'promoting Cambridge as a foodie destination' (AFD1). Again, the idea of 'creative resistance' here manifested as a hoped-for outcome; whereby alternative food providers promote an alternative (and resistant) artisan identity for the city. BROL1 and BROL3 talked about 'power in numbers' and about creating pockets of similar business that occupy certain areas of the city centre, labelling those zones as 'foodie' business areas.

> I think there's just power in numbers. So, the greater the scene gets, the more people (customers) will use it and rely upon it, and support it. And that will attract more people into either districts, the city centre. (BROL3)

Although optimism radiated out of those occupying a central locality, businesses of whom occupy secondary locations outside official boundaries of the city centre (approximately two miles outer ring) were clearly much more defeatist generally, and specifically with respect to the chances of acquiring city centre trading space. 'Out' businesses talked less about fighting back against the chains and more about 'surviving' (IC2) and 'making a living' (DB2) having been locked out of the main city centre marked and remarked that 'I guess [I could] move out to the suburbs, or kind of the villages surrounding Cambridge, I actually think they're becoming more important' (B3), and 'we can afford in smaller areas, we've looked at like Saffron Walden and St Ives' (IC2). Several 'out' businesses realised the need to innovate and market themselves as a separate and alternative foodie 'destination' (B3) in of themselves. The leveragable value of the festival was raised as a vital part of this transition as it is assumed that 'people [consumers] travel to quality restaurants' (DB2):

> I think it's important, if you're really good and you have a good business and good quality produce, people will come to you and you know - you become a destination. You know, so you know they will come. And I think if you can't afford Cambridge, which most people can't, then it's going somewhere else and being good enough to survive there. (B3)

Social media was perceived as a way to contest, traverse and negotiate 'clone' spaces, allowing alternative producers to gain presence and reputation over their competition. Responses were indicative of what Girouz (2003) might have described as cultural struggles within sites of the everyday, and echoes Deleuze and Guattari (1987, p. 33) who claim resistance is 'rhizomatic multiplicities of interactions, relations and acts of becoming', creating unexpected networks, connections and possibilities, and specifically notions of 'creative resistance'. The ability to achieve new opportunities was now possible through physical and digital linkages between producers–consumers as the festival was regarded as an umbrella brand that bridged respective stakeholder groups together in an intermixed physical and digital landscape.

Below, we present a relational model between concepts and context under investigation. Figure 2 illustrates several key features. The paper argues that festivals manifest as a series of short-term and longer term leveragable resources, producing a plethora of digital and physical marketing and communications opportunities that connect the festival, producers and consumers together. In turn, this can be seen to afford producers to overcome and 'creatively resist' their peripheral locality generated by on-going valorisation of urban space and the Clone Town effects found within Cambridge, with generalisable features across a significant number of UK towns and cities (e.g. NEF, 2010). In turn, whilst the on-going gentrification and pricing out of smaller producers indicate a challenging condition of the corporatised, neoliberal city – it has fuelled and sparked an emergent wider 'foodie

Figure 2. Relationships between key concepts under investigation (developed by authors).

movement' that seeks to redistribute opportunities back to smaller producers who may have found themselves marginalised, and serve to open up and democratise urban space affording a plurality of narratives that disrupt the day-to-day naturalised assumptions associated with capitalistic modes of urban development and neo-liberal doctrine.

Conclusions

This paper has suggested festivals can offer a form of open, fluid and 'democratised urban space' – egalitarian in nature and can be conceived of as 'liminoid spaces' which amplifies the voices and commercial opportunity for those of whom are often perceived as having a lower economic worth and contribution toward the vitality of the neo-liberal–touristic city (Raco & Tunney, 2010). We have argued that the central tourist district in an historic city like Cambridge is not always open to alternative food providers given the high costs of rents and the dominance of space by 'clone' commercial interests and large multi-national food chains. Through a complex blend of physical components and amorphous digital presence across popular social media, there is opportunity for a leveragable marketing and communication vehicle for alternative producers. #EATCambridge acts as a food tourism amplifier, providing a temporary opportunity for alternative providers to occupy the 'core' physical space which is then built on and developed using social media. This paper has put forward the 'what' in terms of event leveraging, the 'how' in terms of the use of social media to develop physical and digital spaces, and the 'why' this is being done in regard to local producers engaging in forms of what we have theorised as 'creative resistance'.

We have suggested that the concept of 'creative resistance' (Deleuze & Guattari, 1987) is useful in illustrating specific physical and digital tactics invoked to overcome peripheral locality and leverage event-induced benefits (building brand, presence, reputation, business/consumer engagement and relationships). Though the concepts of resistance and liminoid spaces, we have found that through co-creation with consumers, producer can resist the centre, create new destinations of their own and challenge the dominant spatial orthodoxies in Cambridge. We find that social media offers a parallel digital and virtual space, providing producers with an opportunity to transcend the 'inbetweenness' of core and the peripheral; acting as a form of marketing bridge from their outside location to the 'core' of the city's economic activity. #EATCambridge is an example of an organisation using social media to disrupt 'core' food and drink offerings in the form of subtle resistance against powerful and economic forces.

It is clear that social media linked to a high-profile festival event offers alternative food providers in heritage cities with a powerful tool to create new spaces of consumption. Respondents felt social media facilitated their engagement in positive acts of resistance and provided consumers with a vehicle of critical consumption which helped them achieve greater local sustainability. Events and festivals provide, in this sense, an illustrative process of the democratisation of urban spaces. Collaborative social media approaches built from a central food event is proving vital for protecting local livelihoods, and the cultural identities that comprise the socio-economics of Cambridge's vibrant and diverse locale and regional food and drink scene places and spaces.

Acknowledgement

The authors thank both Heidi Sladen, Director of EAT Cambridge, and Emma Thornton, Chief Executive at Visit Cambridge and Beyond for their time participating and providing access into key stakeholder networks.

Disclosure statement

No potential conflict of interest was reported by the authors.

References

Aching, G. (2010). Carnival time versus modern social life: A false distinction: Social identities. *Journal for the Study of Race, Nation and Culture, 16*(4), 415–425.

Afuah, A., & Tucci, C. L. (2012). Crowdsourcing as a solution to distant search. *Academy of Management Review, 37*(3), 355–375.
Anderson, C. (2007). *The long tail: How endless choice is creating unlimited demand*. London: Random House.
Ashworth, G. J., & Tunbridge, J. E. (2000). *The Tourist-historic city*. London: Routledge.
Bogers, M., Afuah, A., & Bastian, B. (2010). Users as innovators: A review, critique, and future research directions. *Journal of Management, 36*(4), 857–875.
Broadway, M. J. (2017). 'Putting place on a plate' along the West cork food trail. *Tourism Geographies, 19*(3), 467–482.
Caudwell, J., & Rinehart, R. E. (2014). Liminoidal spaces and the moving body: Emotional turns. *Emotion, Space and Society, 12*(1), 1–3.
Centre for Cities. (2016). *Cities outlook 2016*. Retrieved from http://www.centreforcities.org/wp-content/uploads/2016/01/Cities-Outlook-2016.pdf
Chalip, L. (2004). Beyond impact: A general model for host community event leverage. In B. Ritchie & D. Adair (Eds), *Sport tourism: Interrelationships, impacts and issues*. Clevedon: Channel View.
Chalip, L., & Leyns, A. (2002). Local business leveraging of a sport event: Managing an event for economic benefit. *Journal of Sport Management, 16*(1), 132–158.
Cook, I., & Harrison, M. (2007). Follow the thing "West Indian hot pepper sauce". *Space and Culture, 10*(1), 40–63.
Cresswell, T. (2014). *Place: An introduction*. Oxford: Blackwell.
Deleuze, G., & Guattari, F. (1987). *A thousand plateaus*. Minneapolis: University of Minnesota Press.
Duignan, M.B. (2017). *Olympic territorialisation, shocks and event impacts: Small businesses and London's 'Last Mile' spaces* (Unpublished PhD thesis). Cambridge: Anglia Ruskin University.
Duignan, M. B., & Wilbert, C. (2017). Embedding slow tourism and the 'slow phases' framework: The case of Cambridge, UK. In M. Clancy (Ed.), *Slow tourism, food and cities: Pace and the search for the 'good life'* (pp. 197–213). London: Routledge.
Eat Cambridge. (2017). EATCambridge – About us. Retrieved from http://www.eat-cambridge.co.uk/about/
Everett, S. (2016). *Food and drink tourism: Principles and practices*. London: Sage.
Felix, R., Rauschnabel, P. A., & Hinsch, C. (2016). Elements of strategic social media marketing: A holistic framework. *Journal of Business Research, 70*(1), 118–126.
García, B. (2004). Urban Regeneration, Arts Programming and Major Events: Glasgow 1990, Sydney 2000 and Barcelona 2004. *International Journal of Cultural Policy, 10*(1), 103–118.
Getz, D. (2005). *Event management and event tourism* (2nd ed.). New York, NY: Cognizant.
Getz, D. (2007). *Event studies: Theory, research and policy for planned events*. Oxford: Elsevier.
Getz, D., & Page, S. J. (2016). Progress and prospects for event tourism research. *Tourism Management, 52*, 593–631.
Getz, D., Robinson, R., Andersson, T., & Vujicic, S. (2014). *Foodies and food tourism*. Oxford: Goodfellow Publishers.
Giroux, H. A. (2003). Public pedagogy and the politics of resistance: Notes on a critical theory of educational struggle. *Educational Philosophy and Theory, 35*(1), 5–16.
Holt, J., Rumble, J. N., Telg, R., & Lamm, A. (2015). The message or the channel: An experimental design of consumers' perceptions of a local food message and the media channels used to deliver the information. *Journal of Applied Communications, 99*(4), 6–20. Retrieved from http://go.galegroup.com/ps/i.do?&id=GALE|A440822601&v=2.1&u=anglia_itw&it=r&p=AONE&sw=w&authCount=1
Hudson, S., & Thal, K. (2013). The impact of social media on the consumer decision process: Implications for tourism marketing. *Journal of Travel & Tourism Marketing, 30*(1–2), 156–160.
Independent. (2010). Cambridge beats exeter for title as UK's ultimate clone town. Retrieved from http://www.independent.co.uk/news/uk/this-britain/cambridge-beats-exeter-for-title-as-uks-ultimate-clone-town-2079476.html
Kaplan, A. M., & Haenlein, M. (2010). Users of the world, unite! The challenges and opportunities of social media. *Business Horizons, 53*(1), 59–68.
Kim, J., Boo, S., & Kim, Y. (2013). Patterns and trends in event tourism study topics over 30 years. *International Journal of Event and Festival Management, 4*(1), 66–83.

Kim, Y. H., Kim, M., Ruetzler, T., & Taylor, J. (2010). An examination of festival attendees' behaviour using SEM. *International Journal of Event and Festival Management, 1*(1), 86–95.

Kim, Y. H., Yuan, J., Goh, B. K., & Antun, J. M. (2009). Web marketing in food tourism: A content analysis of web sites in West Texas. *Journal of Culinary Science & Technology, 7*(1), 52–64.

Leung, D., Law, R., Van Hoof, H., & Buhalis, D. (2013). Social media in tourism and hospitality: A literature review. *Journal of Travel & Tourism Marketing, 30*(1), 3–22.

Lim, M. (2012). Clicks, cabs, and coffee houses: Social media and oppositional movements in Egypt, 2004–2011. *Journal of Communication, 62*(2), 231–248.

Ma, L., & Lew, A. A. (2012). Historical and geographical context in festival tourism development. *Journal of Heritage Tourism, 7*(1), 13–31.

Mason, J. (2002). *Qualitative researching* (2nd ed.). London: Sage.

Minazzi, R. (2015). *Social media marketing in tourism and hospitality*. Cam, Switzerland: Springer.

Misener, L., Taks, M., Chalip, L., & Green, B. C. (2015). The elusive 'trickle-down effect' of sport events: Assumptions and missed opportunities. *Managing Sport and Leisure, 20*(1), 135–156.

Morse, J. M. (2000). Determining sample size. *Qualitative Health Research, 10*(1), 3–5.

National Audit Office. (2017). *Planning for 100% local retention of business rates*. Retrieved from https://www.nao.org.uk/wp-content/uploads/2017/03/Planning-for-100-local-retention-of-local-business-rates.pdf

New Economics Foundation. (2010). *Re-imagining the high street: Escape from Clone Town Britain*. Retrieved from http://neweconomics.org/2010/09/reimagining-high-street.

O'Brien, D. (2006). Event Business Leveraging: The Sydney 2000 Olympic Games. *Annals of Tourism Research, 33*(1), 240–261.

Office for National Statistics. (2011). *UK 2011 census*. Retrieved from http://www.ons.gov.uk/census/2011census

Pappalepore, I., & Duignan, M. B. (2016). The London 2012 cultural programme: A consideration of olympic impacts and legacies for small creative organisations in East London. *Tourism Management, 54*(1), 344–355.

Pechrová, M., Lohr, V., & Havlíček, Z. (2015). Social media for organic products promotion. *Agris on-line Papers in Economics and Informatics, 7*(1), 41–50.

Peters, K., Chen, Y., Kaplan, A. M., Ognibeni, B., & Pauwels, K. (2013). Social media metrics - a framework and guidelines for managing. *Journal of Interactive Marketing, 27*(4), 281–298.

Picard, D., & Robinson, M. (Eds.). (2006). *Festivals, tourism and social change: Remaking worlds*. Clevedon: Channel View.

Pielichaty, H. (2015). Festival space: Gender, liminality and the carnivalesque. *International Journal of Event and Festival Management, 6*(30), 235–250.

Preuss, H. (2015). A framework for identifying the legacies of a mega sport event. *Leisure Studies, 34*(6), 643–664.

Qazi, J. A., & Selfa, T. L. (2005). The politics of building alternative agro-food networks in the belly of agro-industry. *Food, Culture and Society: An International Journal of Multidisciplinary Research, 8*(1), 45–72.

Raco, M., & Tunney, E. (2010). Visibilities and Invisibilities in urban development: Small business communities and the London Olympics 2012. *Urban Studies, 47*(10), 2069–2091.

Rapp, A., Skinner Beitelspacher, L., Grewal, D., & Hughes, D. E. (2013). Understanding social media effects across seller, retailer, and consumer interactions. *Journal of the Academy of Marketing Science, 41*(5), 547–566.

Sassatelli, R., & Davolio, F. (2010). Consumption, pleasure and politics: Slow food and the politico-aesthetic problematization of food. *Journal of Consumer Culture, 10*(2), 202–232.

Schegg, R., & Fux, M. (2010). A comparative analysis of content in traditional survey versus hotel review websites. *Information and Communication Technologies in Tourism, 2010*, 429–440.

Schulenkorf, N., & Schlenker, K. (2017). Leveraging sport events to maximize community benefits in low-and middle-income countries. *Event Management, 21*(2), 217–231.

Shields, R. (1990). The 'system of pleasure': Liminality and the carnivalesque at Brighton. *Theory, Culture and Society, 7*(1), 39–72.

Shortt, H. (2015). Liminality, space and the importance of 'transitory dwelling places' at work. *Human Relations*, *68*(4), 633–658.

Soja, E. (1996). *Thirdspace: Journeys to Los Angeles and other real-and-imagined places*. Oxford: Blackwell.

Solberg, H. A., & Preuss, H. (2007). Major sport events and long-term tourism impacts. *Journal of Sport Management*, *21*(1), 213–234.

Standing, C., & Vasudavan, T. (2000). The impact of internet on travel industry in Australia. *Tourism Recreation Research*, *25*(3), 45–54.

Starr, A. (2010). Local food: A social movement ? *Cultural Studies? Critical Methodologies*, *10*(6), 479–490. Retrieved from http://journals.sagepub.com/toc/csca/10/6.

Sturiale, L., & Scuderi, A. (2013). Evaluation of social media actions for the agrifood system. *Procedia Technology*, *8*(1), 200–208.

Taks, M., Green, B. C., Chalip, L., Kesenne, S., & Martyn, S. (2013). Visitor composition and event-related spending. *The International Journal of Event and Festival Management*, *7*(2), 132–147.

The Economist. (2016). *Pocket world in figures: 2016*. London: Profile Books.

The Telegraph. (2016). *Cambridge and milton keynes to lead UK growth in 2016*. Retrieved from http://www.telegraph.co.uk/finance/economics/12065319/Cambridge-and-Milton-Keynes-to-lead-UK-growth-in-2016.html

Thomassen, B. (2016). *Liminality and the modern: Living through the in-between*. London: Routledge.

Tikkanen, I. (2007). Maslow's hierarchy and food tourism in Finland: Five cases. *British Food Journal*, *109*(9), 721–734.

Tourism South East. (2010). *Economic impact of tourism: Cambridge. City results 2010*. Eastleigh: TSE Research.

Tourism South East. (2016). Tourism volume and expenditure. Retrieved from http://www.tourismsoutheast.com/services-and-support/research/tourism-volume-and-expenditure.html

Tresidder, R, Hirst, C. (2012). Marketing in food, hospitality, tourism and events: a critical approach. Oxford: Goodfellows Publishers.

Turner, V. (1992). *Blazing the trail: Way marks in the exploration of symbols*. Tucson, AZ: University of Arizona Press.

Turner, V., Harris, J. C., & Park, R. J. (1983). Liminal to liminoid, in play, flow, and ritual: An essay in comparative symbology. In J. C. Harris & R. J. Park (Eds), *Play, games and sports in cultural contexts* (pp. 123–164). Champaign, IL: Human Kinetics Publishers.

VisitBritain. (2016). *Inbound town data*. Retrieved from https://www.visitbritain.org/town-data

Watts, D. C. H., Ilbery, B., & Maye, D. (2005). Making reconnections in agro-food geography: Alternative systems of food provision. *Progress in Human Geography*, *29*(1), 22–40.

Weed, M. (2008). *Olympic tourism*. Oxford: Elsevier.

Weichselbaumer, D. (2012). Sex, romance and the carnivalesque between female tourists and Caribbean men. *Tourism Management*, *33*(5), 1220–1229.

Zeng, B., & Gerritsen, R. (2014). What do we know about social media in tourism? A review. *Tourism Management Perspectives*, *10*(1), 27–36.

Zhuo, X., Wellman, B., & Yu, J. (2015). *Egypt: The first internet revolt? Boletim do tempo presente*. Retrieved from http://www.seer.ufs.br/index.php/tempopresente/article/viewFile/4224/3490.

Ziakas, V. (2014). For the benefit of all? Developing a critical perspective in mega-event leverage. *Leisure Studies*, *34*(1), 689–702.

Ziakas, V., & Boukas, N. (2016). The emergence of 'small-scale' sport events in 'small island' developing states: Towards creating sustainable outcomes for Island communities. *Event Management*, *20*(4), 537–563.

Proximate tourists and major sport events in everyday leisure spaces

Katherine King, Richard Shipway, Insun Sunny Lee and Graham Brown

ABSTRACT
The local and the everyday provide a base resource for an individual to draw upon selectively in the reflexive construction of their leisure lifestyles. Through processes of tourism, however, these everyday spaces can become transformed into tourist products such as through the staging of major sports events. Research often recognises the social impacts sport tourism events can have on host communities yet assume homogeneity across these communities without considering the differentiated leisure lifestyles which characterise them. This paper explores the interplay between the hosting of major sports events and leisure spaces, community and practices of local established sporting communities who are connected to the event through their socio-cultural proximity to the leisure lifestyle and physical proximity to the event setting. The study draws upon qualitative data from interviews with 19 cyclists who live in Adelaide, the host city of the Tour Down Under, an annual professional cycle race and festival. The findings explore the ways in which local cyclists experience the event as proximate tourists drawing upon their knowledge of everyday sporting spaces, local resources and their insider status to inform their identities. The findings examine the ways in which they maintain connections with local places throughout the staging of the event, and highlight some of the tensions this creates in their on-going everyday leisure practices. It argues that organisers of major sports events should utilise the pool of resident participant experts offered through local sports clubs and communities and ensure they benefit from their hosting.

摘要:

地方和日常生活为个人建构休闲方式提供了一种可以选择性利用的基本资源。然而，这些日常空间通过旅游发展（比如举办大型体育赛事）可以转化为旅游产品。已有研究常常认识到体育旅游活动对主办社区的社会影响，却假定这些社区是同质的，没有考虑到他们差异化的休闲生活方式。本文探讨了举办大型体育赛事与当地运动社区的休闲空间、休闲群体与休闲实践之间的相互作用，这些社区由于其社会文化及实质环境赛事场景相近而与赛事联系起来。该研究基于对阿德莱德19名骑行者的访谈获得定性数据。阿德莱德是年度职业自行车赛事的举办城市。该调查探索了当地的骑自行车者作为近距离游客体验这一事件的方式。他们利用对日常运动空间、当地资源和他们内部人的地位来宣告他们的身份。研究结果分析了他们在举办赛事过程中与当地空间保持联系的方式，并强调了在他们日常休闲活动中所产生的一些紧张关系。该研究认为，大型体育赛事的组织者应该利用当地体育俱乐部和社区提供的常驻参与专家，确保他们能从主办城市中受益。

Introduction

Recent debates within tourism geographies have drawn attention towards the relations between the tourism phenomenon and everyday life arguing that in an era of globalised mobility the interplay between these domains is increasingly blurred (Jeuring & Diaz-Soria, 2017). Social and cultural geographers have focused attention on concepts of the exotic and the mundane as tools for understanding the tourism processes which shape understandings of everyday places, identities and culture and sought to rethink these framing dichotomies in favour of a more reflexive approach. Most notably, work on mundane mobilities has examined the regularities of the everyday experience which inform the tourist performance or tourist place (Chen & Chen, 2017; Edensor, 2007; Larsen, 2008; Mikkelsen & Cohen, 2015). A recent issue within tourism geographies (see Jeuring & Diaz-Soria, 2017) introduced the concept of geographical proximity to these debates by focusing attention on the meanings of tourism practices near home (Diaz-Soria, 2017) and the touristic aspects of everyday places and environments (Jeuring & Haartsen, 2016). Physical proximity to settings of everyday practices provides a frame of reference for individuals (Diaz-Soria, 2017). Other works in tourism explore the notion of socio-cultural proximity as 'what people feel and know as part of their personal life worlds, on the one hand, and how they perceive and experience encounters with differences, on the other hand' (Szytniewski, Spierings, & van der Velde, 2017, p. 66). These analyses of proximity highlight the multiplicity of ways in which people make meaning of their environments through tourist experiences and in doing so challenge the conceptual boundaries between the tourist and the local or host community.

Theories on place attachment have been applied to a range of everyday and tourist settings identifying socio-cultural dimensions such as belonging to a group, or collective and physical dimensions such as recreational qualities which act together to facilitate feelings of rootedness and identification with a particular environment (see Lewicka, 2011; Raymond, Brown, & Weber, 2010; Scannell & Gifford, 2010). Of particular interest within this paper are those place bonds which are created through everyday leisure practices and routines.

It is argued that tourism research has prioritised the exotic and exceptional examples of tourism rather than those which are more mundane. A fundamental component of these analyses of proximity to date is premised on the notion of crossing into a tourist space or adopting a tourist identity however geographically or culturally nearby. Less attention has been turned to host communities and the activities, practices and environments which comprise the broad concepts of the mundane, the local or everyday, and their relationships with tourism performances that intersect these. The role of everyday leisure spaces as the context for tourism within tourism geographies are yet to be fully explored.

This paper is concerned with exploring the ways in which local (leisure) communities are connected to tourism processes through both their physical and socio-cultural, or lifestyle proximity to a sport tourism event. Where previous studies have examined the transfer of the life world through the act of tourism this study examines the process by which the space of the life world is transformed through the hosting of a sport tourism event. It contributes to debates on tourism, mobility and the everyday in two ways; First, by exploring the experience of both socio-cultural and physical proximity from the perspective of a host community whereby a space is (temporarily) transformed through tourism rather than an individual or community is temporarily transported (to a tourist place). Second, by providing a more nuanced analysis of socio-cultural and physical proximity which considers the ways in which these interplay in the process of place attachment as part of everyday leisure lifestyle practices and routines.

Leisure, lifestyles and place attachment

The concept of lifestyles captures the 'aesthetic projects' of social actors, organised around habits, rituals, and the consumption of cultural forms, places, styles and practices as part of social identification (Chaney, 1996). In essence, lifestyles are a response to the expanded choice in late modern society and this choice becomes increasingly important in the constitution of self-identity and daily activity (Giddens, 1991). Lifestyles provide a set of props which are embedded within everyday life and the spaces and places we inhabit (Chaney, 1996; Goffman, 1959).

Bennett (2005, p. 64) argues that it is 'through their lifestyles individuals in late modernity exhibit a continued "tiedness" to local spaces in which they live out their everyday lives'. The local provides a base resource for an individual to draw upon selectively in the reflexive construction of their lifestyles. Drawing upon Lefebvre, Gardiner (2000, p. 76) claims that 'it is through our mundane interactions with the material world that both subject and object are fully constituted and humanised'. Leisure in everyday life is one such example which can provide social actors with the raw materials for the formation of meaning, identity and selfhood (Gammon & Elkington, 2015; Henderson & Frelke, 2000). As Crouch and Tomlinson (1994, p. 317) have argued:

> ...the physicality of where leisure happens in late modernity is very real; it contributes to the cultural identity of distinctive leisure practices: people's geographical knowledge is significantly local. The cultural meaning of local places is constituted through everyday leisure practices in a way that resonates with other sources of meaning and identity.

Place attachment refers to the emotional bonds people feel towards a particular place (Lewicka, 2011; Seamon, 2014) and work on place attachment has explored the relationships that sport and leisure participants form with the environments they encounter. Within this literature, attention has been paid to the contribution sport can make to the cultural meaning and representation of places (Bodet & Lacassagne, 2012; Ramshaw & Hinch, 2006; Tonts & Atherley, 2010) and the sense of belonging and connectedness to places of sport that fandom can offer individuals (Bale, 2003; Brown, Smith, & Assaker, 2016; Charleston, 2009; Spracklen, Timmins, & Long, 2010). Yet it is participation in these activities, and the construction of space through the 'doing' of leisure (Crouch, 2000, 2015), in particular that may offer the richest source of analyses. Research has therefore recognised the embodied experience of performing sport and leisure and the lifestyle connections made between participant and place.

In their simplest forms, sport and leisure settings provide the resources necessary to support participation (Hinch & Higham, 2011). Beyond this, significant work demonstrates the interdependencies between participation, space and identity and the intimate connections recreationists can form to those local places which provide the foundations for their leisure lifestyles. Theorists on place attachment have recognised the role of repeated engagement with particular places through everyday activities and routines which take time to develop but result in a feeling of existential insideness (Lewicka, 2011; Seamon, 2014). The lifeworlds of sport and leisure participants facilitate a socio-cultural proximity to local environments such that authenticity can be performed through commitment, local knowledge and experience. (Rickly & Vidon, 2017)

Significant work within lifestyle sports identifies a local scene attached to participants who represent the core of the community and often a coveted sports location. 'Locals' often feel they have more rights to spaces in relation to visiting outsiders who perform the same activity and information about access to these locations can be used as capital by members at the core of sports subcultures to indicate status or insider identity (see Beaumont & Brown, 2016; Edwards & Corte, 2010; Hinch & Higham, 2011; King & Church, 2015; Rickly & Vidon, 2017, for examples). Others observe how the rhythms and rituals performed in everyday sports spaces inform the sense of self (Cherrington, 2014). The work of Bricker and Kerstetter (2000, p. 250) for example, argues that a leisure space which is 'not the focal point of their existence' will limit its integration into the lifestyles of committed recreationists. Therefore for those 'serious' enthusiasts (Stebbins, 2015) in particular, identity politics are played out in the everyday spaces they occupy through their ritualised leisure practices and routines. In these examples, physical and socio-cultural proximity are interdependent in the embodied performance of sporting lifestyles.

Sport events, tourism and host communities

Recent years have seen a renewed interest in urban spaces as settings for global processes of capital accumulation, notably through the emergence of an urban cultural economy. Culture led regeneration policies are commonplace within post-industrial cities, and consequently the hosting of major sports events has emerged as a central strategy for increasing tourism, attracting investors, improving infrastructure and revitalising communities (Gratton & Henry, 2002; Paddison & Miles, 2009). Cities compete in a global marketplace for the hosting of major events as a form of 'urban entrepreneurialism' (Belanger, 2000, p. 380). It is claimed, for example, that sport mega events are part of a 'grobalising vision' for localities which conceive sport as a prominent global platform to instil civic pride, boost tourism and establish their 'global cultural currency' (Sturm, 2014; p. 77) with cities competing to gain a place in the urban status hierarchy of major sport cities (Misener & Mason, 2006; Schimmel, 2006).

The convergence of the global with the local has seen a significant impact on the everyday experience in contemporary society. As local leisure sites become transformed into tourist products through the staging of major sports events, the sense of place felt by residents in these communities is undoubtedly affected (Misener & Mason, 2006). Through the hosting of major sporting events, everyday spaces are branded, commercialised, owned and transformed, largely for the consumption of visiting others. 'In a spectacular society, bombarded by signs and mediatized spaces, tourism is increasingly part of everyday worlds, increasingly saturating the everyday life which it supposedly escapes' (Edensor, 2007, p. 200). Major sports events are the ultimate example of the city as tourist spectacle (Waitt, 2003) as the city becomes an object of and for the consumption of others. Destination marketing and the (re)creation of place identity is also one of the core tenets of the hosting of major events (Getz & Page, 2016). Celebrating the unique cultural qualities of local spaces and selling these to outsiders forms a key component of event delivery and legacy planning (Ramshaw & Hinch, 2006). Sporting events in particular can play an important role in the construction of the place identity of tourist destinations and can enable cities to acquire status and differentiation through hosting them (Mason, Washington, & Buist, 2015; Sturm, 2014). These events can significantly impact the physicality of a city (Miles, 2010).

For local residents whose everyday lives are entwined with these spaces, such spectacular occasions can alter their (mundane) encounters and consequently the place meanings of their local environments. Authors such as Misener and Mason (2006) have therefore argued that in bringing events to cities, the meanings of local spaces are transformed or even replaced with newly constructed meanings linked to transitory and commercial tourism strategies focused on the 'visitor class'. As a result, locals may therefore struggle to assert identity or connectedness to their own neighbourhood spaces.

There is an extensive and growing literature on the purposes and social impacts of sports events for local host communities which, while short lived as experiences, are often embedded within longer term strategies to improve city neighbourhoods and communities (see Chien, Ritchie, Shipway, & Henderson, 2012; Shipway & Fyall, 2012). Socio-cultural impacts can be defined as' the impacts of an event on the day-to-day life of people associated directly or indirectly with that event, and on the values, attitudes, beliefs and traditions that determine or guide that day-to-day life' (Sharpley & Stone, 2012, p. 349). As well as yielding significant economic benefits for the host destination, the social value of sport for enhancing communities is one of the central tenets of the hosting of sport events. It is claimed that sport events can reduce social isolation within communities and increase civic engagement (Jarvie, 2013). For example, Waitt (2003) argues that international sporting events can act to generate patriotism and a sense of community. The success of a region in terms of sport performance can also provide a commonplace identity for local residents (Hinch & Higham, 2011). For local sport and leisure communities, however, it is claimed that processes of globalisation and commercialisation surrounding large scale sports events can see grassroots participants increasingly divorced from the benefits of these occasions (Jarvie, 2013). Despite an established literature on socio-cultural impacts of sport tourism events on host communities, this research assumes homogeneity across these communities without considering the differentiated leisure lifestyles which characterise them, and consequently their experiences of hosting sport tourism events.

Graburn's (2001) theory of secular ritual positions tourism experiences as rooted in the home life of tourists but metaphorically sacred because of the temporality of the connection and their difference from the ordinary routine. Tourists pursue renewed versions of their same selves through a ritual reversal of some aspects of their everyday lives. Experiences of bonding with other participants as part of this liminal state provides a levelling of statuses or communitas. Following Graburn's (2001) work, sports tourist experiences are constructed as liminal (Fullagar & Pavlidis, 2012) with participants less constrained by the roles they adopt in everyday life in comparison to those who are from proximate locations (Smith & Stewart, 2007). It is argued that participatory sport tourists experience heightened feelings of escape and may have more freedom and space to experience existential authenticity and project their true selves than in other settings (Lamont, 2014; Shipway, King, Lee, & Brown, 2016). As in discussions of communitas within tourism experiences (Graburn, 2001), it is claimed events can offer transient versions of participatory communities (Miles, 2010) often cited as a valuable aspect within sport tourism literature for enabling an individual to prioritise and celebrate their sporting identity outside of the constraints of daily life (Lamont, 2014; Lee, Brown, King, & Shipway, 2016). Consequently it has also been argued that events should be designed to enhance the liminality of the setting and help participants to disengage from their daily life (Chalip, 2006; Lee et al., 2016). Sites of urban revitalisation strategies and image building are also, however, sites of everyday leisure and local connectivities. The interplay between ritual and place attachment, escape, and liminality have not been explored from the perspective of placed leisure communities who experience both physical and socio-cultural proximity to the event space through the ordinary patterns of everyday life formed through sport and leisure lifestyles.

This paper explores the experiences of members of the local cycling community during the staging of an international cycling event the 'Tour Down Under' (TDU) in their home environment to consider how local sport and leisure communities assert identity and connectedness to their own localities through both their physical and socio-cultural proximity to these processes. In terms of size, scale, complexity and internationalisation, the TDU fits the categorisation of a major sports event (Jago & Shaw, 1998), as it involves competition between both cycling teams and individual riders representing a number of nations; it attracts significant public interest, nationally and internationally, through spectator attendance and media coverage in South Australia; and is of international significance to cycling and features prominently on the international calendar. Previous research has examined the importance of the TDU in building social capital within the local community (Jamieson, 2014; Mackellar & Jamieson, 2015), while others have argued that the event creates few tangible legacies and causes little disruption to normal patterns of life in the local area (Brown, Lee, King, & Shipway, 2015). This paper will build on these works to consider the ways in which the hosting of a major sports event is experienced by local individuals whose leisure lifestyles facilitate both a socio-cultural and physical proximity to the event and the event space. The interviews for local cyclists who were attending the event were therefore designed around three central research questions:

- What characterises the participation of local cyclists at the event?
- How do cycling experiences differ from daily practice during the event?
- How do local cyclist's interactions with local leisure spaces alter before, during and after the staging of a major cycling event?

Method

The TDU is an annual professional cycling race event in South Australia and forms the context for this study. The TDU is the first event of the annual Union Cycliste International (UCI) series. The TDU is classified as a major event (Tour Down Under, 2016) based in the city of Adelaide and consists of six race stages held during six days throughout the state of South Australia. In addition to the professional race, the TDU also includes a festival of cycling held within Adelaide and surrounding towns including activities such as street parties, charity challenges, tour dinner evenings and family cycle events and a mass participatory ride for amateur cyclists, which in 2014 was called The BUPA Challenge Tour. In 2014, the TDU attracted more than 760,000 spectators, including approximately 40,000 event specific international and interstate visitors (South Australian Tourism Commission, 2014). It has been recognised as the largest cycling event in the southern hemisphere.

During the 2014 TDU, a research team conducted face-to-face individual or paired semi-structured interviews with both visiting and local event spectators. Individuals who attended the 2014 TDU and / or participated in any cycling activities during the 2014 TDU were asked to participate in the interviews. Participants were recruited through a purposeful sampling approach. Four cycling clubs in Adelaide and surrounding towns were contacted, via email in the weeks preceding the TDU to invite club members who were attending the TDU to participate in interviews. In addition, the research team employed an opportunistic approach by recruiting participants for interviews during the event at a range of locations including the start and finish lines of each stage, the Tour Village (the hub of the TDU), local cycle races, and other cycling events held in and around Adelaide during the six event days. All interviews took place during the event, often in a physical event setting such as within the Tour village or while spectating the race and the length of the interviews varied from 30 to 45 minutes. Importantly, situating the interviews in the research context helped to position the research as an extension of the participant's event experience rather than as distinctly separate (Spinney, 2006).

In total, 35 interviews with event participants were conducted as part of a wider study on the event. Nineteen of these participants identified themselves as local cyclists from Adelaide or surrounding towns and form the sample for this work. Table 1 provides a summary of participant details including their age group, gender, distances cycled per week and indications of cycle club affiliations.

This local sample presents a spectrum of 'serious' participants (see Stebbins, 2015). For example, all respondents interviewed claimed to cycle at least 100 km a week

Table 1. Participant information.

Participant	Pseudonym	Age	Gender	Club membership	KM cycled per week
1	David	55–64	M	Club member	150–200 k
2	Jane	55–64	F	Club member x 2	250–300 k
3	Liam	65–74	M	No club	200–250 k
4	Ryan	35–44	M	Club member	100–150 k
5	Sam	65–74	M	No club	No club 100–150 k
6	Ben	35–44	M	Club member	250–300 k
7	Jim	35–44	M	Club member x 2	250–300 k
8	Alice	45–54	F	Club member	200–250 k
9	Rachel	45–54	F	Club member	100–150 k
10	Martin	55–64	M	Club member x 2	300–350 k
11	Mark	35–44	M	Club member x 3	500 k +
12	Arnie	45–54	M	Club member	500 k+
13	Alex	35–44	M	Club member	200–250 k
14	Tom	55–64	M	Club member x 2	200–250 k
15	Ian	64–75	M	Club member	200–250 k
15	Jamie	34–45	M	Club member	100–150 k

with some cycling up to 500 km a week and 13 identified themselves as members of at least one cycle club. All participants were over 35 years with over half the sample aged 55 years or over. Most respondents were male with only three females taking part in the study.

All of the interviews were recorded and consequently the first stage of data analysis was to transcribe the recorded interviews verbatim. Subsequently, research team members explored the transcripts individually to derive general structures, patterns and initial codes as a process of interpretation (Creswell, 2007). Following this process, team members met to discuss their own interpretations employing an inductive approach rather than following a pre-existing theoretical framework or theoretical interest outside of the research questions (Holloway & Wheeler, 2010). The research team adopted differing roles, following the idea that adopting differing methods (in this case, observation and interviewing) may be useful in developing a more holistic and contextually grounded assessment of the phenomenon (Shipway & Jones, 2007). One of the authors, as an 'experienced insider' used their own emic knowledge of the social world under investigation to help illustrate and explain some key issues that may not be apparent to a more 'scientific' approach (Shipway, Holloway, & Jones, 2013). The less experienced members of the research team, however, adopted the role of 'outsiders', critically questioning some of the meanings and interpretations of both the data and event setting, from the etic perspective. A coding framework was developed and applied and three core themes related to local cyclists were identified as place identity; insider experiences; and interactions with the everyday. These are presented in the results and discussion section below.

Results and discussion

Place identity and the proximate tourist

In 1996, the Australian Grand Prix was relocated from Adelaide to Melbourne which resulted in a strong sense of loss of status for the region (also see Jamieson, 2014). The TDU originated as a replacement for the Grand Prix and is now described as

Australia's premier cycling festival (Tour Down Under, 2016). As previously discussed, major sports events such as this often act as image builders and are useful promotional tools for regions seeking to attract visitors within an environment of competitive globalisation (Hinch & Higham, 2011; Shipway & Fyall, 2012). The extract below shows how local cyclists celebrated this positioning of their everyday sporting environment as a noteworthy cycle event setting.

> Mark: To see professional riders, top riders like Cadel Evans and the Australian stars here… to have the top European riders coming over here and race in our state. It's fantastic.

Seamon (2014) describes place identity as a process whereby individuals recognise places as integral to their identity and self-worth. For the local cycling community, hosting a major cycling event attracting both professional sportspersons but also other committed amateur sport tourists to their home environment was a source of self-validation and served to strengthen their place identity. Tom, a member of two local clubs celebrated the regions connections to other prestigious cycling events.

> Tom: The TV coverage gets shown around the world its got to raise the profile of Adelaide a bit and the fact that in Australia we do have a category 1 UCI event it means we're, whilst its only for a week, not 3 weeks, but it means we're up there with France, Italy, Spain, all those better known places.

The status of a UCI event and the representation of the region through national television coverage of the event prompted a reimagination of the everyday environment for local cyclists. For example, the quote below shows how one participant adopts a tourist gaze (Urry & Larsen, 2011) despite being in a familiar environment (Diaz-Soria, 2017).

> Martin: When you see them you realise how brilliant – I mean the TV coverage is very, very good – the helicopter shots I love it out here. I've got everything here I want but it's good to be able to see – when you see the shots on Tuesday of Angaston and they go through all the wineries – just think I'm so blessed to live here. I really do feel that and I know most of my mates do.

Interactions with visiting event attendees also acted to attach status to their home environment in the context of their leisure community. The participant below describes hearing visiting members of the cycling community celebrating the cycling opportunities available in the region in comparison to their usual cycling environment.

> Liam: Some people come over with their clubs so they'll have large groups and they'll ride in the hills and realise how good we've got it. A lot of people come over from Melbourne and, say, "All our races now, we've got to travel at least 2 hours from Melbourne to find a road we can ride on. You guys have it so good y'know?"

Proximate tourism encounters such as those experienced by local cyclists at the TDU complicate the roles of participants as both residents and tourists and consequently the interactions between place and self (Jeuring & Haartsen, 2017). The hosting of the TDU focused the attention of local cyclists on their relationship with their everyday leisure space and the legitimacy of their locality for their sport. Their physical proximity to these spaces facilitated a strong sense of connection which in turn resulted in feelings of pride and self-worth. The next section explores this further by examining how lifestyle proximity in addition to their physical proximity created the role of an event insider in comparison to visiting cycle tourists.

The proximate tourist as insider

Cycling events are sites of sporting significance which promote a sense of collective belonging for participants of the sport (Brown et al., 2015; Fullagar & Pavlidis, 2012). In turn, the hosting of such events imbues everyday leisure space with meaning and currency within sporting communities. The hosting of the event in their home setting was seen to provide participants with insider privileges and these formed an important part of local cyclists' experiences as proximate tourists. For example, Tom described his access to the best vantage points in terms of spectator experiences of the professional race.

> Tom: I had the advantage for quite a few years – well I think the last four, there's been a stage finish just a couple of kilometres from home. And they whip around through my area three times so it's quite a good vantage spot and at one stage they were going past the end of my street. Now you can't beat that!

Sport provides ways to be included, and to attain recognition and status (Vermeulen & Verweel, 2009), as such insider experiences can act as currency to be exchanged or drawn upon within the wider lifestyle community. David below describes the opportunity to demonstrate insider knowledge to visiting members of the cycling community.

> David: I have a nephew from Victoria who comes across, and just on the odd occasion he'll ring me up and say I want to go to a place called Mylor", which is down, it's the other side of Stirling "What's the best way to get there? Do you know any shortcuts or do you know a quieter road?" and obviously I take him because I am able to do that.

According to both Lamont and McKay, (2012) and Shipway et al. (2016) behind the scenes access and chance encounters with professional cyclists at tour events can enhance the perceived authenticity of the event experience. For local cyclists, however these occurrences were not limited to the period of the event itself but intersected their everyday leisure practices. Participants such as Adam below spoke of opportunities to meet professional participants through local contacts or as part of chance encounters, for example, during their everyday cycle practice in the run up to the event.

> Arnie: If you're that keen and you know the stages and you went out on the stages the week before you would bump into them. We saw Trek Racing; we were in the middle of our race going across what they call 'The Range' and they're coming the other way and they all wave at you and stuff like that.

Another cyclist spoke of meeting Cadel Evans, the Australian professional racing cyclist, while undertaking a casual ride along the local coastline in the days leading up to the event.

> Ian: I met Cadel Evans last week... down the beach the other day drinking coffee with all his mates, I just pulled the bike up jumped off, jumped into the middle of the café, how you going Cadel Evans' nice to meet ya, shook his hand, tried to break it, said good luck and took off.

Through their position as proximate tourists, local cyclists developed their own event rituals and routines outside of the packaged or formalised event offer which saw their everyday leisure spaces and practices intersect with the eventscape. Most local participants took leave from paid employment during the week of the TDU and in many ways performed similar activities as visiting cyclists such as cycling out to race stages, spectating and browsing the tour village. Yet the intersecting experience of both physical and socio-cultural proximity gave them access to fringe activities on the local cycle scene which served to reinforce their position as event insiders, blending the ordinary with a ritualised break from routine (Graburn, 2001).

The TDU includes a one day 'BUPA community challenge' which invites amateur cyclists to cycle one of the race stage routes just hours before the professional race riders which has grown in popularity. Previous work on cycle tourists has identified feelings of authenticity and a more empathetic connection with the professional racers evoked by cycling on the same routes as part of the event experience (see Lamont, 2014; Lamont & McKay, 2012; Spinney, 2006). For local cyclists, however, this event was constructed as a 'tourist experience' and one which was avoided by many in the local cycling community. Insider knowledge dictated this as a dangerous and unpleasant space for experienced cyclists:

> Martin: I probably try to avoid the charity ride now... too many people can't ride very well and they have a tendency to make you crash because myself and the other guys I race with we go past a lot of those guys doing double their speed and it tends to freak them out, so then they get the wanders and they cause a crash. It's for the crowds really, it's not something us guys feel we need to do.

In part, an insider identity was enacted through the dismissal of this event particularly for more serious riders who were connected to a network of alternative race events year round. These cyclists chose to shun this official event experience instead constructing their own versions of authenticity through alternative activities that utilised and celebrated their local connections to communities and spaces and the resulting privileges. For example, the participant below describes attending a barbeque with professional cyclists through a local connection:

> Mark: A mate of mine has helped out with a team so he has a barbeque around his place which is just around the corner from my place, but you meet Andre[1] and all these sort of guys, you have a bit of communication issues to sort of deal with but they're all very nice friendly people.....a few beers and stuff with some of the guys, yeah absolutely.

Another popular element of the TDU was a street party, held on the second evening of the TDU in a suburb of Adelaide. Several participants invited the research team to attend an event taking place on the same night at a local race circuit. When asked why they would not be attending the official street party event Alice responded that:

> It's the same every year, it's not for us. It's nothing but cyclists everywhere talking about cycling when you can come here and actually cycle. It's a chance for our club to compete against other clubs who are down this way for the Tour. This is where the real cyclists come.

Socio-cultural proximity to the lifestyle of the cycling community combined with physical proximity to the event spaces and places enabled local participants to pick and choose between the tourist spectacles of the event itself and alternative activities within the local leisure community, with both assuming differing importance at different times.

Beyond the proximate tourist: shaping everyday leisure practice

Active engagement between sport tourists and eventscapes can be various, personal and value rich (Lee et al., 2016). While cycling the same routes as the professional riders during the TDU was an important part of visiting cyclists experiences (see Shipway et al., 2016), local cyclists used their physical proximity to the space to connect with these experiences in different ways. Cyclists drew upon their local knowledge of the event routes to reflect upon the quality of the performance by professional cyclists at the TDU.

> Rachel: You can just see how much training goes into how they do it, and you might be riding up a hill at 12 kilometres an hour and they're averaging, what 40. And you just, you compare that when you're doing it at 12 and struggling and they're just like cruising it at 40, you know.

For local cyclists, however, the process of connection and comparison with the event space and performances occurred after the staging of the event to permeate the everyday leisure experience. GPS technology such as 'Strava' which enables cyclists to record their routes and times and compare them with others was utilised as part of everyday leisure cycling and enabled local cyclists to virtually compete with both professional riders and visiting cyclists on the routes of the TDU at any time of the year. Below, Mark demonstrated to the researcher how he used the times and routes recorded during the TDU on Strava as part of training rides.

> Mark: I've actually gone faster than the pros on that section because I do it all the time. I will show you that one – this is Mount Torrens so the Tour Down Under actually normally goes along this road and that time was in the Tour Down Under last year or the year before and that guy who came second well he was being motor paced but I can ride it anytime I want.

The local cyclist below also described how he could use his knowledge of the conditions and his physical proximity to the route to compete against the performance of both professional riders and serious amateurs on the sections of the TDU at any time of the year.

> Arnie: You go out and you look at the wind and you go man which way is the wind going? Right I am going to hit this section of road today because I know I am going to create a record. As an example last year we did Shepherds Hill and I rode over there with one of my mates in my team and he said I'm feeling pretty good today. I said go as hard as you can up Shepherds Hill. The pros were going up there and my mate was like 6th fastest time out of 3,000 people and he was faster than any of the pros up there in the Tour Down Under.

Hockey's (2004; 2013) work explores how the embodied sense making of athletes which occurs during repeated training runs is employed to evaluate and inform their performance. In this case, however, participants use their embodied knowledge of the familiar terrain to challenge their own performances and compete virtually against the event performances of the elite, as well as visiting cyclists from the wider community beyond their physical presence in their locality. In this instance, the spectacle of the elite event performances intersects with the mundane of the training route to participants' everyday leisure practices and encounters. Therefore while engaging with the eventscape is experienced by visiting sport tourists as extraordinary, for proximate tourists, these became embedded in their everyday leisure routines and rituals blurring the understanding of what is every day and what is not (also see Diaz-Soria, 2017; Larsen, 2008).

Hosting visiting cyclists in their everyday leisure space facilitated a sense of connection to a wider sporting community which also continued beyond the event. During the TDU, cycle clubs invited visiting clubs to locally hosted events to give their own members a chance to compete within a wider pool of talent. Participating in such activities as part of the event helped participants feel more connected to an international cycling community and gave them a focus for training at other times of the year:

> Alex: During the Tour Down Under, the club have a competitive series that's on. We have a road race, a time trial, a hill climb and a criterion race like mid week and we get a lot of people from interstate come so it really spices things up a bit, gives the club a focus that they need to represent during this week, its great for the guys to have that to aim for leading up to the tour.

Cyclists also described how the hosting of the TDU had direct repercussions on their everyday leisure experience after the event had finished. Some participants, for example viewed the visibility of cyclists during the event as a platform for improving the overall cycling experience in Adelaide for local users.

> Ian: It raises the profile of cycling in the community which is a good thing and hopefully it makes people more aware of cyclists on the road. I ride out on the open road and you need motorists to give you a bit of space and its gets a bit scary up there on the roads sometime its only a matter of educating drivers; 1 to be a bit more patient; and 2 to give the riders a bit more room.

It was felt that hosting such a prestigious and well-attended event changed the ways in which local motorists responded to cyclists throughout the year in the sharing of road space between different user groups.

> Jane: Cyclists - They're on the news, they're in the paper, they're on the TV, hopefully motorists will see riders as just normal people that have a legitimate use of the road not something to get angry with and that's going to delay them 30 seconds or something.

Nevertheless, not all participants felt that hosting the event had a positive legacy for cycling in the local area. The sponsored community ride discussed in the previous section was identified as creating lasting problems for local cyclists. Respondents discussed its attraction for novice cyclists who were less likely to understand the road using etiquette embedded in cycling culture.

> Tom: A lot of those people ride on the road like mainly the month leading up to it and then after that they don't ride, but they cause so much agro with the local drivers because a lot of them they just don't ride with common sense that then the day that finishes I've got to deal with that for the next couple of months before they cool down again.

The participant below also describes how the popularity of this event was seen as damaging for relations between road users and local experienced cyclists.

> Ian: Like the traffic round here, it can get pretty hairy and especially around the TDU I think they get fed up with so many of us and that. All the ones who get their bikes out once a year can do real damage to the relationship between car users and cyclists for the rest of the year.

The problematic relationship between cyclists and other road users impacting the ability to participate is well documented (see O'Connor & Brown, 2010). In this case, the relationship between cyclists and other road users is exacerbated by increased numbers of cyclists before, during and after the event itself and the increase of novice participants from the local area is considered to heighten the problems. Local cyclists in this study felt a sense of authority through their own identities as experienced cyclists while also framing their concerns through a strong sense of connection to place (also see Rickly & Vidon, 2017). Such examples highlight the paradox experienced by local cyclists in their hosting of international sports events. While cyclists develop connections and validating experiences during the event, event hosting can also contribute to politicise and contest leisure spaces for local users at other times of the year.

Conclusion

This paper offers insights into the hosting of sport tourism events in leisure spaces of the everyday by considering the impacts of the staging of international sport events on the culture, community and practices of local established sporting communities. The research questions sought to consider the characteristics of participation for individuals who experience physical proximity to the event and subsequent lifestyle identification with both the sporting spectacle and the (everyday) place within which it is located and how these interact with everyday practice and differing temporalities.

This study shows how the distinction between the spectacular and the mundane is muddied for local leisure participants as proximate tourism intersects with everyday practice in complex ways. Indeed to separate event participants into locals and tourists may be too simplistic as the experience of the mundane or the spectacular cannot be assumed (Chen & Chen, 2017; Edensor, 2007). For those whose interconnections with event spaces extend before, beyond and between the eventscape, their locality and their lifestyles, their experiences are deeply invested with both shared and individualised notions of culture, value, community and self.

These findings contribute to emerging work on proximate tourism by considering how socio-cultural insideness to a leisure lifestyle manifests through tourism practices in home environments. For Jeuring and Harrtsen (2017), presenting familiar places from a new angle enables people to reconstruct their own identities and those of the places they inhabit. This study considers how the proximity can be experienced as adding value through insideness and a reflection on the everyday which extends beyond the event itself. For those whose leisure pursuits provide a strong source of identity tourism experiences often provides an opportunity to take time to participate in their preferred leisure activity but in a different setting (Chang & Gibson, 2011).

Participants in this study identified themselves as committed cyclists no less involved and invested in the sporting lifestyle and the opportunities for developing their leisure interests presented by TDU than visiting tourists but had a different experience of the setting itself. Their familiarity with local people, places, and prior knowledge of the sports event itself acted as a further point of reference and insideness which was played out through their interaction with their local spaces at different times. During the event, local connections such as informal social gatherings and local events were chosen over some of the commodified authenticities available as part of the official programme. Yet once the event was over the opportunity to connect with the professional event performances through social media and technology offered a further dimension to their ordinary cycling experience which served to rework their everyday connections to place. Graburn's (2001) work on tourism as secular ritual refers to the liminal state of tourist experiences which provide some inversion of everyday conditions and routines. As proximate tourists, local cyclists developed their own event rituals yet these intersected with their home lives and spaces blurring the entry and exit points of the liminal tourist state. Thus, socio-cultural proximity allows for the utilisation, celebration and reimagination of local connections, communities and spaces betwixt and between the states of host community or visiting tourist.

Diaz-Soria (2017) argues that proximate and visiting tourists share curiosity as motivation but do not have the same points of reference. The findings of this paper suggests that frames of reference are informed by leisure lifestyles of serious participants and as proximate tourists they drew upon their knowledge of everyday sporting spaces, local resources and their insider status developing capital for local leisure participants within the wider visiting tourist community. As Rickly & Vidon (2017) have also argued, leisure participants use their lifestyle commitment as leverage to assert authority, particularly in spaces they see themselves as locals.

In addition to the proximate tourist experience during the event, these findings also show the ways in which the spectacle of a major sports event creates contestation in everyday leisure space beyond its temporality. Increases in casual cycling as a by-product of the event was considered problematic for committed cyclists who negotiate a complex relationship with road users throughout the year. Their lifestyle proximity promoted strong connections to the local environment which informed their attitudes towards its use (also see Rickly & Vidon, 2017). Thus the hosting of major sports events can be somewhat paradoxical for local participants providing greater connections to the sporting community while also creating tensions in their everyday leisure practice.

This paper has sought to situate the performance of everyday leisure alongside the employment of external facing place making strategies in tourism destinations. While consultation and engagement with local residents is an established practice within the planning and staging of major sports events there is little evidence of the recognition of local sport participant communities as a connected and invested stakeholder group with specific place attachments and identities (also see Green, 2001). We suggest future research should consider lifestyle proximity as part of host community experiences of major sports events which may shape the proximate tourist encounter and the experiences of legacy in different ways to those who are less connected to the focus of the event.

Similarly, a focus on social and economic benefits of hosting major sports events on local resident communities is a major area of concern, yet the benefits of hosting an event which has relevance for local sports clubs and communities has not been fully examined. Major sports events organisers should recognise the value connections with local sports clubs could offer as a pool of resident participant experts and ensure they benefit from the hosting of sports events if not materially then socially and culturally. The opportunities provided for facilitating the interaction between local and visiting members of the wider sporting community should also be considered to ensure local sports communities are represented in sport tourism event space.

Note

1. Referring to professional racing cyclist André Greipel.

Disclosure statement

No potential conflict of interest was reported by the authors.

ORCID

Katherine King 0000-0002-9679-3142
Richard Shipway 0000-0003-2811-0546

References

Bale, J. (2003). *Sports geography*. London: Routledge.

Beaumont, E., & Brown, D. (2016). 'It's not something I'm proud of but it's ... just how I feel': Local surfer perspectives of localism. *Leisure Studies*, *35*(3), 278–295.

Belanger, A. (2000). Sports venues and the spectacularization of urban spaces in North America. *International Review for the Sociology of Sport*, *35*(3), 378–397.

Bennett, A. (2005). *Culture and everyday life*. London: Sage. Retrieved fromhttps://books.google.co.uk/books?hl=en&lr=&id=BbGC0FxRqowC&oi=fnd&pg=PP1&dq=Culture+and+Everyday+Life&ots=HWHhdehNE_&sig=DN1LMBtxmGSrl5gE79gOpBiM3rI

Bodet, G., & Lacassagne, M. F. (2012). International place branding through sporting events: A British perspective of the 2008 Beijing Olympics. *European Sport Management Quarterly*, *12*(4), 357–374.

Bricker, K. S., & Kerstetter, D. L. (2000). Level of specialization and place attachment: An exploratory study of whitewater recreationists. *Leisure Sciences*, *22*(4), 233–257.

Brown, G., Lee, I. S., King, K., & Shipway, R. (2015). Eventscapes and the creation of event legacies. *Annals of Leisure Research*, *18*(4), 510–527.

Brown, G., Smith, A., & Assaker, G. (2016). Revisiting the host city: An empirical examination of sport involvement, place attachment, event satisfaction and spectator intentions at the London Olympics. *Tourism Management*, *55*, 160–172.

Chalip, L. (2006). Towards social leverage of sports events. *Journal of Sport and Tourism*, *11*(2), 109–127.

Chaney, D. (1996). *Lifestyles*. London: Routledge.

Chang, S., & Gibson, H. J. (2011). Physically active leisure and tourism connection: Leisure involvement and choice of tourism activities amongst paddlers. *Leisure Sciences*, *33*(2), 162–181.

Charleston, S. (2009). The English football ground as a representation of home. *Journal of Environmental Psychology*, *29*(1), 144–150.

Chen, J., & Chen, N. (2017). Beyond the everyday? Rethinking place meanings in tourism. *Tourism Geographies*, *19*(1), 9–26.

Cherrington, J. (2014). 'It's just superstition I suppose ... I've always done something on game day': The construction of everyday life on a university basketball team. *International Review for the Sociology of Sport*, *49*(5), 509–525.

Chien, P. M., Ritchie, B. W., Shipway, R., & Henderson, H. (2012). I am having a dilemma: Factors affecting resident support of event development in the community. *Journal of Travel Research*, *51*(4), 451–463.

Creswell, J. W. (2007). *Qualitative inquiry and research design* (2nd ed.). London: Sage.

Crouch, D. (2000). Places around us: Embodied lay geographies in leisure and tourism. *Leisure Studies*, *19*(2), 63–76.

Crouch, D. (2015). Unravelling space and landscape in leisure's identities. In S. Gammon & S. Elkington (Eds.), *Landscapes of Leisure: Space, place and identities* (pp. 8–23). London: Palgrave Macmillan. Retrieved fromhttp://link.springer.com/10.1057/9781137428530

Crouch, D., & Tomlinson, A. (1994). Leisure, space and lifestyle: Modernity, postmodernity and identity in self-generated leisure. In I. Henry (Ed.), *Modernity, postmodernity and identity*, 309–321, Brighton: Leisure Studies Association.

Diaz-Soria, I. (2017). Being a tourist as a chosen experience in a proximity destination. *Tourism Geographies*, *19*(1), 96–117.

Edensor, T. (2007). Mundane mobilities, performances and spaces of tourism. *Social & Cultural Geography*, *8*(2), 199–215.

Edwards, B., & Corte, U. (2010). Commercialization and lifestyle sport: Lessons from 20 years of freestyle BMX in 'Pro-Town, USA'. *Sport in Society*, *13*(7–8), 1135–1151.

Fullagar, S., & Pavlidis, A. (2012). 'It's all about the journey': Women and cycling events. *International Journal of Event and Festival Management*, *3*(2), 149–170.

Gammon, S., & Elkington, S. ((2015).Eds.). *Reading landscapes: articulating non-essentialist representation of space, place and identity in leisure*. London: Palgrave Macmillan UK, 1–7. Retrieved fromhttp://link.springer.com/10.1057/9781137428530

Gardiner, M. (2000). *Critiques of everyday life*. New York, NY: Routledge. Retrieved fromhttp://site.ebrary.com/lib/bournemouth/Doc?id=5001620

Getz, D., & Page, S. J. (2016). *Event studies: Theory, research and policy for planned events*, London: Routledge.

Giddens, A. (1991). *Modernity and self-identity: Self and society in the late modern age*. Cambridge: Polity Press.

Goffman, E. (1959). *The presentation of self in everyday life* (1st ed.). Garden City, NY: Anchor.

Graburn, N. H. H. (2001). Secular ritual: A general theory of tourism. In V. L. Smith & M. Brent (Eds.) *Hosts and guests revisited: Tourism issues of the 21st century*. (pp. 42–50). New York, NY: Cognizant Communication Corporation.

Gratton, C., & Henry, I. (2002). *Sport in the city: The role of sport in economic and social regeneration*, London: Routledge.

Green, C. (2001). Leveraging subculture and identity to promote sport events. *Sport Management Review*, *4*, 1–19.

Henderson, K., & Frelke, C. (2000). Space as a vital dimension of leisure: The creation of place. *World Leisure Journal*, *42*(3), 18–24.

Hinch, T., & Higham, J. (2011). *Sport tourism development*, Bristol: Channel View Publications.

Hockey, J. (2013). Knowing the 'Going': The sensory evaluation of distance running. *Qualitative Research in Sport, Exercise & Health*, *5*(1), 127–141.

Hockey, J. (2004). Knowing the route: Distance runners' mundane knowledge. *SOSOL: Sociology of Sport Online*, *7*(1).

Holloway, I., & Wheeler, S. (2010). *Qualitative research in nursing and healthcare*. (3rd ed.). Oxford: Wiley-Blackwell.

Jago, L., & Shaw, R. (1998). Special Events: A Conceptual and Definitional Framework. *Festival Management and Event Tourism*, *5*(1–2), 21–32.

Jamieson, N. (2014). Sport tourism events as community builders—How social capital helps the 'locals' cope. *Journal of Convention & Event Tourism*, *15*(1), 57–68.

Jarvie, G. (2013). *Sport, culture and society: An introduction, second edition*, London: Routledge.

Jeuring, J., & Diaz-Soria, I. (2017). Introduction: Proximity and intraregional aspects of tourism. *Tourism Geographies*, *19*(1), 4–8.

Jeuring, J. H. G., & Haartsen, T. (2016). The challenge of proximity: The (un)attractiveness of near-home tourism destinations. *Tourism Geographies*, *19*(1), 118–141.

King, K., & Church, A. (2015). Questioning policy, youth participation and lifestyle sports. *Leisure Studies*, *34*(3), 282–302.

Lamont, M. (2014). Authentication in sports tourism. *Annals of Tourism Research*, *45*, 1–17.

Lamont, M., & McKay, J. (2012). Intimations of postmodernity in sports tourism at the Tour de France. *Journal of Sport & Tourism*, *17*(4), 313–331.

Larsen, J. (2008). De exoticizing tourist travel: Everyday life and sociality on the move. *Leisure Studies*, *27*(1), 21–34.

Lee, I. S., Brown, G., King, K., & Shipway, R. (2016). Social identity in serious sport event space. *Event Management*, *20*(4), 491–499.

Lewicka, M. (2011). Place attachment: How far have we come in the last 40 years ? *Journal of Environmental Psychology*, *31*(3), 207–230.

Mackellar, J., & Jamieson, N. (2015). Assessing the contribution of a major cycle race to host communities in South Australia. *Leisure Studies*, *34*(5), 547–565.

Mason, D. S., Washington, M. S., & Buist, E. A. N. (2015). Signaling status through stadiums: The discourses of comparison within a hierarchy. *Journal of Sport Management*, *29*(5), 539–554.

Miles, S. (2010). *Spaces for Consumption*. Los Angeles, CA: SAGE Publications Ltd.

Misener, L., & Mason, D. (2006). Developing local citizenship through sporting events: Balancing community involvement and tourism development. *Current Issues in Tourism*, *9*(4–5), 384–398.

O'Connor, J. P., & Brown, T. D. (2010). Riding with the sharks: Serious leisure cyclist's perceptions of sharing the road with motorists. *Journal of Science and Medicine in Sport*, *13*(1), 53–58.

Paddison, R., & Miles, S. (2009). *Culture-led Urban Regeneration*, London: Routledge.

Ramshaw, G., & Hinch, T. (2006). Place identity and sport tourism: The case of the heritage classic ice hockey event. *Current Issues in Tourism*, *9*(4–5), 399–418.

Raymond, C. M., Brown, G., & Weber, D. (2010). The measurement of place attachment: Personal, community and environmental connections. *Journal of Environmental Psychology*, *30*(4), 422–434.

Scannell, L., & Gifford, R. (2010). Defining place attachment: A tripartite organizing framework. *Journal of Environmental Psychology*. *30*(1), 1–10.

Schimmel, K. S. (2006). Deep play: Sports mega-events and urban social conditions in the USA. *The Sociological Review*, *54*(Suppl 2), 160–174. https://doi.org/10.1111/j.1467-954X.2006.00659.x

Seamon, D. (2014). Place attachment and phenomenology: The synergistic dynamism of place. In L. C. Manzo & P. Devine-Wright (Eds). *Place Attachment: Advances in theory, methods and applications* (pp. 11–23). Oxon: Routledge.

Sharpley, R., & Stone, P. (2012). Socio-cultural impacts of events. In S. Page & S. Connell (Eds.), *The Routledge Handbook of Events*, 347–361, London: Routledge.

Shipway, R., & Fyall, A. ((2012).eds) International Sports Events: towards a future research agenda. London: Routledge, 1–9.

Shipway, R., Holloway, I., & Jones, I. (2013). Organisations, practices, actors and events: Exploring inside the distance running social world. *International Review for the Sociology of Sport*, *48*(3), 259–276.

Shipway, R., & Jones, I. (2007). Running away from home: Understanding visitor experiences in sport tourism. *International Journal of Tourism Research*, *9*, 373–383.

Shipway, R., King, K., Lee, I. S., & Brown, G. (2016). Understanding cycle tourism experiences at the Tour Down Under. *Journal of Sport & Tourism*, *20*(1), 21–39.

Smith, A. C. T., & Stewart, B. (2007). The travelling fan: Understanding the mechanisms of sport fan consumption in a sport tourism setting. *Journal of Sport & Tourism*, *12*(3–4), 155–181.

South Australian Tourism Commission. (2014). May 21. Record economic impact for 2014 Santos Tour Down Under. Retrieved 28 October 2016, from http://www.tourism.sa.gov.au/media/record-economic-impact-for-2014-santos-tour-down-under.aspx

Spinney, J. (2006). A place of sense: A kinaesthetic ethnography of cyclists on Mt Ventoux. *Environment and Planning D: Society and Space*, *24*(5), 709–732.

Spracklen, K., Timmins, S., & Long, J. (2010). Ethnographies of the imagined, the imaginary and the critically real: Blackness, whiteness, the north of England and rugby league. *Leisure Studies*, *29*(4), 397–414.

Stebbins, R. A. (2015). *Serious Leisure: A Perspective for Our Time*, New Brunswick: Transaction Publishers.

Sturm, D. (2014). A glamorous and high-tech global spectacle of speed: Formula One motor racing as mediated, global and corporate spectacle. In K. Dashper, T. Fletcher, & N. McCullough (Eds.), *Sports Events, Society and Culture*, London: Routledge, 68–82.

Szytniewski, B. B., Spierings, B., & van der Velde, M. (2017). Socio-cultural proximity, daily life and shopping tourism in the Dutch – German border region. *Tourism Geographies*, *19*(1), 63–77.

Tonts, M., & Atherley, K. (2010). Competitive sport and the construction of place identity in rural Australia. *Sport in Society*, *13*(3), 381–398.

Tour Down Under. (2016). About the Tour Down Under. Retrieved from www.tourdownunder.com.au

Urry, J., & Larsen, J. (2011). *The Tourist Gaze 3.0*, London: SAGE.

Vermeulen, J., & Verweel, P. (2009). Participation in sport: Bonding and bridging as identity work. *Sport in Society*, *12*(9), 1206–1219.

Waitt, G. (2003). Social impacts of the Sydney Olympics. *Annals of Tourism Research*, *30*(1), 194–215.

Mikkelsen, M. V., & Cohen, S. A. (2015). Freedom in mundane mobilities: Caravanning in Denmark. Tourism Geographies, 17(5), 663–681.

Rickley, J. M., Vidon, E. S. (2017). Contesting authentic practice and ethical authority in adventure tourism. Journal of Sustainable Tourism, 25(10), 1418–1433.

Big data and tourism geographies – an emerging paradigm for future study?

Jie Zhang

Introduction

Big data has become a hot topic in tourism and geographic research, as well as in other socioeconomic sciences. The definition of big data remains open with characters of huge in volume, high in velocity, diverse in variety, exhaustive in scope, fine-grained in resolution, relational in nature, flexible and scalability (Kitchin, 2013). Geographers have noted that big data research has seen a shift from a data-scarce to a data-rich environment, resulting in the emergence of a new mode of the data-driven geography (Miller & Goodchild, 2015). In terms of big data analytical techniques, which include the ability to manage datasets that exceed the processing capability of traditional data analysis software, the phenomenon has almost become an all-purpose tool that often substitutes for traditional research approaches. At tourism industry conferences in China, big data companies demonstrate ever expanding technical abilities to monitor and manage the real-time visitor use at tourist attractions, and local government tourism administrators like to show off their cellphone screens with displays of these real-time monitoring tools for tourist sites under their governance. In turn, these officials are paying less attention to traditional data collection methods and models of tourist flows. Big data techniques have clearly brought opportunities and benefits for tourism research and industrial operations. However, does a cell phone display equal the big data? Will big data completely replace the theoretic models of tourist flows and other theories of tourism geographies? How will our understanding of tourism geographies change by big data? What aspects of tourism benefit the most from big data, and to what extent? These are questions needed to be examined properly, or at least thought about in a reasonable manner.

Big data and tourism geographic research issues

Geographical perspectives on the benefits of big data in tourism research mostly focus on the ease of new forms of data acquisition. Big data for tourism can be derived from a variety of sources (or channels), including cell phones, aerial imagery, satellite imagery, online social media platforms, merchandise sales and distribution sources, public monitoring devices (cameras and counters), and industry specific data collection services. New data channels emerge rapidly and provide large quantities of data that have potential applications for travel, tourism and hospitality research, and which can overcome the issues of data shortage that are common in traditional tourism research. More and more research has focused on the relationship between various big data indices and aspects of tourist flow, such as the Baidu index and tourist flow predictions (Huang, Zhang, & Ding, 2013; Li & Zhang, 2013; Sun, Zhang, Liu, & Zhang, 2017). Properly referenced big data can contribute rich information and insights into the patterns and structures of visitation and movement of visitors across geographic areas. A Chinese website company, for example, released a report on the stampede of December 31, 2014 in Shanghai soon after the tragedy based on big data analysis (Yang, 2015). The speed with which this report was issued made public aware that big data has the potential to manage and even prevent such disasters, although some researchers doubt if a credible forecast of that event could have been made based solely on big data.

The realm of the big data research, however, remains fluid and developing, because its definition is closely related to emerging technologies, new abilities in data processing, and innovations in applications. There are no clear thresholds of the absolute volume for datasets for them to be called 'big' data. Some data are bigger than others, and some applications require bigger data than others.

Cyberspace (the Internet) has received more attention than tourist tracking data, and is often described as a metaphor of the real world. The real world counterparts of cyberspace appear in tourism, such as theme parks that are based on virtual worlds created through online gaming and other entertainment media. Conceptually, it might be possible to think of all of tourism as a cyberworld metaphor from a modeling perspective. Software that simulates hotel and airline operations are examples of narrow applications of this type. Moreover, Liu et al. (2015) proposed the term 'social sensing' to describe the ways that big data is collected from various channels, from social media to satellite imagery, to monitor human social behavior.

The concept of big data is based largely on the internet technology, and e-commerce embodies the internet from a business perspective. Anderson (2006) proposed the concept of 'long-tail' e-commerce for customized niche marketing, which has also been applied to the tourism economy (Lew, 2008; Pan & Li, 2011). Using big data approaches, e-commerce can create large markets for niche products. According to the most popular legend, in 2009, students on the campus of Nanjing University in China complained about their single status by proclaiming the 'Singles Day' on 11.11 (Nov. 11th). This was picked up by the Ali-Baba company (China's leading online marketplace company), which turned the Singles Day into a shopping event. On November 11, 2017 the event generated total sales of 168,200 million RMB Yuan (about US$25.300 billion) for Ali-Baba, up from the 52 million RMB Yuan during the same day in 2009 (Xinhua net, 2017), i.e. sales multiply more than 3000 times after 8 years. Thus, a local tiny social event on a college campus was transferred into a global economic phenomenon, reaching consumers in over 200 countries and regions, through big data (in a broad sense) techniques and culture. Meanwhile, the event has also become a social-economic carnival show with live broadcasting by three satellite TV channels and many online broadcast websites, with live showings of peak moments of online sales, such as: 11 second to reached 100 million RMB Yuan, 3 minute reached 10 billion, 40 minute 50 billion, 9 hours reached 100 billion, and 24 hours to reach 168.2 billion (Sina Tech, 2017).

Characteristics commonly associated with big data, as noted above, include volume, variety, and velocity (Kitchin, 2013). Yet are other important features include value (with more valuable finer grain data), vertigo (data redundancy and nonstructural data with uncertainty), and volunteered (social media adding more information). All these big data 'V' characteristics are configuring a new map for tourism research (Table 1).

It is necessary to understand the mechanism and the types of big data for tourism geographic research, to dig or filter the tourism geographic information with big data, and even to create new categories of big data for various tourism geographies. The large

Table 1. Big data related tourism geographic research.

Type of research	Role of big data	Result of big data in research	Big data categories
Big data aided research	Data of traditional tourism conceptual models of analysis: big data with volume, variety, velocity, value, vertigo and volunteer	Expansion of traditional tourism research with more volume and variety of data	Data capturing and mining, filtering, storage, data cloud, analysis, search, sharing, transfer, visualization, querying, updating, social emotion, system robustness, information security, privacy and data source, big data platform for business operation
Big data aimed research	Special method for/of big data, big data itself as object, more sophisticate data system, post big data tech, A.I.	New methods, data mining and capturing, data filter, paradigm shift, system robustness,	
Big data arised phenomena research	New tourism phenomenon arised / driven by big data, e.g., new consumer behavior, new model of tourist decision making	To understand and predict new phenomena arised by big data, etc.	
Big data application research	New model of tourism operation, new tourism spatial model of organization economic value creation	New services and operation of tourism, Longtail market, B2C trade platform, etc.	

variety of research topics and fields related to big data in tourism geography emerges as follows:

1. Identification and description of big data phenomena: to find the critical influence of big data in tourism geographical research and to avoid the abuse and misuse of big data; big data-related socio-cultural phenomena, including how and to what extent big data changes socio-economic organizations related to tourism, and how traditional geographic topics and theories might shift with big data perspectives. For example, in China, there are increasing numbers of local command centers with huge display screens that offer live monitoring of tourist sites, which can also be accessed by cellphone by site administrators. In the Chinese cultural and institutional context, local administrators tend to use this form of big data in tourism management as a way of building reputation in their technological prowess, rather than as any real analytic and management practice tool.
2. Big data and allied technological services in tourism operations, marketplace and marketing: characteristics of mobile online services using big data, for example, accommodations, travel agents and transportation; implications of cellphone position tracing data; long tail and other theories to understand the big data tourism economy; big data supported visitor management and congestion monitoring; and new advertising strategies and techniques using big data mining and filtering for tourism.
3. Big data quality and ownership: The open-source and elicit mathematic descriptions of some popular big data indices issued by commercial companies are still lacking, raising issues as to whether a technical big data 'black box' will cause credibility problems; possible big data monopolies could be problematic for both researchers and industrial uses.
4. Social and technical accessibility to big data knowledge and applications: the technical knowledge gap between potential users and big data suppliers is increasing as new and more complex products are offered; attitudes, perceptions and abilities may vary

among different sectors of tourists and tourism providers toward big data and related info-tech service providers; large portion of the general public face user constraints to big data application, including infrastructure limitations, technical abilities, and psychological barriers. On the other hand, mobile online APPs (such as WeChat and Twitter) are also more accessible for larger numbers of users, and have become new resources or platforms for tourism operation.

Big data and tourism geography methodological and paradigm issues

Methodologically, big data techniques can help promote a more integrated approach to tourism management that encompasses a greater diversity of tourism sector activities, as well as its broader social and economic interconnections. Big data will expand and improve tourism research and by bringing new research topics and methodologies. These include:

1. Big data both as a technical tool to describe the tourism system and tourist flows with new sources of data, data support, and as tools for monitoring and research emerge. Big data mining through social media sensing, for example, has already been widely applied (Satta, Parola, Penco, & Persico, 2015). Big data often possess characteristics of nonstructured data, rather than traditionally structured data, which raises issues that have yet to be worked out.
2. The live (or near live) availability of some big data sources will require new mathematical models of tourism systems to match the fast data updates and feedbacks. Big data allows sophisticated description, such as tourists gathering in limited microspaces, the temporal pattern of visitor flows, and the possible application of short-term forecasting with trend extension hypotheses of various time series scales.
3. New measuring models and indices will be needed for emerging tourism statistics. Beyond simple trend extensions, the 'why and how' questions of tourism geography will become increasingly important for long-term forecasting with big data. Geographic understandings of spatial organization, spatial behavior and place theory can provide basic building blocks for the research, for example, on tourist crowding and congestion.

Big data might face a statistical paradox, since the basic of traditional statistics is to find the character of 'big' data object with small data sampling. The big size of a dataset is not necessarily the advantage of big data. Instead, the widening range of data types and channels for data collection may be its greatest advantage comparing to traditional statistics. In this sense, big data is not only a quantitative promotion, but also offers a qualitative shift (Barnes, 2013). In tourism research, big data techniques provide new and diverse data sources and channels, many of which may inform qualitative aspects of tourism. Social sensing (Liu et al. (2015), in particular, along with other big data techniques provide both quantitative and qualitative big data for tourism research, which might lead to changes in the basic view of the tourism system.

Ontologically, big data brings new tourism geographic phenomena, that is, the big data arised phenomena like newly operation tourism system based on big data. Moreover, big data largely changes human knowledge both in terms of our perception (and cognition) of the world, and in how we organize knowledge itself. Hence, big data becomes a paradigm issue. For example, big data now involves the daily life of the general public. Cellphone-based map applications are changing the human mental maps, spatial behavior and the model of people know and exist in the world. The basic function of mental maps for guiding might not be needed when people have and ever-present big data supported cellphone guidance system. Searching a map-related application, which utilizes big data and AI techniques, matches the user's need more efficiently, while at the same time creating knowledge restrictions. Such restrictions may be intentional user-created filters or filters applied by the app creator or app advertisers. Either way, the user is presented with a more narrowly spectrum of knowledge. The concept and cognition of space and place are different and changed by the context of big data, in comparison to direct (nondigitally mediated) bodily experiences.

Epistemologically, this new mode of understanding human behavior in a tourism world stretches traditional research assumptions in which description is a first step, followed by mechanism of causal relationships. However, under big data, the world is dominated by connective relationships, rather than causal relationships. This creates an image (or illusion?) that people who have big data can do anything in tourism research without relying on underlying structured principles or mechanisms. And just like a constructed descriptive model of gravity can be created by physicists for the precise quantitative relationship without understanding gravity's explicit mechanics, tourism geographers might only need to set up a connective relational model of the tourism system from the big data, and even build a framework of the tourism system from bottom up through big data and without references to traditional theoretical models. Such phenomenon goes beyond the traditional science paradigm that is emphasized in tourism and geographic research.

Concluding remarks

Table 1 suggests four 'A' types of big data research approaches in tourism: aided, aimed, arised, and application. New paradigm of big data research seems to be emerging, and tourism research is gradually shifting in response, from models consisting of phenomenon-mechanism-reality to those that consist of phenomenon-relationship-practical monitoring. Whether such a paradigm would be sophisticated, stable, and explicit, remains to be studied. Yet such a shift still needs to fulfill the basic component of a paradigm, i.e. the assumption and hypothesis of the view of the world (tourism system) and a related epistemology (theory and methodology). Whether the big data paradigm is confined to a narrowly technical context, somewhat like the chaos theory paradigm in the social sciences, or becomes a revolutionary and all pervasive approaches for tourism geographies, it will attract the interests of tourism geographers for at least the near future.

References

Barnes, T. J. (2013). Big data, little history. *Dialogues in Human Geography*, *3*(3), 297–302
Huang, X., Zhang, L., & Ding, Y. (2013). Study on the predictive and relationship between tourist attractions and the Baidu Index: A case study of the forbidden city. *Tourism Tribune*, *28*(11), 93–100 (in Chinese)
Kitchin, R. (2013). Big data and human geography: Opportunities, challenges and risks. *Dialogues in Human Geography*, *3*(3), 262–267.
Li, L., & Zhang, J. (2013). Impact of network information evaluation on tourists' information-related behavior and travel decisions. *Tourism Tribune*, *28*(10), 23–29 (in Chinese)
Lew, A. A. (2008). Long tail tourism: New geographies for marketing niche tourism products. *Journal of Travel & Tourism Marketing*, *25*(3-4), 409–419.
Liu, Y., Liu, X., Gao, S., Gong, L., Kang, C., Zhi, Y., & Shi, L. (2015). Social sensing: A new approach to understanding our socioeconomic environments. *Annals of the Association of American Geographers*, *105*(3), 512–530.
Miller, H. J., & Goodchild, M. F. (2015). Data-driven geography. *GeoJournal*, *80*(4), 449–461.

Pan, B., & Li, X. R. (2011). The long tail of destination image and online marketing. *Annals of Tourism Research*, *38*(1), 132–152.

Satta, G., Parola, F., Penco, L., & Persico, L. (2015). Word of mouth and satisfaction in cruise port destinations. *Tourism Geographies*, *17*(1), 54–75.

Sina Tech. (2017, Nov. 12). Online business volume of Tianmao online marketplace of Ali-Baba reach 168, 200 million Yuan during Single's Day with 1480 million item of business by Alipay. Retrieved from http://tech.sina.com.cn/i/2017-11-12/doc-ifynshev5376614.shtml (in Chinese)

Sun, Y., Zhang, H.L., Liu, P.X., & Zhang, J. (2017). Forecasting tourist flow to tourist attraction based on online attention index – a case study of Baidu index of online service. *Human Geography*, *32*(3), 152–160. (in Chinese)

Xinhua net. (2017, Nov. 12). Volume of business on Ali-baba website breaking 1600, 000 million Yuan during the Single's Day. Retrieved from http://www.xinhuanet.com/2017-11/12/c_1121941917.htm (in Chinese).

Yang, J. (2015, Jan. 27). Behind the stamped accident- big data analysis by Baidu Big data Lab. Retrieved from: http://www.shdrc.gov.cn/fzgggz/sswgg/xwbd/shghwxbs/24762.htm (in Chinese)

The impact of distance on tourism: a tourism geography law

Bob McKercher

In 1970, Waldo Tobler established the first law of geography when he wrote "everything is related to everything else, but near things are more related than distant things" (Tobler, 1970, p. 236). This law entrenched the concept of distance decay into the popular geography lexicon. Basically, distance decay theory demonstrates how demand or volume declines exponentially as distance from a source increases. Its validity has been demonstrated in a variety of contexts, with Greer and Wall (1979) being the first geographers to apply it to recreational tourism. Distance decay has been one of the foci of my research for 20 years.

Distance has a profound, though often underappreciated impact on all aspects of tourism, extending well beyond the volume of tourist movements. It also reflects changes in the types of tourist who are most likely to visit a destination and their subsequent behaviour. This brief will explain how it applies to tourism.

Waters (2017) indicates laws must satisfy three criteria. They must be universal, necessary and synthetic. Universality means it applies to all members of the class. Necessity indicates that the relationship is guided by some underlying principle(s) and is more than just accidental, while the synthetic component joins to concepts. Synthesis in this context elates to consumer behaviour, physical and human geography.

Compliance with the universality concept was verified by a study examining available 1915 origin–destination pairs from 41 outbound markets and 146 destinations (McKercher, Chan, & Lam, 2008). Data were derived from official UN World Tourism Organization figures, and accounted for 77.3% of global tourism when the study was conducted. Distance decay patterns were observed from all outbound countries studied, although the shapes of individual curves were modified by a range of geo-political factors. More strikingly land neighbours account for 57% of all arrivals, while, collectively, destinations within 1000 km of a source market's border attracted 80% of all arrivals, as shown in Figure 1. Global tourism demand declined sharply thereafter, with cumulative shares stabilizing at between two and three percent of departures, with the exception of a small blip between 5000 and 6000 km away. The study determined absolute aggregate demand fell by about 50% with each 1000 km of added distance from the source market.

Compliance with the necessary condition was inferred when a similar pattern was noted in intra-destination movements, or movements within a destination (Shoval, McKercher, Ng, & Birenboim, 2011), suggesting some underlying universal forces must be at work. This study used hotels as the 'home' point and analyzed the proportion of a tourist's total daily time budget by distance from the hotel. Again, most time was spent in the vicinity of the hotel, with the amount of time spent at any one place decreasing exponentially with distance.

But that is not the whole story. In theory, the decaying curve results from both a reduction in demand and a concomitant uniform increase in supply as distance changes (Greer

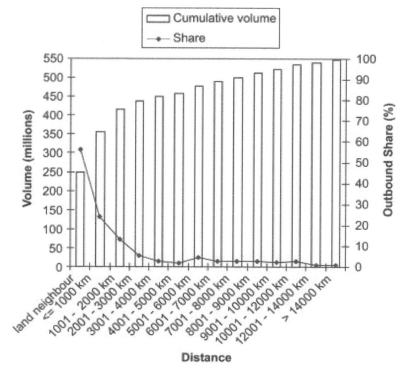

Figure 1. Distance decay in international tourism. Source: McKercher et al. (2008).

& Wall, 1979). Of course, in reality, a range of factors ensure that mean that the global supply of tourism products and access to them is not uniform, leading to the creation of Effective Tourism Exclusion Zones (ETEZ) (see Figure 2) where little or no tourism activity occurs, or where the activity that does occur is of little interest to the source market (McKercher & Lew, 2003). The ETEZ is created by physical geography obstacles, such as oceans and mountain ranges; political geography factors including strained relations between countries that result extreme access limitations; lack of suitable infrastructure and superstructure; or the provision of products that not appeal to the source market.

The impact of the ETEZ on outbound travel demand from Hong Kong was tested (McKercher & Lew, 2003). Substantial differences in travel patterns and tourist behaviour were observed at destinations located before the inner boundary of the ETEZ was reached and after the outer boundary of the ETEZ was crossed. This observation also led to the conclusions that the ETEZ represented the perceptual boundary defining short-haul and long-haul travel. Trips taken before encountering the ETEZ tended to be of shorter duration, often involved repeat travel, usually involved a single destination, had a high proportion of package tour participation and were taken largely for recreation, togetherness and escapism reasons. By contrast, trips after the outer threshold of the ETEZ was passed tended to be longer in duration, involved a multi-destination touring component, were often one-off visits and were aspirational in nature, being motived by a desire to learn and experience different cultures.

The study also suggested the location of the inner boundary in relation to the source market and the width of the ETEZ also distorted the traditional distance decay curve.

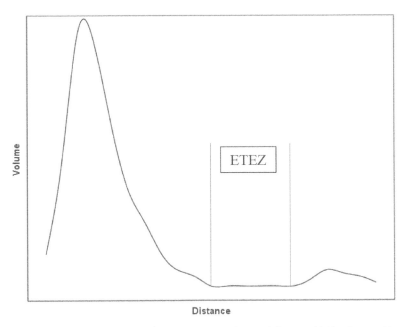

Figure 2. Impact of effective tourism exclusion zones on demand. Source: McKercher and Lew (2003).

Demand was concentrated more strongly in nearby destinations when the ETEZ was located close to a source market, and depending on its width, little travel occurred beyond the outer edge. Alternately, if the size of the ETEZ was small, a fairly large secondary demand peak was observed beyond the outer edge. Little impact is noted when the ETEZ was either narrow or located at a greater distance from a source market.

Moreover, a relationship has been observed between distance and the type of market segments likely to be attracted to the destination, along with subsequent behaviour of markets at a destination. This idea is predicated on the assumption of segment transformation as shown in Figure 3 (McKercher, 2008). Essentially, anyone who can travel can travel short distances, but not everyone can travel long distances. Distance, therefore, may effectively filter out some segments, due to higher time, emotional and financial costs associated with age, travel party size and composition, disposable income, time availability, motives and willingness or ability to enter culturally different destinations. In particular, the Young Office Lady and Young Office Men segments who have limited time availability, families with high transport costs considerations, and those people who are motivated to travel primarily for leisure, relaxation and escape are much more likely to travel short distances. By contrast, older, better educated, higher income earning individuals with long periods of time availability, or younger backpackers with no time constraints are more likely to be found in disproportionate shares amongst long-haul tourists.

The net result is that the short-haul market tends to be more homogenous, while the long-haul tends to be more exclusive. These differences translate into substantial differences in the profile, travel patterns and in destination behaviour (McKercher, 2009). For example, the short-haul market is likely to be younger and composed of a disproportionately larger cohort of women than long-haul tourists. Short-haul tourists are likely to be travelling with friends and children, while the long-haul tourists are more likely to be travelling alone

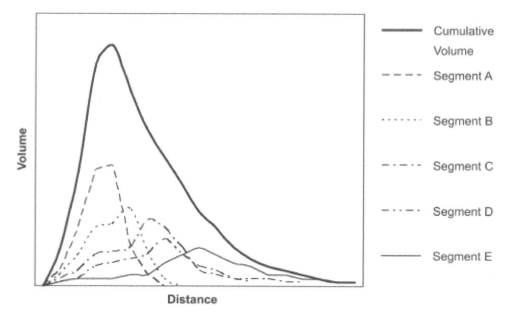

Figure 3. Segment transformation with distance. Source: McKercher (2008).

or with spouses/partners. Importantly, short-haul tourists are far more likely to engage in hedonistic activities such as visiting theme parks, shopping and dining, while the long-haul tourist is much more likely to engage in activities that enable the exploration of a destination's cultural heritage. Interestingly, no significant differences were noted in per capita expenditure, substantial differences emerge in where expenses are incurred, with long-haul tourists spending proportionately more on hotels, dining and purchasing of day tours, while short-haul tourist spent proportionately far more money shopping.

Finally, the synthetic conditions required for the validation of a law represents one of the reasons why distance decay continues to attract less interest from the research community than it deserves. The impact of distance on demand is not a deterministic construct in its own right. No one wakes up and says "I need a holiday but I can only travel 153 km and no further." Instead, distance represents a proxy variable that embodies a range of physical and human geographic conditions and also takes into consideration many consumer behaviour variables.

References

Greer, T., & Wall, G. (1979). Recreational hinterlands: A theoretical and empirical analysis. In Wall (Ed.), *Recreational land use in Southern Ontario, Dept. of Geography Publication Series # 14* (pp. 227–246). Waterloo: Waterloo University.

McKercher, B. (2008). Segment transformation in urban tourism. *Tourism Management, 29*, 1215–1225.

McKercher, B. (2009). The implicit effect of distance on tourist behaviour. *Journal of Travel and Tourism Marketing, 25*(3/4), 367–381.

McKercher, B., Chan, A., & Lam, C. (2008). The impact of distance on international tourist movements. *Journal of Travel Research, 47*(2), 208–224.

McKercher, B., & Lew, A. (2003). Distance decay and the impact of effective tourism exclusion zones on in international travel flows. *Journal of Travel Research*, *42*(2), 159–165.

Shoval, N., McKercher, B., Ng, E., & Birenboim, A. (2011). Hotel location and tourist spatial activity in cities. *Annals of Tourism Research, 38*(4), 1594–1612.

Tobler, W. R. (1970). A computer movie simulating urban growth in the Detroit region. *Economic Geography*, *46*, 234–240.

Waters, N. (2017). Tobler's first law of geography. *The International Encyclopedia of Geography*. Hoboken, NJ: Wiley.

Sensing tourists: geoinformatics and the future of tourism geography research

Noam Shoval

In the last decade, we have witnessed unprecedented advances in the collection and utilization of high-resolution data on tourist mobility. This is a result of a variety of technological developments as well as the widespread availability of tracking technologies such as GPS, mobile positioning, geocoded social media messages, and Bluetooth (Shoval, Kwan, Reinau, & Harder, 2014). Most recently, researchers have also benefitted greatly from the development and widespread use of smartphones, which incorporate several tracking abilities, real-time surveying techniques, and ambulatory sensing have allowed researchers to advance the empirical investigation of the interaction between space and emotion (Birenboim & Shoval, 2015). In parallel, we are witness to growing possibilities for analyzing the huge space-time databases created by these tracking technologies. This is due to the continuous development of geographical information science/systems in particular and to the advances in our computing abilities more generally (Richardson et al., 2013). The opportunities to collect and analyze high-resolution space-time data that cover long periods of time opens up enormous possibilities for initiating new lines of tourism research and formulating new research questions that could not be answered previously.

Digital tracking technologies represent a revolution in terms of the accuracy of time/spatial information regarding the whereabouts of tourists in destinations on different scales, from the tourist attraction to the regional, national, and even global scales (Hawelka et al., 2014). Researchers can collect real-time information about tourists' subjective and objective feelings (Kim & Fesenmaier, 2015; Shoval, Schwimer, & Tamir, 2016, 2017; Zakrisson & Zillinger, 2012); this is a new dimension in our ability to monitor tourists – not only in geographic space but also in emotional space – as they visit a destination. These advances in research are not just theoretical; tourist movement has profound implications for infrastructure and transport development, tourism product development, marketing strategies, the commercial viability of the tourism industry, and the management of the social, environmental, and cultural impacts of tourism. Thus, highly accurate and reliable information in real time represents a great leap forward for research – both applied and theoretical.

Modern smartphones began to appear on the market in the mid-2000s. The launch of the first-generation iPhone on 29 June 2007 and the widespread adoption of the Android operating system one year later signaled a new phase in the history of mobile phones and mobile computing. The implication of the rapid and widespread introduction of smartphones to the market has led to immense availability of information for users at any time and any place; this also has implications on tourists' ability to receive information while touring a destination and changes the paradigm about tourists' knowledge of destinations (Tussyadiah & Zach, 2012). Due to the high roaming prices for phones when crossing international borders, however, the use of such data by tourists was relatively limited in the past. Recently, the use of local sim cards and attractive international roaming programs has made smartphones relevant for tourists in destinations.

Smartphones and other mobile devices, such as tablet computers, incorporate a set of embedded sensors that include various technologies: GPS, cell-tower identification and Wi-Fi positioning, proximity technologies such as Bluetooth and RFID, accelerometer, gyroscope, magnetometer (compass), light sensor, microphone, and camera. In addition, sensors such as the barometer, ambient thermometer, humidity sensor, and pedometer, available in some higher-end smartphones, might become the standard for many smartphones in the near future, furnishing them with even more sophisticated sensing abilities (Birenboim & Shoval, 2015).

There is a growing body of research regarding the implementation of tracking technologies in tourism studies. Naturally many of the early publications were occupied with presenting the feasibility of the different methods in a variety of contexts and with developing methods to analyze and visualize the data. A second generation of papers in this field used new data to discover or measure spatial and temporal phenomena of tourist movement. Some papers deal with research questions per se, using the new technologies and their advantages over traditional tools (Shoval & Ahas, 2016).

There can be no doubt that tracking technologies are giving us new avenues for the advancement of tourism research. Our growing ability to transfer and analyze data in real time augments our prospects for putting the data to practical use in destinations, on one hand; on the other, it makes it possible to gather tourist responses in real time, collecting valuable information about experiences and emotions at destinations. The potential use of sensors will also make it possible to understand objective feelings conveyed by tourists and not only subjective ones, as is the norm; we predict that smartphones that can connect to various external sensors will facilitate this line of inquiry in a very short period of time.

The rapid advances in tracking technologies and the growing possibilities in implementing them for use in different areas in general and in the realm of tourism research in particular leaves no doubt that the future of tracking technologies in tourism will be exciting and dynamic, providing researchers with invaluable insight and information.

References

Birenboim, A., & Shoval, N. (2015). Mobility research in the age of the smartphone. *Annals of the Association of American Geographers, 106*(2), 283–291.

Hawelka, B., Sitko, I., Beinat, E., Sobolevsky, S., Kazakopoulos, P., & Ratti, C. (2014). Geo-located Twitter as proxy for global mobility patterns. *Cartography and Geographic Information Science, 41*(3), 260–271.

Kim, J., & Fesenmaier, D. R. (2015). Measuring emotions in real time: Implications for tourism experience design. *Journal of Travel Research, 54*(4), 419–429.

Richardson, D. R., Volkow, N. D., Kwan, M.-P., Kaplan, R. M., Goodchild, M. F., & Croyle, R. T. (2013). Spatial turn in health research. *Science, 339*(6), 1390–1392.

Shoval, N., & Ahas, R. (2016). The use of tracking technologies in tourism research: The first decade. *Tourism Geographies, 18*(5), 587–606.

Shoval, N., Kwan, M-P., Reinau, K. H., & Harder, H. (2014). The shoemaker's son always goes barefoot: Implementations of GPS and other tracking technologies for geographic research. *Geoforum, 51*(1), 1–5.

Shoval, N., Schwimer, Y., & Tamir, M. (2016). Real-time measurement of tourists' objective and subjective emotions in time and space. *Journal of Travel Research*, 1, 3–16. doi:10.1177/0047287517691155

Shoval, N., Schwimer, Y., & Tamir, M. (2017). Tracking technologies and urban analysis: Adding the emotional dimension. *Cities, 72*(1), 23–42.

Tussyadiah, L. P., & Zach, F. J. (2012). The role of geo-based technology in place experiences. *Annals of Tourism Research, 39*, 780–800.

Zakrisson, I., & Zillinger, M. (2012). Emotions in motion: Tourist experiences in time and space. *Current Issues in Tourism, 15*(6), 505–523.

The more-than-visual experiences of tourism

Tim Edensor

John Urry's focus on the tourist gaze (1990) marks a definitive shift away from hitherto singular, functionalist and ethnocentric theories about what tourists do, understand and feel. His key suggestion is that contemporary tourists typically anticipate visual encounters with cultural and natural sites upon which they subsequently gaze. According to Urry, these visual practices epitomize historically distinctive way of seeing, and in contemporary times he averred, they are embedded within a particularly ocularcentric culture in which images proliferate.

In *The Tourist Gaze* (1990), the most prominent visual practice enacted is the romantic gaze, inspired by historical constructions of the picturesque and the sublime. The enaction of this often-solitary gaze has inspired the promiscuous photographing of scenes viewed at length during 'sightseeing' escapades. Urry claims that this highly normative, extensive tourist compilation of images relies on the consumption of similar images in promotional media before the trip has been undertaken, creating what he calls a 'hermeneutic circle', the endless recycling of similar images through which the representation of tourist sites becomes reified. This emphasis on visual consumption led Urry to identify other distinctive forms of the tourist gaze, including the 'collective', 'spectatorial', 'environmental' and 'anthropological' gazes. Other scholars have subsequently itemized the 'mutual', 'humanitarian' and 'social-mediatized gaze'; I have also identified the 'reverential gaze' and 'pharmacological gaze' (Edensor, 1998). In the updated, extensively revised *Tourist Gaze 3.0*. (2012), Urry and his co-author, Jonas Larsen, acknowledge that the gaze is entangled with olfactory, sonic and tactile oral experiences. However, there remains an insistence that the visual is the dominant organizing sense amongst tourists and that the visual apprehension of sites, landscapes and people is merely supplemented by other sensory experience.

Here, I argue that though the visual is indeed integral to many tourist pursuits, tourism should be more broadly considered as multi-sensual in practice and experience. In opposing the contention that the visual is invariably the predominant sense mobilised by tourists, I suggest that the gaze is frequently accompanied by Scarles (2009) and subjugated by sonic, tactile and olfactory sensations. Indeed, a brief review of diverse tourist practices immediately provokes awareness that there is a wealth of more-than-visual experiences. The beach holiday solicits a range of sensory experiences that include a powerful awareness of the sun's heat on skin, the tactile effects of waves upon the swimming body, the sonic impressions of the crashing rhythms of the sea and the squawk of seabirds, the scents of seaweed and suntan lotion, and the granular irritations of sand in the body's crevices (Obrador-Pons, 2007). And as well as gazing upon the surrounding scenery and the path being followed, the walking or climbing holiday involves periods of time in which aching feet and muscles, shortness of breath and pain eclipse visual experience as dominant sensations (Lund, 2005). These tourist sensations are supplemented by numerous others, and the range and diversity of sensory experiences currently being made available for tourists are expanding.

These proliferating sensations could constitute a response to the contemporary prevalence of regulatory strategies that seek to maintain smooth mobile flows of vehicles and bodies, declutter spaces and reproduce normative aesthetic order. Dissatisfaction with the sterile 'blandscapes' that eventuate from such procedures perhaps instigate the pursuit of unfamiliar kinetic, aromatic, sonic and visual sensations. Yet despite this urge, and although influential accounts characterise tourism as moving from the quotidian towards the extraordinary, authentic or liminal, many common tourist experiences are replete with routine, unreflexive habits performed in serial resorts, themed spaces and enclaves (Edensor, 2007). Such realms accord with highly managed spaces elsewhere in that they are sensually regulated to minimise disruption and provide a comfortable homeliness in which the body is cosseted into relaxation. Themed designs remove disturbing sights, the aromas of incense and aromatic blooms waft through space, harsh sounds are purged and replaced by piped muzak or trickling fountains, silken textures and air-conditioning enclose bodies, and smooth floors encourage seamless movement. Such locations satiate desires for reliability, comfort and unselfconscious relaxation, and encourage shared performative conventions of walking, lounging and consuming. While these spaces cater for the suspension of everyday stress and workaday routines, they instantiate a new set of habits, reiterations and predictabilities and promote the familiar, predictable, comfortable sensory environments that are characteristic of a particular form of serial upmarket tourist space.

However, in addition to these familiar, reliable sensory realms, numerous other tourist practices strive to escape highly ordered space, seeking out visceral, enlivening pursuits in which sensory apprehension is challenged or intensified. The quest for immersive sensation is evident in action sports such as bungee jumping and white water rafting, the white-knuckle thrills sought at amusement parks, and the somatically enlivening endeavours of hang-gliding, mountain biking and canoeing. In depicting an especially radical departure from ordinary sensation, Merchant (2011) reveals how scuba divers learn new sensory skills, notably in developing very different ways of touching and hearing, since the senses that they usually rely upon are unreliable when underwater. Though this may be initially alarming and awkward, such sensations may be thrilling in their alterity, as with other immersive experiences in spa tourism, dance tourism and urban exploration. Exemplifying the sheer multi-sensory entanglements of certain highly immersive tourist occasions, Saldanha (2002) describes a Goan beach rave in which the sounds of music, smells of sweat, kerosene and cannabis combine with the sight of the moon and swaying coconut trees, the tactilities of moving bodies, sand underfoot and humidity.

A more sustained immersion in sensual otherness is also exemplified by forms of space in which backpackers temporarily dwell. Movement through the sensually rich, socially diverse, cluttered materialities of such 'heterogeneous' honeypots solicits encounters with rough textures, undulating pavements and dust. Noises emitted by machines, people and animals, the horrible and delicious smells that emanate from a market, and the disruptive tactilities provoked by dense crowds and uneven surfaces also offer unaccustomed sensory experiences (Edensor, 2001). In seeking sensual otherness, tourists may welcome or recoil from these unfamiliar stimuli. For instance, at the start of their adventures through India and Thailand, many female backpackers embraced the experience of repellent smells, dirt and noise. In signifying an ability to cope with such sensations, these young travellers developed self-pride and acquired cultural capital. Yet over a longer period, they modulated overwhelming and harsh sensory experience with visits to comfortable hotels and air-conditioned restaurants that served familiar food (Edensor & Falconer, 2011).

This demonstrates how tourists typically manage desires for both sensory familiarity and alterity. The cultural conventions through which we interpret what we sense shift across the cosmological, moral, aesthetic and political, and vary enormously across time and space. Yet it is also vital to acknowledge that these interpretations of sensory experience are invariably entangled with the affordances of the world we encounter. As tourists, we tell stories about what we have encountered *after* an immanent, immersive sensory engagement with the world. Accordingly, although tourists seek out specific sensorial qualities, movement through even highly regulated realms cannot always preclude the surprising, the contingent and the unexpected. When such sensory intrusions they emerge, they may be frightening and disturbing, but equally, may be welcomed as memorable, and narrated after the event as momentous. In this way, our sensory phenomenological experiences are thoroughly intertwined with the meanings we attribute during our encounter with the currents and energies of a world-in-formation, with the affordances of the sites and spaces we gaze upon, move through, smell, hear and touch. Furthermore, we cannot escape from the ways in which our distinctively human sensory capacities apprehend how light falls upon the landscape, negotiates the surface of the ground, receive sound from many sources, and smell the scent of leaf mould or perfume. In tourism, as with all experience, sensation is thus biologically shaped, culturally conditioned and subject to more-than-human agencies all at the same time. It is also always more-than-visual.

Disclosure statement

No potential conflict of interest was reported by the author.

References

Edensor, T. (2001). Performing tourism, staging tourism: (Re)producing tourist space and practice. *Tourist Studies*, *1*, 59–82.
Edensor, T. (1998). *Tourists at the Taj*. London: Routledge.
Edensor, T. (2007). Mundane mobilities, performances and spaces of tourism. *Social and Cultural Geography*, *8*, 199–215.
Edensor, T., & Falconer, E. (2011). The sensuous geographies of tourism. In J. Wilson (Ed.), *New perspectives in tourism geographies*. London: Routledge.
Lund, K. (2005). Seeing in motion and the touching eye: Walking over Scotland's mountains. *Etnofoor*, *181*, 27–42.
Merchant, S. (2011). Negotiating underwater space: the sensorium, the body and the practice of scuba-diving. *Tourist Studies*, *11*, 215–234
Obrador-Pons, P. (2007). A haptic geography of the beach: Naked bodies, vision and touch. *Social and Cultural Geography*, *8*(1), 123–141
Saldanha, A. (2002). Music tourism and factions of bodies in Goa. *Tourist Studies*, *2*(1), 43–62.
Scarles, C. (2009). Becoming tourist: Renegotiating the visual in the tourist experience. *Environment and Planning D: Society and Space*, *27*, 465–488
Urry, J., & Larsen, J. (2012). *The Tourist Gaze 3.0*. London: Sage.
Urry, J. (1990). *The Tourist Gaze*. London: Sage.

The end of tourism? A Gibson-Graham inspired reflection on the tourism economy

Patrick Brouder

Tourism continues to grow, with international arrivals now over one billion annually (UNWTO, 2012). Cities, towns, rural and peripheral communities all experience tourism to a greater or lesser extent. The tourism economy is important to many communities but remains a contested realm. Tourism development is not a unilinear process and the complex interactions between stakeholders require careful unpacking. In this article, I draw on feminist economic geographies and evolutionary economic geographies in order to open discursive space for rethinking tourism development. The renowned work of J.K. Gibson-Graham (feminist economic geographies) offers an alternate perspective through which tourism development may be explored. I present a brief reflection on their work to encourage further discussion of community economic development research within studies on the economic geography of tourism. Some epistemological reflection is always needed in order to keep tourism research meaningful to the communities whose space is occupied by it. To better plan for tourism development a more holistic, inclusive understanding of stakeholder agency and stakeholder dissonance is required even if this leads us to 'the end of tourism'.

In this short reflection I discuss the main topics simplistically (admittedly!) and ask the reader to bear with me as this article is not intended as a review piece but rather as a preview of where I believe research on the tourism economy is most likely to gravitate towards in the years ahead. Here, I simply make the connections from the key works on the political economy of tourism (Mosedale, 2010, 2012) and the economic geography of tourism (Brouder, Anton Clavé, Gill, & Ioannides, 2017; Debbage & Ioannides, 2004) to Gibson-Graham's thesis on the epistemology of capitalism.

In their influential book *The end of capitalism (as we knew it): a feminist critique of political economy*, Gibson-Graham set out a clear critique of the traditional Marxian view of capitalism: it is a behemoth, expansive and self-reproducing, and capable of conferring identity and meaning on all it consumes (Gibson-Graham, 1997); the critique being that its image as an invincible force has limited Marxian attempts to overcome it. Their book deconstructs the epistemology of traditional political economy thought in order to liberate spaces of economic difference and allow them to flourish. While some tourism scholars have made inroads by listening to the previously unheard voices in tourism development in order to critique the power relations at play (Reed, 1997), it is also true that the dominant discourse in tourism development has been one in which the inevitability of both tourism and capitalism is assured, for better or worse!

The burgeoning tourism opportunities of recent decades have led to tourism becoming a near ubiquitous element of regional development discourse in a great many places. Government planning documents speak of bed nights and increased tax receipts and tourism promotion documents are near carbon copies of each other while each extols the uniqueness of its own particular region! Much of this has taken place in a 'boosterist' discourse focussing on the joys of growth rather than the pangs of growing (Marcouiller, 2007) and many tourism entrepreneurs who have fallen outside the boosterist line of thinking have found themselves ostracised from decision-making processes, alienated from local networks, and often overlooked by tourism researchers who focus on the centrally-networked stakeholders. This has created a challenge for communities, planners, and researchers, many of whom have found their voice in promoting competing development discourses (Saarinen, 2004) and, ultimately, by developing alternative tourism paths (Brouder & Fullerton, 2015).

I will not belabour (at risk of overdrawing) the parallel between pervasive capitalism and growth-centric tourism but suffice it to say that tourism research today is replete with examples in the spirit of Gibson-Graham (e.g. community-based tourism, etc.) while less research has attempted to bridge the gap between traditional economic approaches to tourism studies and more epistemologically-peripheral approaches to tourism economics (Brouder, 2014a, 2014b; Ioannides, 2006; Mosedale, 2012). While Gibson-Graham's concern that 'economic evolution has become a story of the progressive emergence of ever more efficient, more competitive, and therefore dominant forms of capitalist enterprise, technology, and economic organization' (Gibson-Graham, 1997, p. 115) was accurate at the time of writing, it is not representative of where economic geography is today (Barnes & Sheppard, 2010). Even though evolutionary economic geography, for example, is still burdened by its neo-Schumpeterian (high-growth sector focus) heritage, this has been challenged conceptually (cf. Essletzbichler, 2012; MacKinnon, Cumbers, Pike, Birch, & McMaster, 2009) and even empirically in tourism (Brouder & Eriksson, 2013a, Larsson & Lindström, 2014; Randelli, Romei, & Tortora, 2014). Alternative (tourism and non-tourism) development paths brought forth through community dissonance can be a creative, positive force for community development and need not be subsumed by a boosterist doctrine of economic development in places experiencing increasing tourism opportunities. Basically, there are economic movements that may go unnoticed because of their subtlety or difficulty in measuring them or because they are not growing rapidly. However, there is limited integrated conceptualisation of this in tourism economic studies while case studies of successful dissonance abound. Feminist economic geographies could open this space and therefore lead to new avenues of research of what 'had until now been relatively "invisible" because the concepts and discourses that could make them 'visible' have themselves been marginalised and suppressed' (Gibson-Graham, 1997, p. xi). The challenge which remains is a question of pluralism—how will these new avenues fit with community-based cases and conceptual studies of tourism evolution (Brouder & Eriksson, 2013b; Sanz-Ibáñez & Anton Clavéé, 2014)?

Gibson-Graham asked us to rethink capitalism to achieve its 'death by a thousand cuts' (Gibson-Graham, 1997) and we must ask ourselves, is this what we want for tourism too? I will not conclude by answering that question but by simply noting that a fresh conceptual approach combining (as well as contesting) feminist economic geographies and evolutionary economic geographies will further open the space for alternative perspectives on tourism development.

Acknowledgement

This reflection is based on a conference presentation (with Suzanne de la Barre) at the Canadian Association of Geographers Annual Meeting in Vancouver, Canada (June, 2015) and a number of research discussions with Suzanne de la Barre and Kajsa G. Åberg.

References

Barnes, T. J., & Sheppard, E. (2010). 'Nothing includes everything': Towards engaged pluralism in Anglophone economic geography. *Progress in Human Geography, 34,* 193–214.
Brouder, P. (2014a). Evolutionary economic geography: A new path for tourism studies? *Tourism Geographies,* 16, 2–7.

Brouder, P. (2014b). Evolutionary economic geography and tourism studies: Extant studies and future research directions. *Tourism Geographies*, 16, 540–545.

Brouder, P., Anton Clavé, S., Gill, A., & Ioannides, D. (2017). *Tourism destination evolution*. Milton Park: Routledge.

Brouder, P., & Eriksson, R. H. (2013a). Staying power: What influences micro-firm survival in tourism? *Tourism Geographies*, 15, 125–144.

Brouder, P., & Eriksson, R. H. (2013b). Tourism evolution: On the synergies of tourism studies and evolutionary economic geography. *Annals of Tourism Research*, 43, 370–389.

Brouder, P., & Fullerton, C. (2015). Exploring heterogeneous tourism development paths: Cascade effect or co-evolution in Niagara? *Scandinavian Journal of Hospitality and Tourism*, 15, 152–166.

Debbage, K. G., & Ioannides, D. (2004). The cultural turn? Toward a more critical economic geography of tourism. In A. Lew, C. M. Hall, & A. Williams (Eds), *A companion to tourism* (pp. 99–109). Oxford: Wiley-Blackwell.

Essletzbichler, J. (2012). Generalized Darwinism, group selection and evolutionary economic geography. *Zeitschrift für Wirtschaftsgeographie*, 56, 129–146.

Gibson-Graham, J. K. (1997). *The end of capitalism (as we knew it): A feminist critique of political economy*. Oxford: Wiley-Blackwell.

Ioannides, D. (2006). Commentary: The economic geography of the tourist industry: Ten years of progress in research and an agenda for the future. *Tourism Geographies*, 8, 76–86.

Larsson, A., & Lindström, K. N. (2014). Bridging the knowledge-gap between the old and the new: Regional marine experience production in Orust, Västra Götaland, Sweden. *European Planning Studies*, 22, 1551–1568.

MacKinnon, D., Cumbers, A., Pike, A., Birch, K., & McMaster, R. (2009). Evolution in economic geography: Institutions, political economy, and adaptation. *Economic Geography*, 85, 129–150.

Marcouiller, D. (2007). "Boosting" tourism as rural public policy: Panacea or Pandora's box? *The Journal of Regional Analysis & Policy*, 37, 28–31.

Mosedale, J. (2012). Diverse economies and alternative economic practices in tourism. In N. Morgan, I. Ateljevic, & A. Pritchard (Eds), *The critical turn in tourism studies: Creating an academy of hope* (pp. 194–207). London: Routledge.

Mosedale, J. (Ed.). (2010). *Political economy and tourism: A critical perspective*. New York: Routledge.

Randelli, F., Romei, P., & Tortora, M. (2014). An evolutionary approach to the study of rural tourism: The case of Tuscany. *Land Use Policy*, 38, 276–281.

Reed, M. G. (1997). Power relations and community-based tourism planning. *Annals of Tourism Research*, 24, 566–591.

Saarinen, J. (2004). Destinations in change: The transformation process of tourist destinations. *Tourist Studies*, 4, 161–179.

Sanz-Ibáñez, C., & Anton Clavé, S. (2014). The evolution of destinations: Towards an evolutionary and relational economic geography approach. *Tourism Geographies*, 16, 563–579.

UNWTO. (2012). International tourism hits one billion. UNWTO Press Release 12076.

Index

accommodation 55, 61, 75, 133
Adamiak, C. 7
alternative food providers 95, 105–108
Anderson, C. 95, 132
Asero, V. 46
Ateljevic, I. 4
Aubert-Gameta, V. 19
Aviation Environmental Design Tool 83

Balmford, A. 71
Bauder, M. 71–72
beaches 8, 15–16, 121
Beckley, L. E. 45
Beeco, J. A. 66, 74–75, 80, 83
Bennett, A. 114
Berg, N. G. 18
betweenness centrality 50, 54
big data 84, 131–135; techniques 131, 134
Birenboim, A. 25, 32
Borgers, A. 25
Braunisch, V. 76
Bricker, K. S. 115
Broadway, M. J. 95
Brown, G. 66, 74, 78, 83
Brownlee, M. 80

capitalism 148–149
Chalip, L. 92, 99
Chamberlain, M. J. 79
Chinese tourist flows 42–43, 47–49, 52, 59–60; network 54, 60
Chmielewski, J. M. 6
Choi, J-M. 5
Chris, R. 44
Chua, A. 72
Chung, N. 25
Chung, S. H. 25
closeness centrality 50, 54
Cohen, B. S. 79
community-based tourism (CBT) 3, 5, 19
community social functions 4
consumers 91, 96, 100–102, 104–106, 108, 132
Cook, I. 102
Coppes, J. 76

Covab, B. 19
Crompton, J. L. 44
Crouch, D. 114
cycling 117–119, 122–124

D'Antonio, A. 69, 74, 78
data collection 47, 134
Davolio, F. 105
decision-maker 25–26, 28–30, 32, 35
degree centrality 50, 54, 56
Deleuze, G. 103, 106
Derek, M. 4
destinations 4–6, 24, 26, 38, 43–48, 50, 52, 54–61, 72, 75–76, 92, 95, 106, 137–140, 142–143
Diaz-Soria, I. 126
Doxey, G. V. 4
drink festivals 91, 96
Duignan, M. B. 95, 105

#EATCambridge 90, 100–102, 104, 107–108
economic geographies 148–149
Effective Tourism Exclusion Zones (ETEZ) 138–139
egress destination 55
euphoria 4
Event Leverage Model (ELM) 92
event spaces 117–118, 122–123, 125
event visitor economy 92–93

Fesenmaier, D. R. 24, 44
festival spaces 94
festival tourism 93
first time visitors 75
FIT network 49, 56–58, 60–61
Flogenfeldt, T. 44
food festivals 93, 95, 97, 100
foreign visitors 43
free time 27–28
Freitag, T. G. 5
Fristrup, K. M. 83

Gardiner, M. 114
gateway destinations 53–55

Gehl, J. 6
geographic information system (GIS) 32, 46
Gerritsen, R. 94
Gibson-Graham, J.K. 148–149
Girouz 106
global cultural currency 115
Gozzo, S. 46
GPS data loggers 68–71, 73, 78
GPS tracking 73–74, 77, 79
GPT network 56–58, 60
Graburn, N. H. H. 117, 126
Greer, T. 137
Gross, J. T. 79
Group Package Tourists (GPTs) 47–48, 52–53, 56–57, 60
growth, negative effects of 16
Gu, H. 44
Guattari, F. 103, 106
Gunn, C. A. 44

Hägerstrand, T. 66
Haartsen, T. 125
Hallo, J. C. 75
Halseth, G. 7
Harrison, M. 102
Havlíček, Z. 94
Heffernan, E. 6, 19
Heffernan, T. 6
Hockey, J. 123
horseback riders 69, 75–76, 80
host communities 5, 113–115, 117, 126
Hwang, Y. 46

Ilbery, B. 96
innovative application 69
Isaacson, M. 24

Japan 42–44, 47–48, 52–55, 58–60
Jeuring, J. H. G. 125
Job, H. 76
Jung, T. 25

Kastenholz, E. 5, 18
Keller, R. 80
Kemperman, A. 25
Kerstetter, D. L. 115
Kidd, A. M. 74, 77
Kim, M. 100
Kim, Y-G. 5
Kim, Y. H. 100
Kong, Q. Q. 4
Korpilo, S. 73
Kowalczyk, A. 4
Krukowska, R. 8

Lai, B. H. 25
Lamont, M. 121

Lau, G. 44–45
Law, R. 45
Lehvävirta, S. 73
leisure 27–28, 114–115, 139
Leue, M.C. 25
Leung, X. Y. 45
leverageable resource 92–93, 99, 103
Lew, A. 43–45
Li, G. 45
lifestyles 114–115, 122, 125
Lim, M. 103
liminality 93–94, 104, 117
liminoid positionality 104
liminoid spaces 90, 93, 102, 104, 107–108
line density 70
Liu, B. 46
Liu, F. 46
Liu, Y. 132
Lohr, V. 94
London 91
long-haul tourists 139–140
Lue, C. 44

MacCannell, D. 6
major sports events 112, 115–117, 120, 126–127
Marchand, P. 79
Marcheggiani, E. 72
Maye, D. 96
McHugh, K. E. 44
McKay, J. 121
Mckercher, B. 43–45
Mennitt, D. J. 83
Merchant, S. 146
Miller, A. D. 79
Milne, S. 4
Mings, R. C. 44
mobile phones 72, 142
model formulation 27
Moere, A. V. 72
Montgomery, J. 6
Monz, C. 69, 74, 78
Moore, S. A. 45
multi-objective programming 23

National Audit Office 91, 98
network analysis 45–46, 49, 53, 67
network centralization 50
network patterns 43, 56, 60
network structure 46, 49, 56–57, 59
Newman, P. 74
Newton, J. N. 74
nodes structure 49, 53, 57

O'Leary, J. T. 24
Olson, L. E. 79
Oppermann, M. 44

Oppewal, H. 25
Osaka–Kyoto 52
Overvåg, K. 18

Pan, W. 6
Pappalepore, I. 95
parks and protected areas (PPAs) 66–73, 76, 78–79, 81–82, 84–85
Pearce, D. G. 44
Pechrová, M. 94, 95
physical proximity 113–114, 117, 120–123, 125
Picard, D. 93
Pielichaty, H. 94
Pitkanen, K. 7
place attachment 113–115, 117, 126
place identity 5, 116, 119–120
point density analysis 69–70
potential consumers 102
Prebyl, T. J. 79
Preuss, H. 93
proximate tourists 119, 121–124, 126
public places 3, 6–7, 9–10, 14–19
public spaces 3–4, 6, 9, 14–15, 17–18

recreation ecology 75
Recreation Suitability Mapping (RSM) 80
resorts 4, 8, 10, 12, 15–18, 146
Rickley, J. M. 126
Roberts, E. K. 79
Robinson, M. 93
Rosario, D.A. 46
Rose, J. 80
Ruetzler, T. 100

Saldanha, A. 146
Sassatelli, R. 105
Saukkonen, T. 73
Scarles, C. 145
Schamel, J. 76
Schrijver, A. 26
Scuderi, A. 95
Seamon, D. 120
secondary core nodes 54–55, 58, 60
Servillo, L. 72
Shih, H. 46
Shipway, R. 121
Shoval, N. 24
Smallwood, C. B. 45
social interactions 3, 6, 14, 17–18, 76
social media 72, 91, 94–97, 100, 102–104, 106–108, 126, 132, 134
social network analysis (SNA) 44, 46–49, 59–60
social preferences 80
Solberg, H. A. 93
spatial arrangements 4–5, 7, 10, 12, 14, 17–18
spatial behavior 65–67, 71–74, 77–78, 81–85, 134

spatial diffusion 66–68
spatial impacts 17, 76
Spatial interactions 67–68, 74
spatial research 67, 82, 85
spatial segmentation 67, 79, 81
sport events 115–116, 126–127
sport tourism events 114, 125
Squires, J. R. 79
Stamberger, L. 80
Sturiale, L. 95
Świeca, A. 8

Taczanowska, K. 69
Taff, B. D. 74
Taylor, J. 100
theme parks 23–27, 33, 37, 45, 132
time-budgets 66, 76
time windows 26–27
Timmermans, H. 25
Tobler, Waldo 137
Tokyo–Fujisan 52
Tomaselli, V. 46
Tomlinson, A. 114
'Tour Down Under' (TDU) 117–120, 122–126
tourism destinations 3, 46, 126
tourism development 3–6, 17–18, 148–149
tourism economy 132, 148
Tourism South East 99
tourism system 46, 134–135
tourist destinations 3, 24, 52, 54, 116
tourist flow network 44–45, 47, 49–50, 53–54, 56, 58–61; pattern 47, 57
tourist flows 38, 43–50, 52–53, 55, 57–61, 131, 134; distribution of 52–53, 57, 60
tourist gaze 120, 145
tourists 3–10, 14–19, 24–26, 30–32, 35, 37–38, 43–48, 54–55, 59–61, 71–72, 117, 134, 137, 142–143, 145–147
tourist zones 5, 14, 17–18
tracking technologies 142–143
Travelling Salesman Problem (TSP) 26
Travelling Salesman Problem with Profits (TSPP) 26
Tsai, C. Y. 25
Turner, V. 94

UNWTO 44, 148
urban spaces 98, 104, 106–108, 115

Van Riper, C. J. 80
Vaske, J. J. 79
Vidon, E. S. 126
Virtanen, T. 73
visitors 3–6, 14, 17, 24–33, 35–38, 45, 66–77, 80–85, 90, 93, 95, 100; behavior 74, 78, 82; preferences 29; spatial behavior 69, 71, 75,

82; typologies 74; use 68–69, 75–77, 82; use levels 75, 78, 82; use management 68, 82, 84–85
vitality 6, 17, 107
volunteered geographic information (VGI) systems 73
Vu, H. Q. 45

Waitt, G. 116
Wall, G. 4, 137
Wang, D. 24
Wang, F. 45
Wang, X. G. 4
Waters, N. 137
Watts, D. C. H. 96
waypoints 69–70, 78

Whyte, W. H. 6
Wilbert, C. 105
Williams, A. V. 44
Wohlfart, T. 78
Wolf, I. D. 73, 78
Wu, B. 45

Xi, J. C. 4
Xiang, Z. 24
Xu, H. 25

Ye, B. H. 45

Zelinsky, W. 44
Zeng, B. 94
Zhang, N. 4